C000128535

How Irish reunification took happened afterwards...

Dedication

To Muriel and Pauline, my loves and inspiration. To my friends and family, who tolerate and entertain me. To the many bloggers who have taught me what little I know. To the public figures I have projected upon, and the private lives that have been shared. To my fevered imagination that must be released, and to you, dear reader, for allowing me to impose upon you...

Disclaimer

This future history is a fictional narrative claiming to be written in 2040 and looking back at the history of these islands over the previous 20 years. It was in fact written in the summer of 2023 and all statements referring to events up to that date are factually accurate.

Everything else is obviously fiction, including references to actions taken by real people in relation to events which have not yet taken place, and which may in fact never do so.

The intention is not to praise or defame or, indeed, to accurately predict the future in great detail. Perhaps to project forward based on some broad current trends. But mainly to spin a plausible yarn on the edges of possibility which I hope the reader will find enjoyable, perhaps disconcerting, and certainly thought provoking about how the future might evolve.

Fact is often stranger than fiction. There are many possible futures, and many feel anxious about what may or may not happen. In dealing with the future, it helps if we can first imagine it, or indeed imagine alternative futures. The anxiety is in not knowing...

This is a future history written from the perspective of 2040, 15 years after Irish re-unification. It is written in the form of a memoir by a young English journalist who ends up falling in love with an Irishwoman, Ireland, its people, and its politics. It gives a personal account of how a Border Poll was called, why it was carried, and what happened afterwards. It traces the development of a unified Irish state over a 15 year transition period and looks at how it all turned out, from a variety of points of view in Ireland and Britain.

Dramatis Personae

Jeremy Watson, Journalist
Síle De Buitléar TD aka Sheila Butler
Matt Casey, Politics Editor, The Tribune
Professor Meeken, Environmental Editor, The Tribune
Stanley Richards, HR Director, The Tribune
Sebastian Watson, father of the groom

(Involuntary) Supporting cast:

Rishi Sunak, Keir Starmer, Leo Varadkar, Micheál Martin, Neale Richmond, Eamon Ryan, Pippa Hackett, Peter Kyle, Jeffrey Donaldson, Ian Paisley Jnr, Sammy Wilson, Naomi Long.

Acknowledgements:

To members of my family, who provided technical, moral and emotional support, and my fellow bloggers at Slugger O'Toole who helped, advised, criticised and condemned!

Table of Contents

1. My private meeting with Rishi Sunak 4

2. The Bombshell 12

3. Belfast 25

4. Election Night! 36

5. A Draft New British Irish Treaty 49

6. A tale of two General Elections 64

7. My renewed rugby career! 76

8. The Border Poll Campaign 83

9. The people decide. 95

10. Kidnapped 109

11. The Irish Referendum Campaign 120

12. The First All-Ireland Elections 129

13. Disappointment 139

14. My political career move 147

15. A brave new world 156

16. Our Wedding 163

17. The Ukraine War 170

18. Ambassador Filatov 180

19. Economic and social transformation 189

20. The normalisation of politics 202

21. Scandal 211

22. Transforming the Environment 225

23. Back to the EU 236

24. And so, to conclude... 246

1. My private meeting with Rishi Sunak

My story begins one fine summers day back in 2024 in Chequers, the country home of the British Prime Minister. The PM had just been given a rather ominous briefing on the prospects for the British economy. A general election was in the offing and there was almost no good news for the PM to build a campaign around. I was there as a relatively new reporter for the Tribune, a reputable British broadsheet not known to be overly well disposed to the Conservative government.

Our senior political correspondents had all tied their colours to the mast, declaring the government to be a lost cause and facing inevitable defeat. The government press office had asked for a "more objective" reporter to be sent to a private and confidential press briefing with the PM. Even though I was still very junior, I was the only one on the political staff who wasn't either on holiday or known to be hostile to the government. My editor told me it was my big break and not to f*ck it up.

The British economy had never really recovered from the triple whammy of the disappointing outcome of Brexit, the pandemic, and the Ukraine war. It was the last economy in the G7 to return to its pre-pandemic size. GDP was estimated to be 5.5% lower than it would have been without Brexit, resulting in government revenues being down by about £40 Billion per annum. Investment had dried up, almost 30% lower than pre-referendum trends. Worker productivity had flat lined. Many sectors were still experiencing difficulties with exports. Long Covid had resulted in high levels of sickness absence or people withdrawing from the workforce altogether. Many jobs remained unfilled, hampering the economy's ability to grow.

The Ukraine war had led to shortages of key commodities, supply chain difficulties, and a huge spike in energy prices which had fed into inflation and the cost of living generally. Rising interest rates were feeding into huge increases in mortgage repayments and eating into people's disposable income. Consumer confidence was way down. Strikes were endemic, and even when resolved left a bitter taste. The British people had suffered a huge drop in their standard of living and were not best pleased about it. There was a sense that many voters were waiting in the long grass to give the Conservative party a bloody nose.

So, I was expecting a very upbeat briefing by the PM. Green shoots, corners being turned, immigrant numbers down, government initiatives being rolled out, inflation down, more trade deals in the pipeline, you know the sort of thing. Anything for a few positive headlines during the summer silly season when parliament is in recess and real news is at a premium.

Instead, I was shocked at the PM's tone and demeanour. This was the first time I had ever met Rishi Sunak, or even seen him in the flesh. My previous beat in Ireland had allowed me no such privileged access. A meeting with Neale Richmond, a junior government minister, was the height of my reporting scoops. No wonder I had been recalled to head office! But Sunak seemed unable to shake off the sense of gloom and doom in the briefing he had just been given. I found him to be intelligent and engaging, but surprisingly unable to hide his feelings.

His frustrations were clear. The government finances were under extreme pressure, and there was no cash available for the sort of imaginative schemes governments like to announce when a general election is in the offing. The contrast with Ireland couldn't have been greater, where ministers were busily trying to decide how many extra billions they would allocate to public expenditure increases, tax cuts, paying down the national debt and salting away in a sovereign wealth fund to be used only for long term infrastructural projects or profitable investments abroad.

Trying to empathise with the PMs plight, I asked him a question about how he would far rather be in Leo Varadkar's shoes... only to be shocked by his reaction: "that b*stard", he exclaimed, "he really screwed us on Brexit, and I'm still trying to repair the damage with the EU and the USA!"

I mumbled something about having interviewed Neale Richmond, almost my sole claim to journalistic fame to date, and he had explained to me in great detail how the British had failed to take account of the delicacy of the Northern Ireland situation and the peace process in particular, and that if there had to be a customs border between Britain and the EU, the only practical solution was a border in the Irish sea.

This didn't mollify the PM one little bit. "Who is that little sh*t to tell us how to run or own country! I have enough on my plate without having to deal with the DUP and their allies in the ERG as well. I thought we asked the Tribune to send a more objective reporter?"

"I'm not taking sides in the debate" I spluttered (thinking of my editors warning not to f*ck up this great opportunity to get a journalistic scoop), I'm sure he was only stating the Irish government (and EU) position, but Ireland seems to have recovered from the pandemic and the Ukraine war much better than we have". (Trying to be diplomatic, I avoided mentioning the B(rexit) word...)

"And how many billions in military aid have they given the Ukrainians I might ask? - they can't even defend their own airspace. Neutrality my a*se, they're just freeloading on the rest of us!" the PM retorted.

At this point I wished the ground had swallowed me up. My big chance, and I really had f*cked it up!

The conversation moved on to opinion polls, by-election results, policy announcements and campaign strategies with the other reporters keeping well clear of any contentious comparisons with other countries. "And another thing" he flashed a quick glare at me, "Germany isn't doing much better either!" he said, in response to a question nobody had asked.

As the session wound up, the press secretary reminded us all that this was a background briefing only, there were to be no direct quotes used, and any references could only be to "a senior government official". It was important to get the message across that while the opposition is on holiday, this government is still working hard to build a better Britain!

That was a quote we could use to headline our pieces, she said somewhat sheepishly, I thought, although some reporters seemed to lap it up, scribbling the phrase into their notebooks.

As I prepared to leave, she called me back. "The PM wants a word", she said rather ominously.

I expected a roasting.

Instead, the PM seemed in jolly good form all of a sudden saying that we hadn't met before and was wondering how I had found my stint in Ireland. I began by apologising for bringing it up, but he brushed it aside, and said that he didn't want that other lot (the other reporters) leading with that story because the real issue is how we in Britain deal with the problems we are confronted with, not what some small tax haven, reeling it in at the expense of everyone else, was doing.

I didn't know what to say.

"From my perspective" I stuttered, "I can't understand how Fine Gael and Fianna Fáil are so unpopular when they have the fastest growing economy in Europe, full employment, huge government surpluses, and rapidly declining debt".

"People don't care about that sort of thing" he countered, "it's all just big numbers to them. People worry about making their mortgage or rent payments, they worry about housing, health, childcare and educational services. From what I can see, the Irish government isn't delivering on the basics".

I hastened to agree, anxious to find some common ground with the PM, and hoping that fences could be mended before word got back to my editor that I wasn't to be sent to a private press briefing again.

But it was what happened next that really shook me. "How do you think the Irish government would react, if we were to announce a Border Poll, to be held in, say, 12 months' time?".

"Huh!?! Why would you want to do that?" I stalled for time, "both you and the Irish government are heading into a general election in the next few months, and calling a Border Poll would really set the cat among the pigeons. Sinn Féin would be delighted, because they have been calling for one all along, and it would give them a great boost ahead of the Irish elections.

"Precisely", he said. "I don't owe that Varadkar a thing, and he has been far too effective in uniting the EU against us!"

I tried to reel off all the problems I could think of: "Do you really want Sinn Féin leading the next Irish government? And won't this be a great boost to the SNP campaign in Scotland? And what about Northern Ireland, isn't it unstable enough as it is!"

"Precisely", he said. "That Donaldson chap needs a rocket up his a*se. He keeps creating problems and expects me to solve them for him. I had no end of trouble even getting a meeting with Biden. The Windsor Framework is one of my few successes and he wants to deny me even that. He wrecked Theresa May's career, and he isn't exactly helping mine. And as for the Scots, I don't care if they vote SNP or Labour; the point is they won't be voting for us anyway."

"Eh yes, but isn't calling a Border Poll a bit drastic? Sinn Féin won't be any easier to deal with and couldn't there be violence in Northern Ireland? You won't be thanked if you open that can of worms. And aren't you supposed to wait until opinion polls indicate a clear majority in favour of re-unification?" I countered, still trying to recover my equilibrium.

"We'll call a Border Poll when it suits us. Opinion polls count for nothing in the real world. Just look at my polls now (The Conservatives were 20% behind Labour at the time). And as for Sinn Féin, we have a lot of information on all their leaders which they won't want to leak out into the public domain. I don't anticipate having too many problems with them, to be honest. Anyway, this is all conjecture. I'm not really seriously thinking about it. This conversation never happened. Do you understand?"

"Yes, yes, absolutely, I understand! I knew you were only really testing me out as to what I knew about the Irish situation... no responsible government could consider calling a Border Poll right now. What would be the point? It's hardly going to affect the result of the English general election, is it?" I offered.

"Yes, absolutely", he said. "As I said at the press briefing, we need to focus on what we, as a country can do to improve matters, and not worry too much about what other countries are doing. Labour has no ideas as to how to do things better, and we really need to focus on that".

And with that, the meeting was over.

As she whisked me outside the building, the Press Secretary reiterated that the briefing was private – no direct quotes – and that I had been extremely privileged to have had a few minutes with the PM alone. "Hardly anyone has gotten that treatment in recent times" she noted, and then asked: "By the way, what did you talk about?"

"My lips are sealed", is all I said, with a knowing smile. She must have been wondering why a rookie reporter was sent to an important private briefing, never mind him having a few minutes alone with the PM.

I'm not sure she was all that happy with my answer either, but I didn't care. I felt I had passed my first major test in reporting back in England, and couldn't wait to tell my editor I had had a private conversation with the PM.

"Oh! Huh! What did you talk about?" he chuckled, unable to conceal his surprise. "Oh, just about my experience working in Ireland" I replied "He was interested to know my opinions of the Irish government ministers. He didn't seem too impressed with Varadkar and his gang" I said, delighted with my new role as confidential advisor to the PM.

"Don't be losing the run of yourself" was all my editor had to say. I think he thought I was making a meal out of some small talk on the fringe of the briefing. "Rishi likes to cultivate relationships with reporters. Don't be taken in!" was his final word.

But I was.

I couldn't help thinking whether the PM was flying a kite and really thinking of calling a Border Poll in the run up to two general election campaigns. Did he need a distraction from Britain's economic woes that badly? Was his political situation really that desperate? Why would you call a Border Poll just to stir things up? Wouldn't Labour accuse him of gross irresponsibility? Even the Irish government wasn't calling for one.

And if the Border Poll was lost, wouldn't he be blamed for the break-up of the UK? Was saving £15 Billion on the Northern Ireland subvention really that critical to Britain's economic future?

But then again, the UK left the EU for less, saving about £7.5 Billion per annum in net contributions to the EU. But was this really all about money?

People had bitter memories of Boris Johnson's slogan "We send the EU £350 million a week – let's fund our NHS instead." I could hardly see a similar slogan about Northern Ireland going down well with the English electorate. It would only remind people of the divisive Brexit referendum campaign and Sunak's role in supporting something that hadn't turned out quite as people expected.

I put the matter completely out of my mind. I assumed Sunak was just trying it on with an inexperienced reporter. I imagined him laughing to himself at leading a junior reporter on a merry dance.

My next engagements with the government press office were quite mundane. Some of my more senior colleagues had returned from leave and were grabbing the more important assignments.

I was therefore quite surprised to be invited to another private briefing in Chequers some weeks later. My senior colleagues wondered openly why I had been specifically invited. Was I to become one of Sunak's lapdogs? My report on the first briefing hadn't exactly been earth shattering – just the usual stuff on all the things the government was doing to turn the economy around.

My editor opined, to general hilarity, that perhaps the PM needed some advice from a younger demographic. "He knows he's lost you lot!" I didn't think it was all that funny...

I can't say I wasn't chuffed but had to pretend it was just another routine assignment that my senior colleagues were probably better off missing. After all, they had heard it all before. Many times.

2. The Bombshell

My second private briefing in Chequers in August 2024 wasn't all that different from the first. The rumour was that the PM was considering calling the general election for October. He didn't want to have to reconvene parliament to give Labour a platform to lambaste the Government. Better to get it over with quickly. The public wouldn't start paying attention until September anyway, and memories of a paltry budget were fading.

The economic news wasn't getting any better though. The economy was flat lining. The hoped for rise in consumer spending was being killed off by huge increases in mortgage repayments. House prices were falling at their fastest pace since the Second World War. Independent economic think tanks kept issuing reports saying that the British public had experienced the greatest drop in their standard of living since that war. Real household disposable income per person had fallen by 6% in the previous two years. Britain's tax burden, measured as a share of economic output had risen to 38%, the highest it had been since the war, making the Tory claim to be the "low taxation party" somewhat hollow.

Wages hadn't kept pace with inflation, and the cost of living had stayed stubbornly high, despite much higher interest rates. Higher interest rates had also choked off all marginal or risky investments. Businesses were cutting back on all but the safest and most lucrative investment project proposals. Strike activity had still not died down, resulting in a lot of disruption, bitterness, and division in society even after strikes had been ended.   Crime rates were at a 20 year record high, and there was increasing lawlessness on the streets.

People were cutting back on all but essentials. The numbers in Britain using food banks had increased from 25,000 in 2008 to over 3 million in 2023. Over four million children were living in poverty. Over 270,000 people were officially classed as homeless, including 123,000 children. Seven and a half million people were on hospital waiting lists for routine treatments and of these 400,000 had been waiting for more than a year, the highest figures since records began.

I was fascinated to see how the PM would propose to address all these challenges. Of the five pledges Sunak had made on gaining the top job, he had failed to deliver on three – Growing the Economy, Reducing Debt and Reducing Waiting Lists. Progress had only been fitful on the other two - Halving Inflation and Reducing Illegal Immigration. Blaming the doctors and nurses strikes for the increased waiting lists wasn't getting much traction with the public. It was getting harder and harder to find some good news to sell to the electorate.

The briefing started with the PM in ebullient form listing countless initiatives the government was taking in all areas of public life. It seemed like one long list and certainly gave the impression of an energetic, focused, and determined government. But as reporters started digging into the details, they realised that many of the actions listed were repeats of earlier promises that had not been delivered and many had paltry budgets allocated to them. A few extra million here and there weren't going to go far to address many of the problems itemised on the list.

There was lots of talk of public private partnerships, of the government working in close collaboration with charities, but little clarity as to why most businesses – many struggling to keep afloat – should suddenly become social service providers as well.

The briefing got more and more contentious as time went on with reporters getting increasingly querulous. Having almost gotten burned at my first briefing, I stayed well out of it, feeling that the other reporters were addressing all the important issues and were more clued in on the details of past promises. They had been following these issues for years.

Almost by the way, towards the end of the allocated time, the PM mentioned he had an announcement to make in relation to Northern Ireland. The Northern Secretary of State had, after due consideration and careful analysis of all the evidence, come to the view that there was an increasing likelihood that a Border Poll would result in a vote for a united Ireland. Accordingly, in accordance with the terms of the Good Friday Agreement, he had decided to call a Border Poll to be held no later than 12 months from the date of this announcement.

There was a collective intake of breath in the room, but no one said anything. People seemed dumbfounded. There being no specialist Ireland reporters in the room, I felt I had to ask a question: "Could the prime minister clarify, what new evidence had led the Northern Secretary to come to this conclusion? After all it was 15 months since the last elections in May 2023 – the local elections in Northern Ireland - and while opinion polls since had shown increased support for Sinn Féin, there was no evidence that this would translate into a majority for a united Ireland."

"I'm glad you asked me that", he smiled, almost as if he had planted that question with me himself.

"The Secretary of State will issue a detailed statement later outlining the factors he has taken into account, which I understand include the trend in recent elections, opinion poll data, the census results, reduced popular support for the current devolved government arrangements in Northern Ireland, and some focus group research his department has been carrying out. It is important that we respect the democratic process in Northern Ireland and honour our international obligations under the Good Friday Agreement".

The prime Minster then moved the discussion on to his new Industrial Strategy - which included tax breaks, state aids, grants for productivity improvements and worker re-training – before I could ask any follow up questions. The meeting had already run over its allocated time, but I managed to raise the issue of whether the Irish government had been consulted on the decision to hold a Border Poll. The PM stated that "according to the Good Friday Agreement, it is the Northern Secretary, and the Northern Secretary alone who must come to a determination as to whether a Border Poll is likely to be carried. The Irish government has been informed and the Northern Secretary will issue a more detailed statement later". Next question please – and he pointedly didn't point to me.

All further questions on the topic by other reporters were re-directed to the Northern Secretary and the PM closed the meeting nearly an hour late after answering a few desultory questions on other topics.

The briefing adjourned and some of the other reporters, those who knew of my previous assignment in Ireland, bombarded me with questions as to what this meant for Ireland and, in particular, for Northern Ireland. A scrum gradually formed around me as other reporters – not very well up on Ireland or Northern Ireland – became anxious to catch up with the conversation. The Press secretary had to hoosh us all out of the room saying it was needed for another important meeting.

Outside the building, and trying to be helpful, I said that I imagined the Irish government would be upset as they hadn't asked for a Border Poll and probably didn't want this distraction in the middle of the run up to their own general election, expected to take place in November. Sinn Féin would be delighted, however, I thought. They had been calling for a Border Poll for a long time and would love to fight the upcoming general election on that issue.

As far as Northern Ireland was concerned, I felt sure the decision would be welcomed in most nationalist circles as "clearing the air" after two and a half years of stalemate on devolution, and that there was a feeling that Northern Ireland had to find some other way forward. However, I doubted the decision would be welcomed in most unionist circles as it was likely to be a very divisive and perhaps corrosive campaign.

I suggested that unionism had reconciled itself to Direct Rule as preferable to a Sinn Féin First Minister led Executive and were happy not to have to take responsibility for all the huge public service budget cuts the Secretary of State had been imposing. The Alliance Party would be sure to regard the timing as "unhelpful" I felt, although we must wait and see what the parties actually said.

15

Early reports of the briefing in all the media were dominated by the Northern Ireland announcement with little reference to all the other policy announcements made by the PM. In fact, because reporters couldn't mention him by name – other than as a "senior government source" – most of the reports actually named me and quoted my comments on the announcement. They did so without noting my qualification that "we must wait and see what the parties actually say" and gave the impression that I, a junior reporter from the Tribune, was in a position to authoritatively report on the reactions of all the parties.

Stupidly, I had forgotten that the "no attribution rule" only applied to the PM. There was nothing to stop anyone naming me, especially as I had also been speaking outside the building and outside the immediate context of the briefing.

One newspaper actually led with the headline:

"JEREMY WATSON SAYS BORDER POLL CAMPAIGN WILL BE DIVISIVE AND CORROSIVE".

Who?

It was only some way down the piece that the reader learned that the Jeremy Watson quoted was "the Ireland Correspondent for the Tribune". It didn't mention I had since been replaced in that role. I had to apologise to my successor.

The situation was exacerbated by the fact that there had been no reaction from the Irish government or the Northern Ireland parties to date, and thus my opinions were all that the non-Ireland specialist reporters had to go on and were thus featured prominently in their reports.

It later emerged that the Secretary of State was actually in Dublin informing the Irish government of his decision at that very moment, and that the Northern Ireland parties were also only just being informed by a junior Northern Ireland Office Minister.

When I got back to the office, the news was all over the place. Those staff who actually knew me gave me the thumbs up, although some seemed to have a concerned look on their faces. I found that my more senior colleagues were less than impressed by my sudden rise to media fame. Some asked, rather sarcastically, whether I was now the spokesperson for the Irish government, Sinn Féin, and all the Northern Ireland parties combined.

The Tribune's senior foreign correspondent was particularly miffed. "I understand that, in your considered opinion, the Prime Minister should not have used his absolute discretion to call a Border Poll under the terms of the Belfast (Good Friday) Agreement?" he said, in a rather exaggerated formal posh accent. I apologised for having inadvertently strayed onto his patch. I didn't even dare correct him that it was actually the Secretary of State who was empowered by the Good Friday Agreement to make that decision.

More ominously, my editor said nothing, other than "could I please confine my report of the briefing to the PM's **actual** remarks".

The water cooler gossip was that I had been played by the PM. I didn't get too many sympathetic looks. Some pity, perhaps. More likely, "who does he think he is?"

They were not wrong.

Official reaction followed swiftly from the Irish government and all the Irish and Northern Irish political parties. Thankfully, my fame (or notoriety) was short-lived.

That said, the reactions were much as I had anticipated. The Irish government expressed regret that they had not been consulted or informed beforehand but welcomed the 12 month delay as there needed to be a lot of preparatory work done prior to the vote to ensure all voters knew exactly what they were voting for or against. There was no announcement of an Irish referendum which I presumed would be required to give effect to an all-Ireland government should the Border Poll be carried.

Sinn Féin complained that the government should have been doing all this preparatory work all along, and that they would make it a priority to rectify that as soon as they got into government. It was now imperative that the Irish government call the general election immediately so that the Irish electorate could have their say.

Most of the other parties agreed that the timing was unfortunate and that there should have been much more consultation and discussion before any announcement of the Secretary of State's decision. The Alliance party felt that the announcement was "unhelpful" at this difficult time for Northern Ireland and that all communities must band together to avoid their differences being exploited by extremist parties. The Greens noted that any Border Poll campaign promises should include provision for a more integrated rail network throughout Ireland and that there should be no additional funds for motorways.

The DUP complained that this was one more example of the British Government betraying Northern Ireland, and that "the people" must show their disgust by voting for DUP candidates at the forthcoming general election. The time had come for Unionist Unity in the face of this existential threat to the Union.

The UUP agreed but stated that Unionist Unity did not mean everyone uniting behind the DUP. The time had come for unionists to spread their message to all the people of Northern Ireland as "we all have a stake in maintaining a peaceful and prosperous union". "The UUP", it claimed, "was best placed to unite all those who supported the Union".

All independent analysts expressed their surprise that the Secretary of State should have come to his determination just **before** the general election – when much more up-to-the-minute hard information on voter preferences would have become available after the election.

Some reports suggested that it was actually an attempt to help the DUP get out their vote, and that the quid pro quo might be that the DUP would promise to return to the assembly. That suggestion was quickly quashed when the DUP made it clear that it was pointless even talking about returning to the assembly until the constitutional question had been finally settled.

The use of the phrase "finally settled" led some analysts to speculate that a secret deal had been done whereby the UK government would remove the Good Friday Agreement's provision for repeat referendums (at a minimum of 7 year intervals) if the first referendum result was for a continuance of the Union. They also suggested that unionists had a better chance of winning a Border Poll sooner rather than later and that, once the issue was settled, the way was clear for an indefinite, long term return to Direct Rule, as devolution had clearly failed with "both sides" guilty of the failure to fully implement the Good Friday agreement.

However, it was never explained how a British government could change the terms of the Good Friday Agreement without the agreement of the Irish government or tie the hands of Northern Ireland Secretaries for the indefinite future. Also, why did the DUP not welcome the announcement if they were so confident of winning the Border Poll?

I began to suspect that another private briefing had taken place on the Border Poll announcement that I had **not** been invited to. All of the media reports seemed to be taking the same line and citing the same "senior government official". My senior colleagues at the Tribune assured me that no such private briefing had taken place - at least not to their knowledge.

It later emerged that a briefing had taken place at the Foreign Office to which some reporters had been invited. Strangely, the Northern Ireland Office had little to say, other than issuing a lengthy formal statement detailing the reasons for the Secretary of States determination that a vote for re-unification was "likely". It was the first time I had ever seen "focus group research" given as one of the reasons for a formal government decision.

In the days following, a number of opinion polls were published showing surprisingly high levels of support for the calling of the Border Poll both in Northern Ireland and Britain in response to the question "Should the people of Northern Ireland be given the opportunity to express their views on union with Britain or Ireland?"

Well, doh! Who wouldn't approve of that question when it was put to them like that! Especially independence supporters in Scotland.

What intrigued me was how quickly all these opinion polls were published. Normally it takes at least a couple of weeks to decide to hold a poll, schedule it with the market research agencies, agree a budget, agree the wording of the questions and the scope of the demographics to be included, do the interviews either on line or in-person, collate and analyse the results, and publish the findings – usually spread out over a number of days to maximise the publicity the polling agency and the sponsoring media outlets got for the results.

The first polls showing widespread support for the government decision appeared in a matter of days following the government announcement. The decision became much less controversial after that. Apparently, government spokespersons were briefing that it was important to see past all the vested interests blocking progress and "let the people decide". The government, it seemed, had lost patience with the Northern Ireland parties' failure to implement devolution, and a large majority of the public in Britain and Northern Ireland agreed with them.

Whether by chance or otherwise I was shortly afterwards "promoted" to the position of the Tribune's Climate Change correspondent, a new position which the editor said they had been thinking of creating for some time. There would be no more tilting at windmills for me!

I wrote a final piece describing the government's decision as reckless, without due regard to the sensitivities of the situation in Northern Ireland and driven purely by the government's need to distract public attention away from their appalling economic record. Although the formal decision was couched in lofty terms about the Secretary of State's duty to perform his function under the Good Friday Agreement "impartially", having due regard for the evidence of changing attitudes and voting behaviour in Northern Ireland, with due respect for the democratic process, and with Britain having "no selfish strategic interest" with respect to Northern Ireland, the timing and manner of the announcement made it reasonable to assume that other factors were at play. I mentioned that saving £15 Billion on the Northern Ireland subvention could fund a lot of much needed social services in Britain.

To my surprise, Matt Casey published my piece, describing it as my best yet, and wished me well in my new role. I think I could even detect a smile in his face.

Sure enough, and to no one's surprise, the issue of the £15 Billion subvention soon became a central feature of the debate in England following the announcement of the General election a few weeks later. Analysts noted it was about twice as much as the much-hated net subvention to the EU which Brexiteers has made such play of saving.

Labour were wrong-footed. Soon they were being asked to explain where they would find the many billions they needed to fund their election promises. Everyone knew where the Conservatives were proposing to find the money to fund their promises, although no Conservative spokesperson ever publicly averred it might come from the Northern Ireland subvention. Officially the Tories remained neutral on the Border Poll and solemnly declared that they would respect the people's vote.

When challenged that they were supposed to be the Conservative **AND** Unionist party, conservative spokespersons stressed they were all in favour of the Union, but only insofar as the people of Northern Ireland wanted it.

Spokespersons noted a May 2022 statement issued by The Rt Hon Boris Johnson MP, Prime Minister, which approvingly quoted the 1990 declaration by the then Secretary of State for Northern Ireland, Peter Brooke, arguing that Britain had "no selfish strategic or economic interest" in Northern Ireland. Boris Johnson had emphasized that that statement did not say "no strategic or economic interest" in Northern Ireland, – but "no *selfish* strategic or economic interest". There had been no change in government policy. This was all about letting the people of Northern Ireland have their say.

When challenged as to why they weren't offering a referendum to Scotland, their position was that that matter had been settled by the 2014 independence referendum, and that unlike Northern Ireland there was no internationally binding treaty obliging the UK to hold further referendums in Scotland, even if opinion polls indicated their might, from time to time, be a majority in favour of it. "Opinions polls come and go, but the constitutional settlement is permanent," was the official line.

Spokespersons also stressed that, other than in the specific case of the Good Friday Agreement, referendums were only *advisory* under the UK Constitution, and take place only at the absolute discretion of the government of the day. In their view Britain had had quite enough of referendums in recent times, and they didn't propose to hold another one any time soon. This seemed to be a popular policy in England if the opinion polls were in any way accurate.

During the course of the subsequent election campaign, English voters got the impression that a conservative government would have the money to fund their election promises, whereas a Labour government might not.

Quite how the people of Northern Ireland might be persuaded to vote for a united Ireland and thus relieve the exchequer of this financial obligation was breezily passed over as a matter for the Irish to decide, although independent observers noted darkly that the swingeing cutbacks in Northern Ireland's budget over the past two years might have been a preparation for just such an event, and there was some background talk that the Tories might even be planning to escalate those cutbacks regardless of the Border Poll result.

There was much talk of cutting out "wasteful spending" and "unsustainable subsidies" in the Tory manifesto without any official spokesperson ever conceding that such references applied especially to Northern Ireland, although many inferred that that was indeed the case.

"Waste is waste wherever it occurs" is all that the spokespersons would concede.

However, some reports noted that "the Northern Ireland health service cost far more, and delivered far less, than its counterpart in England, citing recent reports to that effect. This was, apparently, a general problem with public services in Northern Ireland.

Although Labour had supported the principle of a united Ireland by consent since the 1980's, Labour leader Keir Starmer denounced the Border Poll decision as an "electoral stunt" designed to distract people from the governments catastrophic economic record. While pledging to respect the democratic will of the people of Northern Ireland, Labour would be campaigning in favour of the union. Labour stood for a proudly British United Kingdom.

He made the announcement flanked by unionist leader Sir Jeffrey Donaldson, who looked incredibly pleased, and announced that "this showed that the British people are rallying behind the Union" and that "unionists would be supporting the formation of a Labour led government in the forthcoming election".

Starmer's announcement led to an almost immediate and damaging split between the left and right wings of the Labour party, with left wingers denouncing Starmer as "more conservative than the Conservatives themselves".

The charge struck a nerve, leading to angry exchanges between Starmer loyalists and most of the rest of the party. In vain Starmer noted that even the Irish government hadn't called for a Border Poll, and that almost the only people welcoming it were Sinn Féin and dissident republicans engaged in terrorist activities (although there had been no significant recent dissident terrorist activity).

Starmer even visited Dublin to sympathise with concerns that the Border Poll had been called "without due consultation and coordination with the Irish government beforehand".

It is not entirely clear his visit was welcomed by Dublin, however. Sinn Féin was quick to point out that while they had been successful in their campaign for a Border Poll, the "conservative parties in Ireland were siding with the unionists, and that the people of Ireland had to be given an immediate opportunity to show whose side they were on."

Apparently both the Taoiseach and the Tánaiste were indisposed at the last moment, and Sir Keir was met by my old friend , the Junior minister, Neale Richmond, instead. I tried to contact Neale for a comment, but he didn't return my calls. It seems my previous very positive interview with him had left no lasting impression on him.

Opinion polling and focus group research in England found that the public largely agreed with Starmer's claim that this was an electoral stunt designed to distract from the government's catastrophic economic record. But they also didn't seem to care over much as to *why* the government had made the announcement. They were intrigued by the possibilities it opened up for increased public spending in England, and they generally approved of the Conservative's plans to increase spending on the NHS, housing, tax breaks, and programmes to eliminate poverty.

Faced with a newly united Conservative party and a divided Labour party, opinion polls showed a significant swing away from Labour in the next few weeks. However, the primary beneficiaries were not the Tories, but the Lib Dems and the SNP in Scotland.

In my, somewhat cynical, view, the Border Poll announcement had already served its purpose. It had changed the electoral conversation to something more people could agree with and less damaging to the Tories. The fact that the Border Poll wasn't due to take place until long after the general election meant that it could now be kicked into the long grass. If the Tories lost the election, it would be somebody else's problem in any case.

Opinion in Ireland, both North and south, was not quite so sanguine.

3. Belfast

Much has been written about the amazing result of the 2024 UK General Election. As I was now the Climate Change Correspondent of the Tribune, I didn't actually cover the lead up to the campaigns as a professional reporter. However, as an amateur enthusiast I kind of felt I knew how it would all play out, even though I had little hard evidence to back up my hunches.

I write this because I found myself getting obsessed with the political process, even though I was now supposed to be covering the climate change brief full time. My new editor, a distinguished environmentalist, must have been wondering why she had inherited a rugby playing Oxford PPE (Politics, Philosophy and Economics) graduate with no known scientific qualifications or particular interest in Climate Change matters.

For the most part this didn't matter too much. I was not expected to write original content so much as cover scientific conferences on climate change and interview prominent climate scientists. My editor would give me a list of questions to ask and evasive answers to look out for. Even so, she found herself spending an inordinate amount of time editing my copy and asking me why I hadn't asked what to her, seemed obvious follow up questions.

I fancy myself as quite a quick learner, but I could see I was trying her patience. She thought that my critique of the Sunak government resiling from many of its climate change commitments was quite good. I had become an expert in reading between the lines of quite bland (and often over promising) government pronouncements. She couldn't bring herself to read all those "stupid government policy documents," but I became quite good at parsing them and tearing them apart. It was the serious scientific stuff I had difficulties with.

Some weeks later I had a conversation with Julia, a colleague, and about the only other staff member I would count as a friend. If anybody knew the latest office gossip, it would be her! I explained that I was having difficulties with all the scientific jargon in the technical journals I was supposed to read, and felt I was bluffing and hamming my way through my brief. She told me on the qt that the word was my new editor was not best pleased to have been "dumped" with me. She had been looking for an assistant junior reporter for quite some time but had in mind a writer who was at least a post-doctoral student in Climate science.

My heart sank.

I did not want to be a charity case. I wasn't used to being totally incompetent at my job. Julia suggested I speak to HR and maybe they could sort something out for me. This suggestion took me quite by surprise. HR did not have the reputation of being there to help people. More likely they would be involved in hiring and firing.

However, I resolved to take the bull by the horns. If there was a problem, I was going to have to confront it sooner or later. I asked for an appointment with the Head of HR, a rather smooth, urbane operator by the name of Stanley Richards.

It was with some trepidation that I approached his office at the appointed hour. The secretary motioned for me to go on in. I knocked on the door and a rather peremptory "come in" boomed from within.

Mr Richards, I'm Jeremy Watson, sir, I asked to see you...

(I have absolutely no idea why the word sir crept into that sentence. Perhaps the scene reminded me, at some subconscious level, of being hauled in front of my old school headmaster.)

He snorted, beckoned me to sit down, and continued reading a file he had in front of him.

After a while he peered above his glasses, and said something like, "ah yes *that* Jeremy, you seem to have had quite a varied career in your short time working for us."

It wasn't really a question, so I said nothing. I was very conscious that nervous people tend to babble too much.

After a while, he continued, "I see you went to Uxbridge Public school, got a rather mediocre second-class honours in PPE from Oxford, played a bit of Rugby, and ended up as a sports reporter for the Wolverhampton Echo. I thought we had recruited you as a sports reporter. How did you end up in Ireland?"

"Well Sir," (damn, that word again) "I played a lot of rugby at Oxford, got an academy contract with Sale Sharks, and started writing a lot about rugby for the local rag. When my academy contract wasn't renewed after year one (I had spent quite a lot of it injured), I managed to pick up a junior reporter job with The Wolverhampton Echo, did reasonably well, and was then offered a job here."

"Yes, Yes, Yes, he harumphed impatiently, but why Ireland, and how the politics desk?"

"Well, eh" (I just about managed to avoid saying Sir), "Ireland had just done ever so well at the Rugby World Cup, and as our Ireland correspondent was on maternity leave, I was sent over to cover the local reaction to it. You know the kind of stuff, colour pieces about the players and fans having a great time afterwards. The team were invited onto the Late Late show and to receptions with the Government and President, and I kind of milked it and stayed on for a couple weeks because I slightly knew some of the rugby crowd from playing against them and was able to get some good gossip and inside scandal.

The features Editor was quite pleased with my stuff and the politics editor said that I seemed to be quite good at making contacts and would I like to cover for our Ireland Correspondent while she was away on leave."

"Ah yes, I remember it now" Mr. Richards said. "So, you spent a few weeks in the sports department, moved over to features for a few weeks, then moved to politics for the Ireland job and now you're in Climate Change. Quite a rapid move through our organisation, I should say. You don't let the grass grow under your feet!" "Well, no point in harming the carbon capture process," I joked rather weakly, trying to emphasize my new environmental credentials… He didn't laugh.

"So why have you come to see me?"

"Well Sir (drat, that word again) I don't think I'm doing very well in my new brief. I think Professor Meeken (my editor) had in mind recruiting a more scientifically qualified reporter."

"Well yes, but needs must… what other job did you have in mind?"

"I heard a rumour we were thinking of appointing a Northern Ireland correspondent to cover the election and the Border Poll there" I said hopefully.

"My, my, word does get around. We only discussed it a couple of days ago. You seem to have your ear close to the ground!"(I had been chancing my arm. I thought it would be logical for the paper to appoint someone to cover the Election and Border Poll campaign in Northern Ireland but had no idea they had actually formally discussed it).

"I'm not sure that would work out. You'd be working for Matt Casey (my former Politics editor) again, and I'm not sure he has entirely forgiven you for the Chequers fiasco. Mind you Bill Featherstonhaugh, (the senior Foreign Correspondent I had offended) hasn't really been on the ball recently. He missed that Foreign Office briefing on the Border Poll announcement, and everyone else had that story bar us. You at least gave us some profile on that story, and I gather the advertising department were very pleased. We haven't had so many clicks on our web site in a while and I gather your name peaked in google search statistics."

I had no idea HR followed all that stuff.

"Not that they would have found anything. You don't have a Wiki page and are just listed as staff with no particular title on our personnel page. We'll have to rectify that. Leave it with me."

Some days later my former editor Matt Casey asked to see me. He was quite pleasant. He said he felt that I had been hard done by because of the Chequers episode and that anybody could make a mistake. "At least you actually showed up for the press briefing and made a bit of a splash. There's too much cosy background chats and nods and winks going on. We need someone to tell it as it really is."

Well, that's Bill Featherstonhaugh seen off, I thought to myself.

"I've done a deal with the sports department. You are to cover rugby in Ulster and Ireland as well, as Irish rugby has such a high profile nowadays. Our current Ireland correspondent hasn't got a clue about rugby and can't get behind the scenes as you did for your post-World Cup coverage. But your main brief is the politics, and you will be working mainly for me. Your rugby, public school, and Oxford background should be quite useful in opening some doors, especially on the unionist side. They can be quite difficult to get any information out of. But for God's sake be careful who you talk to. We don't want **you** to become the story again like what happened in Chequers."

I got the message, **loud and clear**.

So, there I was, back on more familiar territory even if I had never been to Northern Ireland. I was told the Tribune wasn't widely read in Northern Ireland and was somewhat distrusted by Unionists because of its generally left of centre stance. But with Unionists now formally allied with the Labour party it seemed a good time to build a deeper relationship. At least they knew what the Tribune was, and if I was the Tribune's Northern Ireland Correspondent, that was more than all the other British titles who now covered Northern Ireland from London, Glasgow, or Dublin.

I was told I was following in the footsteps of some very distinguished Northern Ireland political correspondents – David McKittrick, Ed Moloney, Simon Winchester, Henry Kelly, Conor O'Clery, Tommie Gorman, Henry McDonald, and Cathal Mac Coille - but that the Northern Ireland newspaper scene was in sad decline since their heyday during the Troubles. Circulations had collapsed with The Belfast Telegraph and Newsletter print editions now selling less than 20,000 copies a day.

Only the Irish News was holding up relatively well and was now the second highest selling regional daily in the UK. Of the non-local titles, only The Irish Times still maintained two journalists based in Belfast, Freya McClements, and Seanín Graham although The Irish Independent and the Belfast Telegraph were both owned by Mediahuis and shared quite a lot of copy between them.

Being a political reporter for a British daily based in Belfast was going to be a lonely place. I could understand why some in the office sniggered when I told them I was going to be our Northern Ireland Correspondent. I might as well have been posted to report from Kabul, as far as they were concerned. After such brief previous stints on the sports desk, features, Ireland, the political desk, and Climate change, it was obvious they felt I was being squeezed out of the paper altogether.

Arriving in Belfast was a bit of a culture shock. I didn't have a clue about the cultural and political geography of the city. I wasn't quite as bad as Karen Bradley, a former Secretary of State for Northern Ireland, who admitted in 2018 that she hadn't realised that "nationalists didn't vote for unionists and unionists didn't vote for nationalists" and that "she was slightly scared of the place".

But it was close.

She had been appointed to the Cabinet position by Theresa May as "a safe pair of hands" at a particularly sensitive time in Northern Ireland on a previous occasion when the devolved Executive had collapsed in the wake of Brexit and local scandals like the Renewable Heat Initiative and an Irish Language Act. Imagine having a government collapse over a language issue in England! She said it was "very different to asking voters in Labour held Staffordshire Moorlands to switch to voting Conservative."

I at least knew of the seemingly irreconcilable differences between the two communities and that protestants and unionists lived mainly in east

Belfast, and Catholics and nationalists in west Belfast. But what were the differences between unionists and loyalists, and nationalists and Republicans? And did political affiliation always correspond to religious belief? Having been raised Church of England in a largely agnostic society, I was surprised by the number of churches of many different hues and had difficulty following the accents.

I had booked myself into the Europa Hotel which seemed appropriate as I was a committed European (I admit to having been a Remainer!) and learned it had been bombed throughout the Troubles. Some claimed it was the most bombed hotel in Europe although I didn't see that highlighted on the Hotel website! My first task was to find a place to live. Expenses didn't cover hotel living after the first couple of weeks, but where should I live? I soon discovered that Belfast was also divided into middle class and working-class areas and that class divisions could be as sharp as the sectarian divide.

The Tribune didn't have an office in Belfast so I decided to locate myself close to the university sector near Queen's where I hoped to find a lot of students and academics to talk to who could fill me in on the local flora and fauna. (I had learned a lot of words in my brief stint as Climate Change correspondent!). But it was now October and all the student haunts seemed already fully booked up. I eventually found an apartment in Ballyhackamore in East Belfast on the fringes of a loyalist area but also not far from the middle-class areas of Knock, Campbell College, and Stormont. It had good WIFI and a spare room for an office, and that was all I really needed. I didn't realise it at the time, but it was also in the heart of the East Belfast Constituency which had become the epicentre of the battleground between unionism, loyalism, and Alliance.

I was soon down in the pub trying to make conversation with the locals. Apparently, my name gave me away as "a likely protestant" and my slightly posh English accent confused many. I soon found myself developing a northern lilt and adopting some of the local patois. Apparently, I came "from the mainland" or was "an English bastard" depending on your point of view. My rugby background marked me down as middle class, but my PPE degree meant my political affiliations could be a little dubious. I tried to keep people guessing for as long as I could. I don't like being pigeonholed. When asked was I "a Prod, a Mick or a Taig" I just replied I was English, and that seemed to settle the matter.

I encountered very little hostility whatsoever, especially in nationalist areas, which surprised me. In fact, it was difficult to reconcile all the friendly people I met with the sharp and vituperous divisions in politics I was expecting. There was lots of banter, of course, and no little "slagging." But I fancy myself as being well able to handle that sort of thing. In fact, it is an aspect of Irish life I was beginning to enjoy. I am not blessed with the middle-class English penchant for politeness and reserve.

I was soon engrossed in meeting every politician who would talk to me and found my calling card "Northern Ireland Correspondent of the Tribune" opened many doors for me. Unionists, in particular, were keen to influence the coverage of their politics on the mainland. They were also very keen to get my take on how the mainland election campaigns were playing out.

Anxious to give them a quid pro quo for all the information I was hoping to get from them, I was as forthcoming as I could be. Besides, I like talking politics and it was important to build up relationships. I had little first-hand information from my colleagues back in the Tribune head Office, but Julia kept me in touch with the stuff I couldn't read in the papers.

Those campaigns were now in full swing, with Labour, marginally, still ahead of the Tories by about 5% - a big drop from their former 20% lead. But interestingly, most of those lost voters seemed to have drifted to the Liberal Democrats rather than to the Tories, who remained at rock bottom. Voters disappointed by Starmer's many about turns in response to Tory about turns still couldn't bring themselves to vote Tory, it seemed.

In retrospect it seems quite logical for the majority of voters, who now regarded Brexit as a mistake and most of whom even wanted to re-join the EU, to vote for the only major English party who had consistently supported EU membership even when the Brexit fever was at its height.

In contrast, Starmer wouldn't even commit to re-joining the Single Market or to "dynamic alignment" on product standards, and it was unclear what he meant by "a closer trading relationship with the EU" and why the EU would agree to it.

As far back as 2023, Sunak had performed one of his many about terms on Brexit and re-instated the EU "CE" [Conformité Européenne] product quality assurance marking for British businesses all but abandoning the Johnson Governments proposals for new UKCA ((UK Conformity Assessed) and UKNI (for products intended solely for the Northern Ireland Market) quality assurance marks which were to enable British and Northern Irish products to depart from European standards for products not intended for the Single market.

So much for "**Taking Back Control!**" Businesses could obtain a CE mark for their products only by paying an accredited agency in an EU country to test and certify their product as conforming to EU standards. "Dynamic alignment" in all but name because they would also have to align their standards with any changes in EU standards on an ongoing basis. It meant that even products produced for and sold in Britain would continue to be tested and certified by agencies in EU countries, as companies were hardy likely to produce the same products to different standards for the British market.

As might be expected, The Mail was apoplectic, accusing Sunak of "yet another Brexit climbdown," but there was remarkably little backlash from Brexiteers. Businesses were ecstatic, of course, because many had already incurred considerable costs preparing their products to meet two or perhaps even three different standards, and many simply did not have the resources to do so. "What was so bad about the CE standards in the first place" was the reaction of one business source who asked to remain anonymous, "it's a pity they didn't make this decision a while ago, because it cost a lot of time, created a lot of uncertainty, and hampered business investment".

What my new unionist contacts didn't appear to realize, however, was that this also meant that "the border down the Irish sea" would be much less significant. Products with the CE mark didn't need to be checked because they had already been certified as Single Market compliant by an EU certification agency. I thought they would be thrilled and was shocked when my DUP contact declared that this didn't matter. It was the principle of being subject to EU rules that was wrong. "We can't have that EU Papist conspiracy and the Irish lording it over us."

I had never thought of the EU as Catholic or Irish!

I quickly changed the subject back to the UK election campaign... I didn't mention it to my new unionist contacts, but I didn't think Starmer's stance in favour of the "Union of Britain and Northern Ireland" was doing Labour any favours on the mainland. People simply didn't have strong feelings about it and were much more exercised about how Labour were going to fix the damage to the NHS, social and educational services. Reporters constantly queried how Labour would fund all their promises, and Labour didn't seem to have clear answers.

Whatever the reasons, it was clear that the Tories were in big trouble, even if Labour had lost its big lead. (Julia said it was also because of the preponderance of people of colour in government leadership positions didn't go down well in the shires). The Liberal Democrats were doing very well in former Tory strongholds, and Labour seemed to be having some success in recovering ground in some "red wall" seats.

The Scottish National Party was cleaning up in Scotland despite their recent scandals as voters were outraged at the holding of a referendum in Northern Ireland and not in Scotland. The Greens and some leftwing Corbynista anti Starmer candidates seemed to be doing well in some constituencies, but overall, the picture was very confused.

Some opinion polls began to show Labour, the Conservatives, and even the Liberals running neck and neck, but nobody seemed to know how that would play out in terms of seats. Most UK election models simply don't cater for a situation where there are three parties with almost equal support in England. The first past the post system means you can win a seat even with less than a third of the vote if the remaining votes are split badly enough.

Election night was going to be some night!

4. Election Night!

I was out and about at various voting centres in Belfast on election day in October 2024 being careful to divide my time between protestant, Catholic, middle class and working class areas. Most people were happy enough to chat, though some gave me the middle finger. Reactions were sharply divided with many unionists saying they were protesting against "Sunak selling out our country when it isn't even his to sell!"

Nationalists were saying it was a dress rehearsal for the Border Poll and they had to show what the "majority in this country really wanted." Few expressed much interest in the election on the mainland although some mentioned that they had to get the Tories out.

I asked them about how they felt about not really having much say in who formed the next government in Britain. Reactions varied, but many were along the theme of "sure it doesn't matter, they're all the same anyway!" Nobody mentioned that the DUP had once had considerable influence over a British government and had caused the downfall of Theresa May. Some were more interested in what was happening in Scotland and expressed surprise that the SNP seemed to be doing so well despite all the scandals, if reports were to be believed.

So far, I hadn't met a single journalist from a British daily and so I had no one to compare notes with. I didn't know whether I was getting a representative sample of opinion but had to file a report anyway. My editor, Matt Casey, had been on to me several times looking for updates. At that stage I had been submitting mainly analytical pieces on the elections as a whole and was only beginning to get a handle on how things looked from a Northern Ireland perspective. To my surprise he had published most of them even though I was hardly a senior analyst on his staff. He seemed to like my stuff, all of a sudden.

To my shock, that evening I was also invited onto the BBC Northern Ireland election programme panel to give my views on the election as a whole from an English perspective. I didn't even know what to wear.

Suit? Shirt and Tie? Too formal? It was to be a late night programme. The producer who invited me suggested an open necked shirt was fine. It was to be an informal chat rather than a formal news programme. I think she was trying to put me at ease.

It was my first time on TV, and I was extremely nervous, and I probably talked too much. My editor's warning never to let myself become the story was ringing in my ears. I had better not be too controversial, but there was no point in waffling – I wouldn't be asked again if I did. But news from the polling centres was slow to come in and they were happy to have someone to fill in the airtime. I was introduced as the reporter who had broken the Border Poll story and asked to give a considered view of how the election had unfolded in Britain.

So, for what it's worth, my analysis, delivered in a stream of consciousness and with only a few prompts on a sheet of paper in front of me, was on the following lines, edited for brevity. It wasn't all delivered in one go, of course, but the presenter held off interruptions from fellow panel members Sammy Wilson and Michelle Gildernew, and kept prompting me to go on: I felt I might be digging a hole for myself, but whatever: In for a penny, in for a pound:

> "Almost as soon as the election was called, Labour's commanding 20 point lead in the opinion polls began a rapid decline. Analysts dispute the precise importance of the various causes, but most are agreed the Tories focus on eliminating wasteful spending hit a nerve. Families were being put to the pin of their collar to make ends meet and saw no reason why government should lavish huge sums on projects and services not of direct benefit to them.
>
> Northern Ireland was barely mentioned in the campaign in England, but few doubted where the Tories thought most of the potential savings would come from. It didn't trouble them unduly because many could never quite understand the place in the first place. For all the unionist protestations of "Britishness," they didn't feel very British from an English perspective.

There was also a natural suspicion of "those who protest too much." True brits are expected to take adversity on the chin and exhibit a stiff upper lip at the same time. There was already quite enough concern that standards in public life were slipping throughout the UK, and Northern Ireland politicians didn't seem to raise the standard appreciably.

Labour's cause was not helped by Keir Starmer appearing to be more conservative than the conservatives themselves. Having endorsed the Tory decision to cap children's benefit at two children, Labour were then completely wrong footed when the Conservatives announced they were confident they could find the money to lift the cap to three children if not more, and that the increasing evidence of rising child poverty demanded such a policy change.

Labour rather sheepishly followed suit soon after, but not before looking completely asinine and spineless for having endorsed a policy totally at variance with their historic commitment to the welfare state.

Further Tory announcements of health service enhancements soon followed, to be followed rather rapidly by "me-to" statements by the relevant Labour spokespersons.

To the casual observer, generally disengaged from the political process, it almost looked like the Tories were leading the charge to improve public services with Labour always one step behind.

In vain, Labour spokespersons pointed out that the Tories had actually been in power for the past 14 years and were primarily responsible for the cutbacks in the first place. The disengaged voter heard only the usual arguments about the past. What they were really interested in was what was going to be done to fix all these problems in the future. And many of them felt Sunak was presenting a more positive and dynamic message.

Every time the conversation veered to Brexit, the pandemic or other past external factors Sunak would simply declare he wasn't interested in blame games about the past, he was razor focused on building a better future, and argued that it was the Tories who had the better ideas and policies, and the energy to implement them.

Whenever the topic of Northern Ireland came up, Sunak was quite dismissive: It was up to the people of Northern Ireland to take responsibility for their own future and not always be looking to others to solve their problems. They had, he declared, the same opportunities as anyone else in the UK, with the added benefit of being next to a quite dynamic economy in Ireland. There could be quite a lot of synergies on the island if that was the way they wanted to go, but he would not dictate a choice to anyone. (He didn't mention that Northern Ireland also had the advantage of full access to the single market).

Independent observers took this to be a coded message that Northern Ireland should hitch its wagon to Ireland, although nobody quite said that and no great controversy at those remarks ever erupted in England. Even the European Research Group (ERG) Tory allies of the DUP were very focused on winning their own seats and anxious to promote an image of Tory unity throughout the campaign. In their view, Donaldson had rather burned his boats by cosying up to Starmer, even if they could understand why.

Come back to us after the election was their response to DUP entreaties to hound the government to robustly reaffirm its commitment to Northern Ireland with increased spending plans. A review of cutbacks in Northern Ireland has been promised, but as we all know, these reports often end up gathering dust on shelves, and are generally promised to frustrate and deflect criticisms of decisions already made...

Of course, the DUP are absolutely apoplectic about all this, but as this is so often their standard operating procedure, the general English public barely noticed. Unionist rallies in Northern Ireland have been well attended but have received scant attention in British and global media. A genuine effort has been made to ensure there was always a strong unionist unity candidate in every constituency, with huge anger directed at the Alliance Party for refusing to play along. However, in practice, where a realistic choice was available, it was always the harder line unionist who ended up getting the unionist unity nomination.

This only drove more moderate unionists into the arms of the Alliance Party. In a couple of constituencies, Alliance and the SDLP had even discussed having a joint "constructive engagement" candidate pledged to respect and implement whatever was the outcome of the Border Poll. This only increased unionist accusations that Alliance were part of a "pan nationalist front." In vain Alliance proposed to "balance their books" by suggesting they and the UUP might agree a joint candidate in a couple of constituencies, particularly Fermanagh South Tyrone, but the UUP refused to play ball, insisting on backing a unionist unity candidate instead.

This refusal to "reach across the aisle" to broaden the base of support for the constitutional status quo surprised outside observers. In most political systems the party which successfully manages to straddle most of the centre ground tends to lead the poll and form or lead the next government. However, the single seat first past the post electoral system tends to encourage polarisation into two large opposing parties and some smaller regional or special issue parties on the margins with little or no hope of forming part of the government.

Strangely, in Northern Ireland, this appears to happen even in multi-seat single transferable vote local and assembly elections, which tend to reward moderation and "transfer friendliness" and usually deliver a much closer alignment of seats won with votes cast. It seems that in very polarised societies, the focus is always on maximising turnout of your own voters rather than reaching across the aisle, because any such "reaching out to" or "accommodating" voters beyond your own party base tends to be seen as "fraternising with the enemy" and puts your own core vote at risk.

This is all fine and dandy if your natural constituency exceeds 50% of the vote. But in a polarised society where neither of the two poles can command 50% of the vote, the battle for the centre ground proves crucial in determining the outcome. This is the ground that Alliance has successfully occupied and expanded in the years leading up to this election, and the attitude of this demographic will prove crucial in determining the outcome of the Border Poll.

However, that same phenomenon may also have badly damaged the Labour party's chances of achieving power in Westminster. Firstly, Sunak's calling of the Border Poll (for I believe it was he who called it, not his rather hapless Secretary of State) handed the initiative back to the SNP in Scotland, aggrieved at being denied a Border Poll when many in Northern Ireland did not even want one. Labour's revival in Scotland amongst moderately nationalist and non-nationalist voters was killed off by that act.

Secondly, in "reaching across the aisle" so strenuously as to nullify any potential Tory attacks against him, Keir Starmer demoralised his own base. Union members couldn't see the point of voting Labour when Starmer sacked shadow cabinet ministers for supporting strikers seeking to protect their living standards by seeking only wage increases in line with the cost of living. Vote Labour, get Tories became the catch phrase on the left, inspiring many leftwing labour candidates to stand as independents and split the potential Labour vote.

Thirdly, while Starmer's stand beside Jeffrey Donaldson in support of a British UK was rarely mentioned again in England, it did have the effect of splitting the Labour party. Many activists refused to canvass for the official Labour candidates and supported Corbyn's decision to stand as an independent Labour candidate (having been expelled from the party) and supported other left wing candidates in Labour strongholds. This had badly damaged the Labour vote. Tory newspapers were able to portray Labour as once again riven by disputes and rivalries and dominated, in their view, by left wing radicals, who got most of their publicity despite not being part of the official Starmer led Labour Party.

So, what was Starmer thinking? Being seen to support a British UK may have made for a good photo op, but few if any voters in England were going to change their vote based on his stance on Northern Ireland. Being seen to cosy up to Jeffrey Donaldson may also have contributed to a perception that Starmer lacked confidence that Labour would win an overall majority and was already setting up potential coalition options. He was also noticeably conciliatory towards the SNP on his trips to Scotland, without ever meeting their central demand of a second independence referendum. This led to Tory charges of "Vote Labour, get an unstable coalition of Labour, SNP, Lib Dems, and Unionists."

It was not a vote winner."

OH SHIT! It hit the fan. Coming from an English background, with a relatively posh English accent, I had been anxious not to appear a Tory or a unionist stooge. I couldn't take sides in the political divide in Northern Ireland, so I couldn't be too positive about Donaldson's considerable coup in getting Starmer on his side. Starmer seemed to have lost the plot to some degree anyway, and it was showing in the opinion polls. I was only repeating what I had read or heard people say many times anyway, but somehow these were not the things a visiting Englishman on the panel was supposed to say.

I was immediately accused of being a Sunak Stooge by Sammy Wilson, the DUP representative on the panel, who was in the process of being re-elected. "You don't have a clue about what you are talking about! There is huge concern in England at the way in which Sunak is SELLING OUT THE UNION, and he was going to be unceremoniously turfed out by all true BRITISH PEOPLE!"

"True," was my somewhat cowed response, but it doesn't look like Keir Starmer is going to reap any benefits from his alliance with the DUP," was all I could get in before an enormous row broke out in the panel. Michelle Gildernew, the Sinn Féin MP who was in a tight contest in Fermanagh South Tyrone seemed to be terribly pleased with my exposition. In vain, the Chair tries to calm things down by stating that the election was over, all the votes had been cast, and the participants weren't going to be winning any more on the night!

It was to be a long night.

Although the programme was broadcast only in Northern Ireland, news of the controversy filtered back to England. Julia was in the room when one of the senior political correspondents showed it on his TV monitor. "He's at it again!" Seemed to be the highly amused collective response. "Trust Matt Casey to send a bull into a China shop!"

I was dreading my next call with him. Would this be the last of my several short assignments with the paper?

Instead, he was quite charming. Apparently, I had raised the profile of The Tribune in Northern Ireland no end. It wasn't even available in shops in some nationalist areas and now it might be. Apparently hits on our website from Northern Ireland had greatly increased. I may have said a few things that people didn't want to hear, but there was no point in not being clear in our communications as to how we see each other. We had to tell it as it is. "Just make sure to cover lots of unionist reactions to the election results," was all the advice he gave me.

Prior to the counts starting to report, TV election analysts had been noting that turnout seemed to be exceptionally high. They noted that there had been a secular decline in turnout in UK elections, from a high point of 84% in 1950, to 67% in the previous 2019 election. Many people had simply switched off from politics and politicians altogether, no longer believing they are there to address their needs. Even in the historic Brexit referendum, the turnout only reached 72 percent. This, in spite of the fact that there are no "safe" constituencies in a referendum where voting becomes almost pointless because the result was a forgone conclusion. Many people had simply switched off from politics altogether.

So, what were the reasons that were driving people to the polls on this occasion? Exit polls and Vox Pops were saying it was time to get the Tories out. Some were saying that Labour were just as bad as the Tories so they didn't know who to vote for. Many felt they had to get out and vote in protest at what they thought was "the terrible state the country is in, where nothing works anymore." Some said they were voting Liberal because of their support for the European Union membership, but many just seemed to want to vote for anyone but the Tories.

Turnout in Northern Ireland Westminster, European and Assembly elections had averaged only 61% in the 55 years prior to the 2024 General election, although the downward trend was not as dramatic as in Britain. That still means that 39% of the electorate are not engaged despite (or perhaps because of) the extreme polarisation and politicisation of everything in Northern Ireland. Had many of them voted, and would they vote in the Border Poll? And if so, how would they vote?

I have to admit that while I felt the election in Britain would be a close call between Labour, the Conservatives, and the Lib Dems, with Labour still in the driving seat, I had no idea how the elections in Northern Ireland would pan out. I simply hadn't spoken to enough people. I had a vague hunch that Alliance would do well, but maybe I had been speaking to too many middle class people. So, the results, as they came out weren't much of a surprise to me, even if many people were truly shocked.

The early results were soon coming in and the BBC predicted the following outcome, based on the exit polls, which turned out to be extraordinarily accurate:

National Prediction: Labour short 36 0f Majority

Party	2019 Vote %	2019 Seats	Predicted Votes %	Predicted Seats
CON	44.7	376	27	107
LAB	33	197	29	290
LIB	11.8	8	28	181
Reform	2.1	0	2	0
Green	2.8	1	5	1
SNP	4	48	4.3	49
PlaidC	0.5	2	0.5	3
Others	1.1	0	4.2	1

The extraordinary unfairness of the UK First Past the Post Single Seat Constituency electoral system is illustrated by the results table above. For the first time ever all three national parties all came in under 30%, but Labour, on 29% got more seats than the Lib Dems on 28% and the Tories on 27% combined. They were still 36 seats short of a majority, however, and couldn't form a majority government without the support of either one of the other major parties or the SNP. The Greens got no extra seats, despite almost doubling their vote and the SNP improved marginally by one seat. Despite almost quadrupling their vote, independents and others got only one seat. Jeremy Corbyn would remain in the Commons to be a thorn in Keir Starmer's side.

Prominent Tories like the Prime Minister, Rishi Sunak; prominent Brexiteers Stephen Hammond and Damian Green; Northern Ireland man

Conor Burns; former leaders Ian Duncan Smith and Theresa May; former Northern Secretaries Theresa Villiers and Julian Smith; former cabinet ministers John Redwood, Jacob Rees-Mogg, Liam Fox, Kwasi Kwarteng, and Chris Grayling; cabinet ministers Kemi Badenoch, Suella Braverman, Jeremy Hunt, Michael Gove, Grant Shapps; and Northern Ireland Office Minister Steve Baker were all projected to have lost their seats.

It may not have been a slaughter of the innocents, but it was some slaughter, nevertheless. The British people had had their revenge on those who had misled them on Brexit.

But, given how close the big three parties were in terms of votes, how this can pass for democracy is beyond me!

Naturally, the Prime Minister, Rishi Sunak, announced his immediate resignation as Conservative leader, although he had to stay on as caretaker Prime Minister until a successor was elected.

Back in the studio, Sammy Wilson was in fine form and couldn't hide his satisfaction. "This is what happens to Prime Ministers who betray our precious union!" he announced, looking extremely pleased.

This was before the Northern Ireland vote projections came in...

Northern Ireland Prediction: Alliance gain 1 seat from DUP

Party	2019 Vote %	2019 Seats	Predicted Votes %	Predicted Seats
DUP	30.6	8	24	7
SF	22.8	7	30	7
SDLP	14.9	2	12	2
Alliance	16.8	1	20	2
UUP	11.7	0	10	0
Green	0.2	0	0	0
Others	3.1	0	4	0

In stark contrast to England, there was very little by way of change in Northern Ireland in terms of the seat count, with only Gavin Robinson (DUP) losing his seat to Alliance Party Leader Naomi Long. This was despite Sinn Féin increasing their vote hugely from 23 to 30% and becoming the largest party in terms of the vote in Westminster elections as well. The DUP lost almost 7% of their vote mainly because they were held responsible for the outcome of Brexit, the collapse of devolution, and the calling of the Border Poll. The SDLP held on to their two seats by the skin of their teeth.

Nationalists were cock-a-hoop to have extended their lead over Unionists to 42 percent to 34 percent, or a margin of 8 percent. Unionists were dismayed. It seemed the DUP's collapse of the institutions was being blamed, in part, for many of the expenditure cuts the Secretary of State had been imposing without effective opposition by an Assembly and Executive. There would now be huge pressure on the DUP to end their boycott.

Jeffrey Donaldson said it all depended on Keir Starmer delivering on his promises. No one was too clear on what Starmer had promised, beyond calling on people to "Support the Union" in the forthcoming Border Poll. But Donaldson could be happy that he had backed the winning horse for once. Even if only just by a short head.

With no party having a clear Majority in Westminster, the formation of a new government was going to be very difficult. The King asked Sir Keir Starmer, as leader of the largest party, to take on that task.

5. A Draft New British Irish Treaty

Keir Starmer was in a tricky position. With 290 seats he was 36 short of an overall majority and only two ahead of the Lib Dems and the Tories combined. Only the SNP could give him an overall majority, and they refused all entreaties to support his government unless he would agree to a second independence referendum to be carried out within 12 months.

He might even have been agreeable to that had they not also insisted on a Treaty between Britain and a newly independent Scotland which would transfer all British assets in Scotland to the new Scottish state, together with only a small portion of the UK national debt proportionate with its population.

Scotland was to be free to join the EU, the Eurozone, and the Single Market. The "Border down the Irish Sea" would extend to the Scottish English border, although the border between Scotland and Northern Ireland would disappear. Provisions based on the Windsor framework would apply at the Scotland England border unless England changed its relationship to the Single Market.

Several attempts to form a government were defeated in the Commons and it looked like a second election would have to be called. The Tories didn't even have a leader and the Lib Dems were anxious to consolidate their newfound position as part of the duopoly of power created by the first past the post electoral system. All their new MPs needed time to establish themselves in their constituencies and learn the parliamentary ropes. One slip and a few percentage points lost, and they would be back to their old role as mere appendages to a system dominated by Labour and the Tories. They had, however, lost some of their enthusiasm for a proportional representation electoral system now that the shoe was on the other foot.

However, the Tories were in dire straits, having lost not only their leader, but virtually all of their experienced parliamentarian and ministerial cadres. Leadership elections would take some time to organise, and they really didn't want an election any time soon. That might have finished them off completely or reduced them to a UKIP like rump.

The recriminations in the party were venomous. Sunak, of course took much of the blame. He was still in Number 10 on a caretaker basis but looked like he couldn't get away fast enough. Apparently, he was in line for a major business appointment.

It was even difficult for Starmer to find someone to negotiate with in the Tory party as Sunak had lost all authority. Eventually Starmer managed to persuade an interim Tory parliamentary party leadership to support his government on a "confidence and supply basis" for the next 12 months, in return for a range of promises to implement much of their policy agenda.

Critics complained that Starmer wanted to implement much of their agenda anyway, but one particular policy issue was a potential deal-breaker: The Tory election manifesto had promised to leave the European Convention on Human Rights (ECHR) in order to deal with the illegal immigration issue. Sunak had justified the decision to call a Border Poll to Tory backbenchers on the need to renegotiate the Good Friday Agreement in any case, as it tied the UK into membership of the Convention.

If Northern Ireland voted to stay in the Union, he would be in a much stronger position to negotiate with the Irish Government in order to have that aspect of the Good Friday Agreement removed. If Northern Ireland voted to leave the Union, Britain would be free to leave the ECHR. For many hard line Brexiteers, leaving the ECHR was a bigger issue than Northern Ireland leaving the Union, and this helped to ensure their support for the calling of a Border Poll.

However here Keir Starmer drew the line: Labour would not leave the ECHR regardless of the Border Poll result. In the end, when another election seemed unavoidable due to the deadlock on this issue, the Tories announced that they would support a Starmer government "strictly on a confidence and supply basis, for a maximum of six months, this being a time of national emergency" but reserved the right to vote down specific measures they disagreed with. Even then, only a little over half the remaining Tory parliamentary party actually supported the confidence vote installing Starmer in office, but it was enough.

In all this time, and despite the prominence of the ECHR issue, Westminster had almost forgotten it had promised to hold a Border Poll in Northern Ireland. I was having difficulty getting any copy published because the news was simply dominated by events in London. There wasn't space in the printed paper for stories from Northern Ireland, and my stories could only be found in the online edition several layers down the menu system under "Regional News" within the Politics section.

Jeffrey Donaldson was making speeches demanding that the Border Poll should only be held if the DUP's Six Demands were met. Demands they had only just formulated.

The SIX DUP DEMANDS were that no Border Poll should be held unless:

1. All Public Service cuts were restored.
2. The Government committed £1 Billion per annum in increased infrastructure Capital Spend.
3. The Barnett Formula was guaranteed and enshrined in constitutional legislation.
4. The Windsor Framework was reformed to "dramatically reduce" all barriers to trade within the UK.
5. The Act of Union was strengthened and updated to guarantee Northern Ireland the same rights as England within the Union.
6. Even if a Border Poll showed a majority for re-unification, there must be no Transfer of Sovereignty to Ireland without a new Ango-Irish Treaty guaranteeing Unionists the same Rights within Ireland as in Britain.

It was the first time the DUP had even conceded that a Border Poll for re-unification was conceivable.

It was unclear how the new Secretary of State, Peter Kyle, could somehow undo his predecessor's determination that a vote for a united Ireland was increasingly likely, and that he was therefore obliged to call a Border Poll under the terms of the Good Friday Agreement. The general election in Northern Ireland had, if anything, reinforced the view that such a vote was likely, with nationalist parties outpolling their unionist counterparts by 42% to 34%.

However, opinion polls continued to show voter intentions to be finely balanced, often with slight majorities in favour of the Union, but generally within the margin of error.

The results of individual polls often seemed to depend on the precise question asked, whether the poll was online or face to face, the nature of the sample polled, and the political situation at the time of the poll.

For instance, the question: "How would you vote if the poll was held tomorrow" generally had lower responses for a united Ireland than "If a poll was held in 5- or 10-years' time". Face to face polls seemed to have far higher percentages for "don't knows" and respondents claiming to be supporters of non-aligned parties. Results for polls of "likely voters" had higher percentages in favour than polls for the entire adult population. When a no deal Brexit had been in prospect, or more government cutbacks were in the news, poll results in favour of a united Ireland spiked.

It was also unclear how the transfer of sovereignty over Northern Ireland from Westminster to Dublin could be held up for, or made conditional on, a new Anglo-Irish Treaty being negotiated and ratified. The Good Friday Agreement specified one condition, and one condition only, and that was a simple majority in a Border Poll.

Rishi Sunak, now safely on his way to becoming the CEO of a major global investment firm, didn't help matters by saying, in a post-Downing Street interview, that he now regretted calling a Border Poll. Surely that should have been entirely a matter for the Secretary of State to determine based on his objective and impartial assessment of voter intentions?

But nobody in Westminster seemed to be paying a blind bit of notice to the DUP's SIX DEMANDS. They were all too busy trying to get the new government up and running. Political speculation was dominated by who was getting what jobs and what Labour policies would have to be sacrificed to secure Tory support in the Commons.

Things had however moved on in Ireland.

The Irish government had not called an election for November as expected because of the turmoil across the water and because Sinn Féin had soared in the polls to an unprecedented 40%, making it very likely they would lead the next government. The government insisted that it would run its full term until March 2025 and that maximum stability was needed "at this difficult time". Sinn Féin accused the government parties of "running away from the people" and having no idea about what to do about Northern Ireland.

Stung by this criticism, the government released a 400-page white paper documenting, in great detail, how any transfer of sovereignty would be implemented, what transitional arrangement would apply, how the finances would all work out, and how this would affect ordinary people in terms of their pensions, taxes, jobs, and access to public services.

People were astonished at the level of detail contained in the document. It was clearly the product of many years work and some very deep thinking. It also made quite a few proposals relating to what the British government would do, and there was much speculation that the document had had considerable British input.

I placed a call to Bill Featherstonhaugh, our senior Foreign Affairs Correspondent, to see if there was any substance to these rumours, and for once he came good. After a couple of hours, he rang me back to say that the word was there had been "some informal discussions" at "official level" without senior ministerial involvement, and that there had been "considerable common ground" found in those meetings. However, "nothing was agreed, until everything was agreed," and, as there had been no senior ministerial involvement, there was effectively no agreement.

I asked him could I quote "senior officials" as having confirmed all this and he hummed and hawed. "Well," he said, "we'd have to be careful about upsetting that apple cart. Some officials may have taken the discussions a little further than their ministers intended. But why don't I submit a draft of my report to him, and he would look at it and perhaps add some perspective. We could publish it under our joint byline."

Yea right. I would do all the work and he would share the credit. But fair enough I supposed, he was far senior to me, and he had come up with that inside information.

I was intrigued by the reference to "*Senior* Government Ministers" and "officials had perhaps taken the discussions a little further than ministers intended." Both implied there had been at least some ministerial involvement and at least some awareness of what was going on at senior levels. Senior Ministers wouldn't necessarily get involved in long term contingency planning in any case.

I placed a call with my old interviewee, Neale Richmond, a Church of Ireland Minister of State at the Department of Enterprise, Trade and Employment and Minister of State at the Department of Social Protection. He could have been centrally involved if *junior* ministers were indeed involved. To my surprise, he called me back almost immediately.

Speaking under guarantee of no attribution, he confirmed that discussions between officials of the Department of Foreign Affairs and the UK Foreign Office had been ongoing for several years with some ministerial involvement and that the 400-page white paper had indeed been the fruit of those discussions, especially those aspects which related to the UK government's role in the proposals.

However, he confirmed that the UK Cabinet had never seen or approved the complete draft and that it must be regarded as only as set of proposals at this stage, to be finalised following the period of public consultation which had now begun.

I sent my report to both Bill Featherstonhaugh and Matt Casey, my editor, and they both agreed it was excellent. It was published, barely edited, under Bill's and my byline, as the front-page lead story the next day: The first time a Northern Ireland related story had made the front page since the election. It began by highlighting the main points of the Irish Government's 400-page white paper:

1. A Formal Transfer of Sovereignty will take place within 3 months of a Border Poll being carried and the necessary changes having been incorporated into the Irish Constitution.
2. A new British Irish Treaty providing for the following will be agreed prior to an Irish Referendum being held:
3. There will be transitional arrangements for up to 20 years including ongoing close cooperation between the two governments on security, policing, civil service transfers, pensions, and all matters of the former Northern Ireland public administration.
4. The Good Friday Agreement, having no sunset clause, will continue to be in force for the transition period. This means the devolved administration in Stormont and the North South, and East West institutions of the Good Friday Agreement will continue to operate "for as long as all parties wish that to be the case, and in any case for the duration of the 20-year transition period."
5. The British government, as co-guarantor of the Good Friday Agreement, will have a role in ensuring that the rights of all British citizens in Ireland will be protected through the East west bodies – the British–Irish Intergovernmental Conference, the British–Irish Council, and an expanded British Irish Interparliamentary Body.
6. There will be a formal mutual defence Treaty concluded in due course covering matters such as intelligence sharing,

cybersecurity, radar/sonar installations, air protection, and maritime surveillance etc.

7. Britain and Ireland will commit to the development of an integrated electricity grid to maximise the opportunities for wind and solar renewable energy utilisation, demand management, load sharing, and nuclear baseload generation.

8. The Free travel area between Britain and Ireland will be maintained.

9. The Windsor Framework will apply to all trade between Britain and Ireland subject to the agreement of the EU.

10. Consultations will take place with Unionist parties as to whether Ireland should join the Commonwealth.

11. Official state Flags, Anthems, and Emblems will be the subject of consultations with all parties represented in the expanded Irish Parliament. There will be no law passed preventing British flags being flown on private property, or by legitimate organisations dedicated to fostering closer British Irish ties by peaceful means.

12. Northern Ireland will join the EU and be entitled to representation in the European Parliament.

13. EU Law, and particularly the European Charter of Fundamental Rights will apply, with final adjudication by the European Court of Justice.

14. All Northern Ireland Civil Servants, who wish to transfer to equivalent posts in Britain will be facilitated in doing so.

15. All Northern Ireland Civil Servants, who opt to stay in Northern Ireland, will come under the authority of Irish government ministers or the devolved administration. They will retain all rights and pensions entitlements accrued under their service to date, payable by the British government. However, any pension rights accrued after the transfer of sovereignty, will be payable by the Irish government.

16. All public assets owned by the British state in Northern Ireland, will become the property of the Irish state. There will be no transfer of public debt from Britain to Ireland.

17. Having regard to the increased costs to be borne by the Irish government with respect to Northern Ireland, the current UK Exchequer subvention, under the Barnett formula, will become payable by the Irish government. However, the UK government will contribute to that cost according to a sliding formula evenly spread over 20 years, whereby the UK government will contribute 95 percent in year one and 90 percent in year two, until the contribution is entirely eliminated in year 20. For the purposes of this exercise the current Barnett formula subvention will be estimated at £15 Billion.

That last point was the kicker. The UK would not be saving £15 Billion in year one, but only £0.75 Billion, rising by that amount every year for the next 20 years. The UK would still be saving £150 Billion at 2024 prices over 20 years, but it would take some years to build up to really substantial amounts. It would not be an immediate panacea for the British Government's budgetary woes.

Both UK and Irish sources later pointed out that the savings to the British exchequer could be far greater, as the Barnett subvention had been rising rapidly year on year. And could easily double or treble in the next twenty years if drastic remedial actions were not taken.

Equally, Irish sources were quick to point out that, should Ireland be able to develop the northern economy to be as successful as the south, there might be no need to subsidise the former Northern Ireland, in which case the continued UK contributions could be a net benefit to the Irish Exchequer.

That would be a big "If" of course. But there was no doubt that Irish officials were confident that, if the right policies were applied, there was no reason why the Northern Ireland economy could not become just as successful as the south, if not more so, within the 20-year timeframe of the UK contributions.

Moreover, they were confident there could be significant savings achieved through the elimination of duplication between north and south public services, and through their integration and transformation into "world class" services that would compare well with public services anywhere in the world.

Irish sources stressed it would not be a case of southern services "taking over" northern services, but rather that both would be combined and transformed into world class "best practice" services, taking in the best elements of both to build a better, higher quality, and better value for money service for all. Services would continue to be devolved to local areas as appropriate.

Irish sources also stressed that, where a better service was available in the north, that it would be retained and gradually extended to all of Ireland. Free GP consultations for all was the main example quoted, although sources stressed that might take some time to achieve, as GP resources were very stressed and stretched on both sides of the border at present.

Social welfare and state pension payments, currently much lower in the North, would also be gradually harmonised with those in the south, but again, that could take time, depending on the budgetary situation. However, all harmonisation processes should have been completed within the 20-year timeframe.

There would be a renewed focus on integrating primary and secondary schools throughout the island and all non-fee paying state funded schools would come under the direct control of a "Joint Educational Council" which would standardise rules, curricula, examination and assessment processes, and the overall ethos of the educational system.

Discrimination on the grounds of religion, ability or disability would be outlawed, although special provision would be made for pupils and students with special needs or disabilities. Schools which did not meet these standards could be de-funded.

The PSNI would be retained, at least for the 20-year transition period, as a regional police force, although it too, would be gradually integrated with An Garda Síochána, with processes being standardised in accordance with best practice throughout the world.

The legal systems and statue books would also be gradually harmonised and standardised across the island, although sources stressed that this could take many years because of the complex issues involved. The Law societies later produced voluminous reports highlighting the degree of divergence that over 100 years of different legislative processes had created.

---oo0oo---

Reaction in Ireland, both North and south, was generally positive, although the credibility of many of the proposals were questioned by unionist sources, who pointed out that the British government had never considered, much less approved the proposals, and as such they were "so much pie in the sky."

Reaction in the UK was much more mixed. "Why on earth would the UK continue to fund a state over which it had no sovereign jurisdiction and only very limited consultation powers under the East West bodies of the Good Friday Agreement?" the Daily Mail thundered!

It was to be some time before that question was answered.

The British Government merely "noted" the publication of the Irish white paper, and stated they would have discussions with the Irish government on the proposals contained therein in due course. There was no guarantee that the two governments would ever see eye to eye on all the matters discussed and that a compromise set of proposals would have to be agreed.

But the publication of the White Paper steadied the ship as far as the Irish government was concerned. They had answered the Sinn Féin criticism that they had not prepared for the possibility of a Border Poll. Sinn Féin expressed dismay at the length of the transition period, and the references to the Commonwealth and a mutual Defence Treaty. Nevertheless, Sinn Féin refrained from rejecting the white paper outright.

There was, however, increasing optimism that a Border Poll could be carried in Northern Ireland if such a comprehensive set of proposals could be agreed and incorporated into an international treaty with the UK.

Some groups such as Aontú and smaller parties in the south expressed their opposition to aspects of the proposals, particularly those on educational reform, and stated they would campaign for a NO vote in an Irish referendum. Strangely, they made no reference to campaigning for a NO vote in the Northern Ireland Border Poll and were sensitive to criticism that they were acting in league with "unionist hardliners."

Analysts noted that the Irish government had still not given any indication that it would hold the referendum required to formally incorporate Northern Ireland into the Irish state if the Border Poll was carried. Commentators presumed that was because the Irish government did not want to be seen to be taking a positive vote for granted. Officially, the whole process was entirely dependent on the Northern Irish people choosing re-unification, at least in the first instance.

The Alliance party, crucial to achieving a majority for re-unification in the Border Poll, was studiously quiet on the proposals. They welcomed its publication, commended the Irish government for the detail contained therein, but stated that they would have to study the proposals in much more detail and achieve clarification on many points. Its chief concern was whether "the Irish government could afford the proposals" and questioned whether the UK government would agree to co-fund the subvention for a further 20-year period. It proposed setting up a number of study groups within the party, to liaise with both governments and consider the proposals in more detail.

While suggesting that the transitionary period should be no longer than 5 years, Sinn Féin was broadly positive, or as positive as an opposition could be. It didn't want to be picking holes in the document and doing the unionists' work for them. Analysts argued Sinn Féin had been wrong-footed by getting the detailed plan it had asked for.

The SDLP welcomed all the consensual, consultative, and gradualist aspects of the proposals. Unification couldn't happen suddenly. It was a long-term process of building trust and winning hearts and minds. People had to be given time to get their heads around it and accommodate themselves to the changes that were bound to happen. They pointed out that many changes were inevitable, even if the UK retained sovereignty over Northern Ireland, and not all of those changes would necessarily be positive under either jurisdiction. They gave the example of water charges being likely to be introduced regardless of whether Ireland or Britain was sovereign.

Unionists noted that while the proposals looked detailed on paper, in practice they left many questioned unanswered. Would there be reductions in public service job numbers? What happens when the southern Irish tax bonanza comes to an end and the Irish economy crashed as it has done many times before? Who was going to pay the price then? Wouldn't everyone then be worse off? It was better to be much more closely linked to the seventh largest economy in the world than a "sclerotic EU" and an Irish economy built on sand. EU resources were far more likely to be directed towards Ukraine than Northern Ireland, and the balance of power in the EU was tilting eastward.

Behind the scenes Jeffrey Donaldson was fiercely lobbying the British government to come up with counter proposals to increase investment in Northern Ireland over and above the Barnett subvention formula. Starmer had promised to support the union, and the time had come to "put his money where his mouth is." Supporting the union required more than a photo op during a general election campaign. He sounded almost as if he had done Starmer a big favour by standing beside him and announcing that the DUP would support a Labour government.

The reality was somewhat different. Analysts gave many reasons for the dramatic fall in Labour support during the election campaign, including Starmer's many U-turns on traditional Labour policies. This had led to Corbyn's successful re-election campaign and at least 3% of the potential labour vote leaking to left wing independent labour candidates. But there is no doubt Starmer's stand with Donaldson and reneging on Labours traditional support for a united Ireland had divided the party activists, demotivated some of its voting base, and encouraged many to vote for other candidates.

Starmer was now even more open to the charge of being "more conservative than the conservatives themselves" because he was obliged to implement many Conservative party manifesto policy priorities by the confidence and supply arrangement and his dependency on conservative votes in the House of Commons to get any legislation through. If anything, the charge was that he was far more competent at implementing conservative policies than the conservatives had ever been.

The last thing Starmer needed, therefore, was to split the party further by emphasizing his support for a pro UK vote in the Border Poll. He tried to avoid the issue entirely, saying only that he respected the right of the Northern Irish people to make up their own minds on the issue, and expressed confidence that they were well able to do so. Donaldson was entirely frustrated in his efforts to get Starmer to make far more concrete and positive financial proposals to encourage Northern Ireland voters to vote for the Union. He only visited Northern Ireland once, on a largely ceremonial occasion, and spoke to party leaders and the media hardly at all.

But neither did he make any further comment on the Irish government white paper, and there seemed to be hardly any substantial further discussions on the Irish White Paper by officials from both governments. Had they had their fingers burned by going too far in their initial discussions? Was the British government now considering reneging on some of the proposals, and particularly on the co-funding of the Barnett subvention for 20 years? The Tories made great play of the costs involved, while ignoring complaints that the proposals had first been developed under their watch.

Starmer's position was further complicated by the fact that he was desperately trying to get a better trade deal with the EU. The Trade and Cooperation Agreement between the UK and EU was "paper thin" and applied only to manufactured goods, when 70% of the UK economy was in services. The City was slowly losing ground in its position as a leading global financial services centre.

How on earth had Johnson not insisted that financial services be part of the deal? There had, effectively, been "No Deal" on services, despite the City being part of Johnson's home base.

But there was no point in blaming the Conservatives now. Starmer had campaigned on the basis of making Brexit work better. And to get a better deal from the EU he needed Irish government support. They, in common with all EU member states, had a veto on any revised trade deal. And Dublin wasn't being noticeably proactive in its support. Brussels wasn't showing any great urgency either. Everyone appeared to be playing a waiting game.

But time was running out. The Christmas recess came and went. Labour was losing even more ground in the polls because the economy wasn't showing any noticeable improvement. The Conservative's had a new and energetic leader in former Home Secretary Priti Patel who was making noises about the confidence and supply agreement approaching its "best before date." Wry observers were wondering if it might also lose its CE mark!

Virtually every problem Starmer faced had been created for him by the Conservatives, but that cut little ice with the electorate. They wanted solutions. They wanted them now. And it was his responsibility to deliver them.

6. A tale of two General Elections

The Irish government was getting increasingly desperate. The publication of the White Paper had cut into Sinn Féin's lead – it was now down to 35% - still close to the highest it had ever achieved, but perhaps not enough to form a government as it would have difficulty attracting sufficient coalition partners.

But rumours continued to circulate that if Fianna Fáil did badly, it would dump their leader, Tánaiste and ex Taoiseach, Micheál Martin, and install a leader more amenable to cutting a coalition deal with Sinn Féin. Others felt that would spell the death knell for Fianna Fáil. The Irish electorate had traditionally dealt harshly with junior coalition parties. Some never recovered. Why vote Fianna Fáil, when you end up getting Sinn Féin? You might as well vote for the real thing.

Leo Varadkar wasn't helping coalition stability by continuing to go on solo runs on the need for tax cuts and providing incentives for people to work harder and longer. "To much marginal income was being taken away by high marginal tax rates kicking in below the average industrial wage". Fianna Fáil didn't necessarily disagree with him, but it resented him trying to steal all the political credit.

It became clear that everyone was holding back until progress was made on the UK agreeing to the White Paper as published by the Irish government. The Irish government couldn't hope to win the general election without assurances that the UK would support the deal. They were not even committing to holding a referendum on Irish reunification if the Northern Poll was carried until a satisfactory "phased transfer of obligations and funding" was agreed with the UK government.

This raised the nightmare scenario of Northern Ireland voting to leave the Union, and yet not being incorporated into the Irish state. Northern Ireland would become a sort of "no man's land," a pariah territory nobody wanted and with a hard border with Ireland if only for security reasons. The political vacuum and insecurity would almost certainly guarantee that large scale violence would break out, and that would make any referendum in the south even more difficult to carry. That situation had to be avoided at all costs, but everyone seemed to be waiting for everyone else to blink.

Eventually, the Irish Government could wait no more. It had to call a general election for March at the latest. Without a deal they were likely to lose to Sinn Féin.

Starmer was looking down the barrel of a gun as well. If new Tory party leader Priti Patel pulled the plug on the deal over the ECHR issue, he was anything but certain to win re-election. Illegal immigration had become an incendiary issue in Britain, and Patel had made it the centrepiece of her successful leadership election campaign.

The Labour Party hadn't become any less divided in the meantime, Corbyn was being lionised by the press, and there was a growing leftwing chorus of opposition to his policies from the many ambitious people he had left out of his government. Starmer loyalists were becoming thinner on the ground after all the compromises he had had to make with the Tories to secure election as Prime Minister.

Starmer wasn't making much progress with Brussels and a Sinn Féin government seemed sure to pursue a harder line on any "phased transfer of obligations and funding" deal. They weren't making helpful noises on the Brussels impasse either.

If former Tory leadership contender, Michael Howard, was said to have had "something of the night about him," Sir Keir Starmer could be said to light up a stage only by getting off it... He wasn't going to win an election based on his charismatic leadership or inspirational oratory. He had to have some concrete achievements to show for his albeit brief period in office.

A deal therefore had to be done. But it had to be better than the tentative proposals prepared by civil servants under the oversight or lack thereof of Conservative Party Ministers. Patel was disowning the phased transfer of sovereignty proposals saying she had never seen them "in their totality" and would have vetoed them if she had.

A summit was called between Varadkar and Starmer for February 21st, 2025, in Armagh. Starmer used the occasion to make good his pledge to support

> "a continuance of the Union between Northern Ireland and the United Kingdom for as long as the people of Northern Ireland wished it to continue, but that if they chose to leave it was important that it was done in a phased, ordered, and structured way so that the continuing rights of British citizens living in Northern Ireland were safeguarded. Britain would continue to play an active role in protecting those rights through the Strand 3 institutions of the Good Friday Agreement, and the protections of the ECHR would continue to apply."

Starmer left Northern Ireland immediately following the press conference after the summit, but Varadkar took the opportunity to stay overnight in Belfast and take in an Ulster rugby match against the Cardiff blues the following day. There he was seen to loudly cheer an excellent performance by the Ulster team. There was a mixture of cheers and boos every time his image appeared on the large screen in the stadium, but to my ear, the cheers slightly edged the boos, particularly when he stood to enthusiastically applaud a rather excellent Ulster try.

Some wags noted that he had taken care not to wear a blue shirt for the occasion. Indeed, he was wearing an Ulster Jersey with the number 14 emblazoned on it in seeming reference to Ulster right wing Robert Baloucoune. Far be it for him to be seen in a left winger's jersey! It made for a handy reference point for my column on the match (as I presume was intended by his handlers).

The Summit agreed the draft treaty, as contained in the Irish government White paper, with one major change. Instead of being tapered over 20 years at £0.75 Billion per year, the subvention payment would be tapered by £1 Billion per year over 15 years. This would save the UK

£37.5 Billion and end their subvention contributions 5 years earlier. Language was added to the White paper to address some of the criticisms unionists had directed towards it, but its core proposals remained substantially the same as I had summarised them in Chapter 5 here and in my lead article in the Tribune at the time of its publication by the Irish government.

The agreement was hailed as a great negotiating coup by Starmer and his allies. Patel denounced it as "facilitating the break-up of the United Kingdom" and stated that the £37.5 Billion saving was "trivial in the context of 15 years", and that it was "beneath the dignity of a major power like Britain to be selling out its birthright for such a sum."

In vain I searched for the last time Patel had actually visited Northern Ireland. All I could find were numerous references to her remarks about how the Irish might starve if their insistence on a backstop led to a no deal Brexit and a restriction on Irish food imports through the British land bridge. Her remarks had been widely condemned as an uncomfortable reminder of the Great Irish Famine which took place under British sovereignty while food was continuing to be exported from Ireland to Britain.

My report also noted that 99% of the deal had been negotiated by British civil servants acting under the authority of a Tory government, even if that government had never formally considered the deal. That detail was omitted in most of the Tory press reports of the Summit.

The deadlock in Brussels over a deal for UK financial services was magically broken soon afterwards. Starmer called a general election for March 28th. "to end the instability in British Politics" (and to avoid having to call one after becoming "the PM who broke up the UK").

He promised to "heal the divisions in the labour Party once they were no longer obliged to implement Conservative policies through the confidence and supply agreement". He made peace with Corbyn by readmitting him into the party and endorsing his candidacy for the general election as an official Labour candidate. He took credit for negotiating a good deal and better choice for the people of Northern Ireland, and a great deal for the City and British financial services with Brussels.

The Irish government now also had a concrete deal they could sell to their electorate both in the general election and in any subsequent referendum campaign. Leo Varadkar had chosen March 14th. as the election date, two weeks before the UK general election. For the first time in recent history, all of Ireland would go to the polls within the same month.

The government parties suggested that it would be far easier to win the Border Poll if the DUP no longer had the bogeyman of Sinn Féin in Government to frighten unionist voters. Some wag even suggested that unionists could now have the option of serving with a conservative Irish government rather than a Sinn Féin First Minister. It did not go down well in Sinn Féin circles.

The Varadkar Starmer deal, combined with steady economic growth and an improving fiscal, inflationary, and housing outlook enabled the Irish government to head off the challenge of Sinn Féin and win re-election by a narrow margin as the government "which had brought Irish Reunification on an agreed basis several steps closer."

Sinn Féin increased its vote and seat count but mostly at the expense of independents and minor parties. Varadkar and Martin again agreed to rotate the Offices of Taoiseach and Tánaiste between them, as Fianna Fáil and Fine Gael had again finished almost neck and neck. The Greens were disappointed at not having done better but put this down to their Green issues being overshadowed by the Northern Ireland Issue. They again agreed to join the Government and Micheál Martin was narrowly elected Taoiseach for a second two and a half year term of office.

This result denied the DUP one of their primary weapons in the UK general election campaign of casting "a likely Sinn Féin led Irish Government" as a bogeyman determined to destroy Ulster unionists' identity. The Varadkar Starmer deal had made it more difficult to maximise fear and uncertainty over the transfer of sovereignty process and reduced doubts about the Irish government's ability to fund re-unification.

There were still plenty of opportunities to provoke fear and uncertainty in their base by spreading misinformation on an industrial scale, but Irish government ministers, ably abetted by the SDLP and to a lesser extent by the Greens, Alliance, and Sinn Féin, were very effective in launching information campaigns dealing with any misunderstandings about the proposed new British Irish Transfer of Sovereignty Treaty.

Unionists bitterly resented all this "electoral interference" by a "foreign power," but the UK government and Northern Ireland Office Minsters didn't seem to have a problem with it. In fact, they regularly hosted "Information sessions" and detailed "clarification talks" followed by press conferences with Irish government cabinet ministers on aspects of the deal within their specific ministerial responsibilities.

Many independent observers commented that they had never seen so much actual policy discussion in a Northern Ireland election before. Nationalist complaints that the 15 year Transition period was far too long were blunted by the obvious complexity of the many issues which had to be tackled if the transition process was to be managed smoothly and the people of Northern Ireland were to have "the best of both worlds."

The sober tone of these sessions, often live on radio or TV, contrasted strongly with the increasingly rabid tone of unionist politicians at the hustings. Irish Ministers seemed to be better informed on the myriad details of the Transition Plan than many unionist party spokespeople. Even hostile questions at public question and answer sessions didn't seem to faze them, and if they did come across a question they couldn't answer, they were quick to promise to come back with an answer within days, and generally did so.

Southern observers were moved to comment that "Ministers were being forced to seriously up their game" in response to all the intense questioning and grilling they received in northern press conferences and debate sessions. I attended virtually all these press conferences and grilled ministers at every opportunity in an effort to restore my credibility with unionist parties.

I was also frequently asked to appear on TV and Radio talk shows discussing the details of the Transition plan to give "the English perspective". The fact that the British government often didn't field a spokesperson for these programmes led to my being seen, increasingly, as a spokesperson for the British government. (I fancied my next job could be in the No. 10 press office. I had seen, at first hand, how they operated, after all!)

I was often accompanied on these shows by representatives of Scottish newspapers who seemed incredibly enthusiastic about the draft British Irish Treaty, believing it to be a template for an agreement they hoped to achieve with England prior to any second Scottish Independence referendum.

With no official spokesperson for the British government generally on the programme, it was often left to me to point out that Treaties are generally between powers that are already sovereign, and that the Good Friday Agreement was an international treaty between the UK and Ireland which had no sunset clause. However, it made no provision for what happened after a Border Poll was carried and how Sovereignty would be transferred. Hence the need for a new Treaty to clarify matters.

The general drift of my comments was that the British government was maintaining an air of studious impartiality on the proposed new British Irish Treaty in order to leave the final decision to the people of Northern Ireland themselves. Starmer had promised to "Support the Union" in the Border Poll, and the fact that Labour was running official candidates in Northern Ireland for the first time in many years indicated that he was hoping to mobilise support for that policy from beyond committed unionist party voters.

However, many observers noted that this was more likely to split the pro-union vote and wouldn't be helpful to unionist candidates in a general election. Some analysts had suggested that some left of centre unionists might vote Labour because of their disillusionment with DUP social policies and who might otherwise vote Alliance. But strangely, Labour had not nominated a candidate in East Belfast where a strong Labour candidate might have done maximum damage to Naomi Long's campaign to retain her seat against Gavin Robinson (DUP). Naomi Long seemed to be popular among supporters of the new British Labour Government.

So far so good. My comments on the Northern Ireland elections weren't regarded as particularly controversial. It was when my comments turned to the elections in England that the fireworks flew:

> *"The Elections in England aren't about Northern Ireland or its place in the Union at all. Opinion polls indicate that most voter's priorities are with fixing the British economy and regard the Irish re-unification issue as a done deal. They don't particularly like the idea of paying for the subvention for another 15 years but seemed happy they would be saving over £100 million over the next 15 years on the subvention they are currently paying in any case.*
>
> *Most voters that thought about the matter at all, thought that the Northern Irish people would be mad to turn down the Irish offer. They would be part of the EU and a dynamic Irish economy. Many resented the fact that Starmer wasn't giving them the option of re-joining the EU and thought that his Brussels deal would benefit mainly rich types in the City...*
>
> *However, Scottish nationalists were following Northern Ireland elections intently, as a successful Transfer of Sovereignty process would be a great precedent for Scotland to negotiate a similar deal..."*

I was going to go on to qualify my remarks somewhat, but it was too late. A rather large constitutional tome flew in my direction, narrowly missing my head, and pandemonium broke out. Ian Paisley jnr., a fellow panellist, had lost the rag...

I was dreading my next call with Matt Casey.

I had done it again and started a minor riot. It had made the news in the Telegraph and some other papers not well disposed to the Tribune. The BBC had shown excerpts on the main news in Britain.

Instead, he was of a rather sunny disposition, congratulating me on my dexterity in moving my head at the last moment. "It must be all that rugby you used to play... I knew it would come in useful some day!" "Yes, I once trained against Owen Farrell" I replied. I think my reference to the former English captain's predilection for head shots was lost on my soccer supporting editor.

He continued by noting that nothing I had said was particularly controversial in Britain and could be evidenced by the results of various opinion polls. If the DUP didn't like it, that was their problem. Our job was to stick to the facts and tell it like it is. He all but said "keep up the good work!".

For the DUP and their unionist allies, this election was now critical to establishing some momentum in advance of the Border Poll campaign. Brexit, the Windsor Framework, the lack of devolved institutions, and government cutbacks were no longer the issue. This was all about protecting the protestant identity within a British sovereign state.

It didn't really matter what the Irish government were offering. It was a foreign government which had no place in the hearts of genuine unionists. Sovereignty was about identity, not economic advantage. They denounced those traitors who "would sell out their heritage for a few pounds more," in reference to better state pension and social welfare rates in the south.

For the first time the unionist parties, and particularly the beleaguered UUP, also made serious well-funded efforts to "reach across the aisle" to "lapsed unionists" and other undecided voters who might not normally vote unionist, or even vote at all. This worried the Alliance party no end. The UUP was trying to eat into their natural base.

To fend off these threats, the Alliance Party refused to get off the fence as to whether they supported the Irish Government white Paper proposals as amended by the Starmer Varadkar deal. They had a pathological fear of losing part of their base by appearing to take one side or the other. They stuck to their line that there were still a lot of details to be worked out, and that Naomi Long would be the best person to cut the best deal for Northern Ireland with either or both governments regardless of how the Border Poll turned out. It was time for "Northern Ireland politicians to engage constructively with both governments in order to get the best deal for everyone". Shouting NO and NO SURRENDER" had gotten Northern Ireland nowhere.

In the end it was all a lot of "sound and fury, signifying nothing". The Northern Ireland General election results ended up much as before. Official Labour party candidates got a derisory two percent of the vote and didn't have any material effect on the outcome in terms of seats. If you added in the Labour party's two percent, parties supporting the Union had managed to narrow the gap between nationalism and unionism to 5 percent – 41 to 36 percent. The Border Poll was going to be keenly contested after all.

Starmer won an overall majority of 30 seats with the Lib Dems falling back slightly but maintaining their lead over the Conservatives. The Conservatives went into another period of near meltdown and elected a safe, white, Eton and Oxford educated, leader. That had worked out so well the last time it was tried… Starmer included many of his left wing critics in his cabinet in an attempt to unify a party that now no longer had to implement Conservative party policies.

Westminster's attention gradually turned to Northern Ireland again. To keep to the original Sunak pledge, the Border Poll didn't have to happen until August 2025, but it was felt that it had to happen in advance of the marching and bonfire season. Consequently, it was scheduled for June

2025, less than 3 months after the general election. It was best to get it over with quickly, one way or the other.

There were to be a few twists in that tale yet.

I reported on all this from my eyrie in Ballyhackamore on the Newtownards Road.

Although my reports dealt increasingly with matters beyond Northern Ireland, centred in Dublin or Westminster, Matt Casey seemed to have no difficulty publishing them. I was no longer the greenhorn who was to confine his reports to "strictly what the PM actually said." A Northern Ireland political correspondent was allowed to comment on things beyond the border.

The BBC also seemed to feel it was worth their while having me on a panel when an English perspective was required. It helped being the Northern Irish Correspondent of the only mainland paper which actually had a correspondent based in Belfast.

I tried very hard not to upset Sammy Wilson, Ian Paisley, or their DUP colleagues quite so much in my subsequent appearances on TV. But the thing was, most of the DUP Westminster MPs seemed to be available only occasionally for panel discussions based in Belfast.

When Sammy Wilson berated me (once again) for knowing nothing about Northern Ireland, I almost felt like saying to him: "well at least I spend more time here listening to what Northern Irish people are really saying than you do!

I don't think that would have gone down very well, coming from a young English reporter...

I was even asked to appear on a Slugger O'Toole panel at the John Hewitt international Summer School in Armagh later that summer. I was savaged by the audience, some of whom seemed to have been waiting in the long grass to get at this opinionated arrogant git who kept telling Northern Ireland people they weren't at the centre of the universe anymore!

Thing was, Northern Ireland *was* becoming the centre of *my* universe. I ate, drank and slept its politics in hostelries and pubs throughout the province. I even picked up a girlfriend over time.

But Sin Scéal Eile, as part of the community here would say!

7. My renewed rugby career!

Shortly after I moved into my apartment in Ballyhackamore I made a point of visiting local rugby clubs in my role as a rugby correspondent and to get to know various local areas better. Rugby camaraderie can transcend all boundaries and I also needed to recover some fitness. My apprentice professional rugby career had been ended by a serious anterior cruciate ligament injury but that was three years ago now and I needed to lose some weight. I had no plan to play rugby anyway seriously again, but it seemed a good way to make some friends and get to know Northern Irish society better.

I played down my previous rugby playing experience, but my cover was blown when a former opponent recognised me from my Oxford playing days and knew about my subsequent academy contract with Sale Sharks. Soon there were several clubs vying for the signature of a star player! I decided to join Malone because they played in the All Ireland League, and I wanted to get more exposure to clubs in the south. After all, I was supposed to be the Tribune Irish Rugby Correspondent as well as my primary political responsibilities.

After only a few training sessions and long before I felt I was ready for serious rugby again I was pushed into their First XV because their regular out half was injured. It's only division two of the league I reasoned, well below even apprentice professional level, or so I thought! The match was against Old Crescent down in the heartlands of Limerick and Munster rugby, and I was soon disabused of that illusion after I had been caught in possession a couple of times and hammered in the tackle.

However, some things are like learning to ride a bicycle and you never quite lose the knack. I kicked a few penalties and conversions, and, late in the game, was fast enough to receive a pass out wide and score a try in the corner. My basic speed had always been my greatest asset as an out half, and I was faster than many wings. The result hinged on my kicking the difficult conversion, but somehow, I managed it. The wind was blowing quite strongly in our favour by that stage and the ball swung in between the posts even though I had aimed for outside the far upright.

I was an instant hero. Beating a Limerick club in their den was a rare feat apparently, and I was forced to drown many a pint bought by teammates and opponents alike. I even got used to the taste of Guinness after the first few. Our hosts were very magnanimous and enquired where Malone had dug out this unknown No. 10. Our regular out half was a natural left footer, and they had been completely wrong footed by some of my moves off my right foot. I couldn't help but notice the overwhelming friendliness and camaraderie between everyone despite the obvious differences in accent and background.

I felt I needed to delve more deeply into the history of Irish rugby for the Tribune.

Irish rugby is quite a unique phenomenon in the world. Despite being predominantly a protestant and unionist sport in Northern Ireland, it never allowed Partition to interfere with its all-Ireland structure. Unlike other sports like soccer, it never set up a separate Northern Ireland Union. This was probably because it was then an overwhelmingly middle and upper class rather than a working class sport, but also because there was a strong camaraderie amongst rugby players and administrators throughout Ireland. Class bonds and loyalties had been stronger than national or sectarian ones.

Ireland had played its first rugby international against England in 1875 and had been competing against England, Wales, Scotland (and later France and Italy) on a regular basis since 1883, so the traditional rivalries ran very deep. For many years Ireland struggled to achieve the same standard as England, Scotland, or Wales, so it was probably just as well that the Union never split into Northern Ireland and Republic Unions, because neither would have been very competitive at international level.

The game was built around clubs playing in provincial leagues with occasional poorly attended matches between the provinces. The provinces did however provide a natural structure for the game when it went professional. The game was just big enough in Ireland to support four quality professional sides. Unlike Wales, there was a pre-existing provincial structure and rivalries to build on covering the whole island, rather than just the south of Wales.

Unlike Scotland, who shut down their Border Reivers professional club when finances were difficult, Ireland did not shut down Connacht, even when it was reliant mainly on players from outside the province. In time, club rugby in the province flourished and started to provide more and more indigenous talent. Neither Scotland nor Wales have a professional club with regional loyalties in huge swathes of their countries.

Munster built on the strong working class tradition of rugby in Limerick and spread its talent development network throughout the province into traditional Gaelic Athletic Association (GAA) football and hurling areas. Having two primary centres in Limerick and Cork was difficult, but the Munster identity was strong enough to make it work.

Leinster, traditionally very reliant on private fee paying schools in Dublin, also spread their net throughout the province competing with the GAA and soccer for footballing talent. It helped that rugby could provide the lure of international sport, and a reasonably lucrative professional career if you were good and dedicated enough.

Throughout the Troubles, Ulster rugby had remained relatively strong and united, albeit centred mainly around unionist areas on the eastern side of the province. Over the years Ulster provided some of the outstanding global stars of the game in Jackie Kyle, Willie John McBride, and Michael Cameron Gibson who were revered throughout the game. Some players of a nationalist background also played the game and there was never a problem with Ulster Rugby remaining part of the Irish Rugby Football Union (IRFU).

Playing God Save the Queen at rare international matches in Belfast and Ireland's national anthem Amhrán na bhFiann (The Soldier's Song) at international matches in Dublin was controversial. Especially so after three Ulster Irish internationals, David Irwin, Philip Rainey, and Nigel Carr were injured by an IRA roadside bomb on their way to training in Dublin, ending Nigel Carr's brilliant international career. (The bomb had been intended for, and killed, Northern Judge Maurice Gibson and his wife, by chance travelling in the next car).

To overcome these tensions, the IRFU commissioned a rugby anthem called Ireland's Call by the world famous northern musician Phil Coulter to be played at all Irish international matches, home or away. Amhrán na bhFiann is still played at home matches in Dublin, but only as a Presidential salute. New Zealand and some of the Pacific Islands have their Haka. Ireland's distinctive contribution to world rugby culture is to have a separate rugby anthem for a team based on players from two sovereign states.

For many, the way Irish rugby has handled the divisions in politics and society on the island is a beacon for how things might be handled in a united Ireland. Gradually, the standard of Irish rugby had risen to the point where Leinster, Munster, Ulster, and Connacht were competing at or near the top end of all competitions they played in, and the Irish team rose to be ranked number 1 in the world.

This was despite France and England having far more elite professional clubs and, together with New Zealand and South Africa, a very competitive semi-professional second tier club competition as well. Could a united Ireland do as well in other spheres was a question lurking at the back of my mind.

There was some concern in Ulster that it was slipping behind the standards of Leinster and Munster and sometimes losing to Connacht as well. Some dated the decline back to 2018 when Irish internationals Paddy Jackson and Stuart Olding were acquitted of rape charges in court but condemned on social media for some WhatsApp messages that were presented as evidence at their trial. Apparently, sponsors were alarmed, and their contracts were terminated for "bringing the game into disrepute". They were forced into exile to continue their club careers in France and England and never played for or in Ireland again.

I felt it was very unfair. If they had been found guilty in court, they would have served their sentence and been rehabilitated in the eyes of the law. Lots of people had been found guilty of far more heinous crimes and yet been re-integrated back into society. But there was no appeal against the judgement of social media and no way of making restitution. Their private WhatsApp messages, written in the aftermath of an end of season drinking binge had been exposed to the world. Their behaviour had been reprehensible, but which of us hasn't done things in private we would rather not remember, never mind have to answer for in public? Can there be justice if there is no means of appeal, making amends, or rehabilitation?

The IRFU was still a very male dominated organisation but was sensitive to claims that it still tolerated a very laddish culture with sexist attitudes towards women. Women's rugby was still in its infancy and had far less resources made available to it. Initially the IRFU tried to justify this on the grounds that virtually all its income was generated by the male international game.

Eventually, in response to protests, and in recognition of the rapid increase of female participation in the sport, they started offering professional contracts to elite women international players as well as improving the coaching and support facilities for women's rugby generally. But women's rugby still had a long way to go before any sort of parity or even competitiveness in the rapidly developing world of women's rugby could be achieved.

I found out the hard way that standards in Ireland's amateur second tier club competitions were improving as well! I continued playing for the club whenever my journalistic commitments allowed, and they gave me some leeway when I was forced to miss training sessions or even matches. Travelling around Ulster and Ireland playing away matches was a very good way of getting to know much of the country.

I was even asked by an Ulster scout if I would consider a trial training session with the Ulster professional team. I thought it would be a good way of getting some background information for any articles I might have to do on Ulster or the Irish team. Playing out half or number 10 in a rugby team is a bit like being the quarter back in American Football or the midfield general in soccer. You are basically expected to call the plays on the pitch within an overall gameplan agreed with the coach and senior players beforehand.

I may have missed three years of playing rugby, but I fancied I was a little bit older and wiser now and had spent much of those three years thinking and writing about the game and how it was evolving at the top level. I knew how Ireland and Ulster wanted to play the game and was keen to see how my thinking about the game tied in with their current coaching philosophy. I really enjoyed training with the Ulster squad and felt I had made a contribution to their discussions after training sessions.

The coaches quite liked my ideas, but the problem was that my strength and conditioning and overall fitness wasn't up to scratch. What was good enough for the second division of the All Ireland League was nowhere near good enough for professional rugby. I knew as much from my academy training days. The coaches were concerned there wasn't any outstanding young talent at out half coming through the academy and said they would consider giving me an academy contract if I hit some very stretching strength, fitness, and conditioning targets ahead of the next season.

I felt I was past all that. I was still in my mid-twenties and young enough to play the game at a top level, but I couldn't bear the thought of starting on that treadmill all over again. Even if I stayed injury free there was no guarantee I would ever make the senior squad and see much game time. Although academy players were expected to combine their training with a third level degree course, combining it with a full time career in journalism was another matter. I had no objection to trying to get a lot fitter but baulked at the targets they set for me. I said I would see how things went but, in my heart, knew I would never make it.

When I was playing in the Sale Sharks academy my ambition had been to make it to the top and play for England. However even before my serious injury, I had doubts about whether I would even make it as a senior club player. There always seemed to be someone else ahead of me in the pecking order. When you have youth on your side you feel it is only a matter of time before you will make the breakthrough into the First XV. I now felt that my promising future was all behind me.

I was therefore shocked to get a call from an Ulster coach some weeks later. There was no way I was even close to the fitness targets they had set me. Apparently, there was an injury crisis among the number 10s in their squad and would I train with the team again. I had been playing quite well with Malone. I was determined not to get my hopes up but couldn't resist the challenge. I trained with the squad and was named for the substitutes bench for the next match. They didn't have another experienced place kicker if their starting out half got injured. As luck would have it, or as fate conspired, that was a European Champion's Cup match against Sale Sharks in the AJ Bell stadium in Manchester.

I thought I might meet some of my old comrades in arms there, but it turned out nearly all the coaching and playing staff had changed and hardly anyone recognised or remembered me. You sweat blood and shed tears for a place, and this is the thanks you get! Ulster played well and were well on top by the time I got onto the pitch in the 75th. minute. My five minutes of fame were remarkable only for the fact that I had to kick a gimme conversion from in front of the posts, catch a couple of passes and kick for touch. It was all about just seeing the team through to full time. I didn't make any mistakes, but neither was my tactical genius required.

I continued to train with the Ulster squad until the end of the season, but my heart wasn't really in it. It was far easier to write about rugby, and the training sessions were beginning to interfere too much with my journalistic duties. I couldn't just cry off for a training session as I had done with Malone.

The border poll was looming.

8. The Border Poll Campaign

The Border Poll campaign felt like one long slog. It seemed Northern Ireland had been in continuous election mode forever. The October UK General Election, The March Irish and UK General elections, and now the June Border Poll. When you combine that with the 2022 Assembly and 2023 Local elections, Northern Ireland certainly didn't lack for elections.

The thing was: they always seemed to produce remarkably similar results. A few seats might change hands here or there, but the politics always remained the same. The constitutional question seemed to be forever unsettled, and it unsettled the whole community, all the time. And it usually dominated everything else.

I say the whole community advisedly. People talk about two communities all the time. But I was still trying to figure out the differences. They seemed to me to be like two sets of football supporters, supporting different teams, wearing different jerseys, shouting abuse at each other, threatening revenge for past defeats. But at the end of the day, they were all just football supporters, sharing a passion for the game.

Catholics didn't seem to be very Catholic anymore. Some I met were more virulently anti-Catholic than any protestant I ever met. They hated their own community's church with a passion. They had felt utterly betrayed by the child sex abuse scandals and the treatment of women and gays by the church.

Sheila Butler, a young Sinn Féin activist and candidate in a mainly unionist area I met was particularly scathing:

> *"It not just that there were sex abusers in the Priesthood. Sex abusers exist in all walks of life, even if the Church insists priests are consecrated and therefore absolutely special, personally in touch with God. It was that the Church had protected the abusers. Lied about their abuse. Failed to report the abuse to the*

criminal investigation authorities. Kept their files on the abusers under lock and key even when the police came to investigate."

I couldn't help noting the irony of a Sinn Féin candidate complaining about Catholics failing to cooperate fully with the RUC, and now the PSNI. She brushed that aside.

"The Church refused to compensate the abused or at least adopted a very adversarial legalistic attitude to them when the abused sought relief. They left the general taxpayer on the hook for the costs. They claimed it was all in the past when social attitudes were very different – when it was the Church that had created and shaped those attitudes in society in the past.

It was the hypocrisy of it all. That Bishops could give lofty sermons condemning all sorts of abuses in public and private life when they themselves were protecting the abusers and allowing them to abuse again. That a Cardinal could say he had a "mental reservation" which allowed him to deliberately mislead people without actually lying, was the last straw. People felt that the church had lost the plot. The Church had always opposed Irish freedom fighters anyway".

That was all in the past, I ventured.

"These same Church leaders are claiming they can condemn the sin without harming the sinner, when gays had been subjected to abuse, torture, and death for many centuries in societies that had been dominated by churchman. Women are still not allowed to be priests and gays are still being bullied and assaulted".

"Irish people, led by Catholics, literally overthrew the church and passed constitutional amendments explicitly against church teaching on contraception, divorce, same sex marriage, and abortion".

"It didn't even matter if they themselves had doubts about the merits of artificial contraception, divorce, same sex marriage or

abortion. The point was that the power of the church to impose their teaching on people had to be overthrown. Right or wrong didn't come into it. People would have to make those decisions for themselves. The Catholic Church had lost the right to make that call."

"In many ways, Irish Catholics became more protestant than the protestants themselves. Indeed, many protestants retained very conservative moral beliefs, and were much more in tune with Catholic Church teaching than the majority of cultural Catholics."

"But weren't there abuses in protestant churches as well?" I offered, well aware of sex abuse scandals in England and in places like the Kincora boy's home in Belfast.

"It wasn't so much that abuses in the protestant churches didn't happen, it was that there wasn't the same hierarchical organisational superstructure that justified and enabled the suppression of the truth. The failings of protestants churchman remained their failings, and they were on their own if they had to face the rigours of the law, even if the police often failed to investigate crimes by protestants properly".

"What drove many young protestants away from their parent's churches wasn't so much any abuses that were uncovered, but that they simply couldn't sustain the literalist interpretations of the bible they were being asked to believe. When science came into conflict with church teaching, they chose science and were not a little embarrassed that they had ever believed in the church teaching in the first place."

"They may have been somewhat resentful at the way in which they had been indoctrinated, but the same level of bitterness, anger, and vituperous rejection of the church wasn't there. They just put it down to the ignorance of the older generations which had been overtaken by science."

It had been quite the diatribe, and I was shocked to be hearing it from a Sinn Féin candidate speaking to a visiting Englishman. I said I was amazed at how open she was to an Englishman about divisions in her own Church and Community. Weren't the English supposed to be the root of all evil in Ireland?

> *"Don't flatter yourself!"* She countered. *"We kicked you lot out of three quarters of our country over 100 years ago, and the final quarter will follow shortly. We are our own worst enemies most of the time now. Sure, didn't Sunak make it clear England would be well rid of us!"*

"Ah yes, but Starmer said he was standing by the union, and didn't he end up the new PM?" I suggested.

> *"That had nothing to do with the Northern Ireland issue. In fact, he would have won an overall majority easily if he had kept well out of it, instead of standing with that idiot, Donaldson, who the English can't abide".*

"Well, they can't understand him much anyway", I agreed, "those who make the effort to try".

Trying to summarise her comments for my report I tried to reflect her views back to her:

"So younger protestants have drifted away from their inherited faith, while younger Catholics had bitterly rejected theirs. And still we have two communities described as protestant and Catholic, at loggerheads with each other, when often the divisions within are more acute?"

> *"Not as much as you might think"* she replied, *"I would estimate that at least 500 of my 2041 votes in the election had to have come from Protestants. There simply aren't enough nationalists in my Constituency to give me 2,000 votes".*

"So why did you bother standing?" I asked. You had no chance of winning, and you nearly scuppered Naomi Long's incredibly tight victory.

"I have absolutely no problem with Naomi. She is going to be incredibly important in the new Ireland. But more and more of Alliance votes are coming from people who might otherwise vote for candidates supporting Ireland, and its time the Alliance party recognised that."

"So, you did months and months of hard canvassing, pounding the pavements in often hostile areas, for 2,000 votes when you had absolutely no chance of winning? What was the point?"

"Those 2,000 votes are going to be incredibly important in the Border Poll, where they will count the same as votes in the Ardoyne. It's the same as your Brexit poll. People living in safe constituencies who never bothered to vote before because it would make no difference to the result came out and voted in protest at the establishment and a system which gave them no effective voice."

"So, you approved of the Brexit vote?", I asked, my Remainer hackles raised.

"I approve of a system where people can actually have a say, as in our Border Poll?" She countered.

"So, you will accept the result of the Border Poll, whichever way it goes?"

"We can always have another poll in seven years' time, the younger generation is overwhelmingly pro-Ireland, and they are coming of age all the time. Unionists have to win every battle. We only have to win once and the war is over, decided in our favour".

"Do you really think loyalists will accept that?"

"Some won't, but we are fighting a long war which won't entirely end with the Border Poll. It only marks the end of English interference. The task of truly uniting Ireland will only just have begun. As I said before, we are often our own worst enemies, and that applies to protestants as much as Catholics."

I was astonished at her long term strategic vision. She seemed to have a plan stretching many years ahead, and it didn't feature herself in a lead role. I asked her why not a leadership role for herself?

> *Any unionists who agree to work with the government in a united Ireland will be fêted and lionised and offered cabinet positions. Working class nationalists like myself will be ignored. Ireland is, after all, primarily a class society.*

"But will there not be violence?"

> *"Of course, there is violence in all class societies. Some political systems are just better at disguising, hiding, containing, or suppressing it. Loyalists are the dupes here. They think we are their enemies. In fact, it's the posh middle class unionists who really hold them in contempt. I got quite a positive reception on some loyalist doorsteps when I explained what I was really for – stuff like better community infrastructure, less drugs, better educational opportunities, better jobs, a fairer distribution of income."*

"Did you really canvass for Sinn Féin in loyalist heartlands?"

> *I canvassed for myself. The Sinn Féin logo wasn't very prominent. I focused on the bread and butter issues. If anyone drew attention to the united Ireland issue, I said Ireland has its inequality and unfairness issues as well, but at least we could have a much greater say in addressing them than we have with a government in Westminster. That seemed to strike a chord".*

I expressed my astonishment that she had the chutzpah to canvass in Loyalist areas. "You are very brave" I said, barely able to conceal my admiration.

> *"Oh, I had a couple of lads in a car following me at a discrete distance in case I had to make a quick getaway. We had to scarper on a few occasions when the local UVF people became aware of my presence. However, I was even invited into the*

house for a cup of tea on a couple of occasions, and that had my minders really worried. They ended up knocking on the door to make sure I was alright!"

"You really worked hard for those 500 votes!"

"Well, it was more than Gavin Robinson (the DUP candidate) did. I heard he hadn't been seen about the place except at election time. Anyway, the unionists were more worried about Naomi Long. I hear she was really harassed all over the place. They possibly had no problem with my candidacy as any votes I got only split the anti-DUP vote."

"So, you were really working for the DUP candidate then", I said mischievously.

"As I said. I have nothing but admiration for Naomi. Any woman that stands up to that amount of abuse would get my vote. But I was going for mainly working class voters who weren't going to vote for Naomi anyway. I didn't care if they were loyalist or republican. Naomi winning was a great fillip for women and for the Ireland cause. It showed that unionism was in retreat even in its own back yard. But ultimately the general election didn't matter anyway. It was all about the Border Poll. And I was hoping to deliver at least 2000 votes from my constituency for Ireland, and the more loyalist votes that included, the better."

"But surely no self-respecting loyalist would vote for a united Ireland".

"You'd be surprised. They're famously thrann, and their thinking is not as uniform as you might think. A few of them said to me on the qt that they thought a united Ireland was inevitable, sooner or later, and that they might be better off to get it over with sooner rather than later. It was going to be too late to make much difference to their lives, but they were hoping for a better future for their kids. Some of their kids had gotten into trouble with drugs and loyalist gangs. There had to be a better way."

I have to say I was astonished at our conversation. I felt like I had made a friend for life. I wrote a long piece on our conversation for the Tribune, anonymised at her request, which I was surprised Matt Casey published. I was waiting for an angry reaction from some of my unionist contacts, but they seemed not to have heard of the piece. Political conversations were still dominated by the outcome of the Westminster elections.

People like Sheila Butler were still working under the radar. I wondered how many Sheila Butlers there might be, working in every constituency for a pro-Ireland vote.

> *"Oh, there's a lot of us, she said. We're seen as political no hopers and losers because most of us don't get elected. But that's not the point. The point is to change the system entirely, and every vote counts, if not now, then in the Border Poll and in a future united Ireland.*

Strangely, I never heard of unionists canvassing for votes in nationalist areas. They seemed to be focused on bringing out the vote in their own areas. There was lots of flags and bunting. Lots of rallies and early bonfires. They were often very well attended, but they always seemed to be preaching to the converted. Loyalist and unionist politicians preached fire and brimstone and doom and gloom if republicans prevailed. Their traditions and Britishness were under threat, and it would be the end of civilisation as they knew it.

I wrote quite of few stories on these gatherings, but most ended up on Matt Casey's spike. It led to accusations that my reporting was one sided. Some of my unionist contacts started treating me with suspicion. They expressed extreme scepticism at opinion polls showing voting intentions in the Border Poll to be extremely close – often within the margin of error. Unionists had never been so united, they claimed, and a lot of previously unaligned voters were coming round to the view that the devil they know is better than the devil they don't.

Their job was to put the fear of God into undecided voters that everything they took for granted was at risk. It didn't help that the new

Labour Secretary of state, Peter Kyle, was seeming to put a lot of that at risk by announcing still more budget cuts and service cutbacks. It seemed strange to me that a Secretary of State with a doctorate in community development should be presiding over so many cuts in community services. I managed to get an interview:

> *"It's not that I want to introduce all these cutbacks, but the UK budgetary position leaves me with no choice. The PM has committed to balancing the books and reducing our national debt. The cuts in England are just as savage, as I know from my own constituency of Hove. Donaldson has been trying to get me to delay the announcements until after the Border Poll, but I really can't take sides in that debate or attempt to put my foot on the scales, one way or the other."*

"But I thought Starmer was all for standing by the Union?" I asked...

> *Yes, absolutely, but that means treating Northern Ireland the same way as the rest of the UK. Otherwise, Scotland and Wales will be holding us to ransom. I can tell you my constituents in Hove are pretty angry at all the cutbacks there and feel everyone else is getting special treatment at their expense.*

"But you are happy to take money from the Irish government for student loans, nurse training, and infrastructural projects like roads, bridges and college facilities?"

> *I'll take money wherever I can get it. Our economy is in a pretty desperate state and our tax revenues have collapsed. Anything which can help maintain services and investment without damaging our balance sheet is a godsend, frankly. When I was younger, I worked as a British aid worker in war torn areas of Eastern Europe. It feels strange now that the boot is on the other foot, but don't quote me on that!*

"Some small businesses are announcing their closures, citing difficulties in getting supplies from Britain and an increased administrative burden. Some owners I interviewed said their sales had been declining anyway, and it simply wasn't worth the hassle anymore. They blame the British government and the Windsor framework, but some added sotto voce, that the DUP weren't blameless either. It seemed to be mostly unionist owned businesses serving unionist areas that were closing."

> "Businesses have a great opportunity to expand their horizons to the Irish and European markets, but some are too small to take advantage or have managements very set in their ways. I have quite a bit of experience of businesses in Hove having difficulties with Brexit as well.
>
> As you know I was a Remainer and advocated having a second referendum on the terms of the Brexit deal. We only lost that vote by 12 votes! It's standard practice in trade union circles to have a poll on withdrawing your labour, and a second poll on whether to accept a proposed settlement deal.
>
> I don't think people ended up getting the Brexit they thought they were voting for but at least the Starmer Varadkar deal gives people here great clarity on what a transfer of sovereignty would look like, and I support that.
>
> The Irish have been great at attracting foreign direct investment (FDI), but I don't think all the political instability here has been helpful. Personally, I think it's best to leave the decision on sovereignty entirely up to the people of Northern Ireland. Some are so contrary; they wouldn't take our advice too seriously anyway. We only got 2 percent in the election here."

Matt published my report on the interview, but it didn't seem to cause much of a stir, even after a sub-editor headlined it with "**How can a party with 2 percent of the vote claim the Secretary of State role?**" I gradually stopped doing stories on the economic side of things because they didn't seem to be getting published. The headline political news was all about what the political leaders were saying – Jeffrey Donaldson, Michelle O'Neil, Naomi Long , Doug Beattie and Colin Eastwood.

Westminster leaders didn't seem to be saying very much at all. Quite a few Brexiteer and Tory politicians came over to Northern Ireland to give speeches and interviews. Most had lost their seats and were regarded as being on the extreme right of the political spectrum. They were rather annoyed when my reports on their statements didn't get published. They were yesterday's men and women as far as the British media were concerned.

Nigel Farage got quite angry when I told him that my editor said his utterances weren't very newsworthy in England anymore. "This is the same as the run-up to Brexit" he declared. "The establishment media didn't report my comments until after we had won the Brexit referendum. I'm sure that the British people in Northern Ireland will rise up once again and tell the establishment what they really wanted. It's time to tell the EU and the Irish to bugger off and mind their own business."

But politicians coming from the mainland didn't seem to have their ears very close to the ground in Northern Ireland. I was finding more and more pockets of people from a unionist background who seemed to have an open mind on the Border Poll and who were very interested in what the Irish government had to say.

Matt Casey seemed to be very interested in stories about what those people had to say. Most of them didn't feel their Britishness was under threat and were positively disposed towards Ireland. Their decision would be a pragmatic one based on whoever they thought might provide the better governance. The last thing they wanted was to be ruled by vigilante gangs, whether loyalist or republican. Some seemed very re-assured that Sinn Féin had failed to lead the southern Government.

Others pointed out that Presbyterians had once before, in 1798, been allied with Catholics against the British and Anglican establishment. 30,000 of them had been slaughtered by the English for their involvement or sympathy for the rebellion in the aftermath. There was a whole history of Scots Presbyterian dissenters aligning with Catholics swept under the carpet. It later became inconvenient to recall this history once discrimination against dissenters ended, and they changed their allegiance to the English Anglican establishment. But they had always regarded themselves as Irish. This emphasis on the "Britishness" of northern protestants was a relatively recent invention.

Opinion polling was showing that the "don't knows" were still always much larger than the gap between the pro and anti-united Ireland voters in the referendum. How they ended up voting, if they voted at all, would determine the outcome.

It was still all to play for.

9. The people decide.

The more I spoke to people, the more confused I was getting. The situation seemed to be infinitely more complex than the simple protestant versus Catholic, unionism versus nationalism, loyalist versus republican narrative that seemed to be the staple of most reporting about the province in the mainstream mainland media. Yes, they did note that the battle was for the centre ground, but most seemed to have little idea of what the centre ground consisted of. It seemed to me to be even less homogenous than either the unionist or nationalist camps.

There were also a lot of seeming contradictions: Sheila had highlighted the contradictions within Catholicism and nationalism. There seemed to be an infinite number of strands within Protestantism and unionism as well. But it was the class divisions that really interested me. Working class protestants and Catholics seemed to have far more in common with each other than their middle class counterparts.

And the same applied to the middle classes in reverse. Middle class protestants seemed to be far more embarrassed at the antics of some of the unionist leaders than their Catholic counterparts, who often just shrugged their shoulders, "what do you expect?" Both were equally horrified at the antics of the paramilitaries, and it didn't seem to matter which side the paramilitaries claimed to be on.

You had the weird combination of many Catholics feeling that the IRA had done more harm to the prospects for Irish re-unification than the protestants ever did, and the protestants now feeling that the DUP had done more to help the cause of Irish re-unification than any Catholic politician or party.

And yet the DUP and Sinn Féin had become the dominant parties in their respective communities all but destroying the erstwhile dominant political parties, the UUP and the SDLP, which had ended the conflict and brought 25 years of relative peace through negotiation and compromise.

People were voting for the war mongers and punishing the peace makers who had not exactly become the sons of God as claimed by the beatitudes, certainly not if the Kingdom of God was ever to be built on this earth.

These sorts of things were seriously taxing on the mind of a young English reporter trying to get to grips with the dynamics of Northern Irish society. How could all these myriad complexities and contradictions always crystalise around "British" and "Irish" identities and whether or not the British or Irish governments should be sovereign?

Having observed the actual operation of the British and Irish governments at relatively close hand, I cannot say there are any great differences that should attract such devoted allegiances. Many Irish live under British sovereignty in Britain and increasing numbers of British live under Irish sovereignty in Ireland, and it doesn't seem to affect their sense of self, identity, self-esteem, culture or belonging to a community over much.

The exercise of sovereignty is the practical outworking of government – who you pay your taxes to, who you get your public services from, which laws you have to obey, and what politicians you elect. Is that really oh so different in Britain or in Ireland?

It used to be the colour of the post boxes that differentiated Britain from Ireland. But the postal delivery was much the same. Now it may be the emblem on the website where you order your public services card.

Why is it only in Northern Ireland that you can only express your identity through that identity being embodied in the state? Can you not wave your flags, go to your churches, march in your parades, and support your football team regardless of whether those same flags fly on city hall? And cannot both sets of flags fly on city hall and let us be done with it?

Must we turn society in two giant teams wearing different colours kicking lumps out of each other? Is that the only way we can get our kicks? Why not keep the football for the football pitch

It was with these sorts of mixed thoughts and confused feelings that I sought to make sense of the Border Poll campaigns. On the one hand a united Ireland was being painted as a Nirvana that would solve all ills. On the other it was being painted as the devil's handiwork, scheming to lure you in to your own certain and painful death.

I simply could not understand how either vision could bear any resemblance to the boring, mundane, fraught, capricious, and chance processes of government I had seen in action. If the Border Poll was carried, one side was going to be very disappointed, and the other mightily relieved. But would it really make all that much difference to the work you had to do, to the services you had to access, and to the lives ordinary people had to live?

Changing the colour of your jersey is not as difficult as some seem to think. You can support the other team and enjoy the football match just as much. Although sometimes it can be more fun to be on the team that's winning. Having been on the receiving end of pastings by some excellent Irish rugby teams, I know which team I would like to join, had I ever made it as a professional player.

Northern Presbyterians used to be on the same team as Catholics when 30,000 of them were slaughtered by the English after the 1798 uprising. They quickly switched teams when the English offered them the prospect of emancipation. Too bad their Catholic allies had to be left behind. They spent two centuries trying to suppress those memories, as recounted in Claire Mitchell's" The Ghost Limb". Perhaps the time has come to change jerseys and switch teams again.

I, as an Englishman, certainly couldn't blame them. Other than the Barnett subvention, it didn't seem that England had been doing them too many favours in recent times. Having been, by far, the most prosperous part of Ireland prior to partition. It was now the poorest region of the UK with a standard of living falling rapidly behind the Republic. The public service cuts begun under the Tories had continued under Labour. All the news I was getting from back home was that the real economy was in a terrible state and that previously comfortable people were having trouble making ends meet.

It didn't seem to me that Northern Ireland was being singled out for special treatment. The Starmer government, now with an overall majority, was having a terrible time trying to keep the economy afloat. The Tory press was blaming all this on the alleged left wingers Starmer had brought into his government after the March general election, but in reality, they were inheriting problems which had had their origins many years before.

I certainly couldn't see the Border Poll in either the apocalyptic terms painted by unionism, nor the idealistic terms painted by northern nationalists. The southerners of all stripes I met painted it in much more critical colours. But at least it wasn't facing the immediate meltdown which seemed to be the mood in Britain. At least unionists had a choice, something that could not be said for the people of Scotland, England, or Wales.

There was a lot of discontent, and a general air of crisis in Britain. Few seemed to have much confidence that the Starmer government had the situation under control. And even if Labour were showing a renewed sense of unity and purpose, the Tories were a shambles and the Lib Dems were only beginning to learn the ropes of how to be a serious opposition. They seemed to be more concerned with staving off any potential Tory revival than with replacing Labour in government.

Despite the imminence of the Border Poll, things seemed a lot more settled down south. On my few visits to Dublin I got the sense that the government was at least trying to tackle the housing and healthcare crises. They may have been re-elected by a very narrow majority and faced an energetic and increasingly confident opposition in Sinn Féin . But they also seemed to have a handle on issues relating to the north.

Numerous meetings were taking place with anyone who would meet them to clarify any aspects of the 400 page white paper that needed fleshing out following the Varadkar Starmer Agreement. More and more discussion documents were being issued giving great detail on how pensions issues, civil service transfers, corporate taxes, income tax, and differences in current social welfare contributions and entitlements would be tackled. Many of these papers were seriously boring, but at least they gave the impression of much hard thinking being done on how systems could be harmonised, and concerns addressed.

Micheál Martin was back in the Taoiseach's seat following a power sharing agreement between Fianna Fáil and Fine Gael. He was a conciliatory figure who exasperated northern nationalists to distraction but was hard to paint as a bogey figure for unionists. He kept focusing on the practical nuts and bolts of public service sharing and infrastructural projects that could benefit both parts of Ireland. He wasn't so much interested in taking over Northern Ireland, as working with the people of Northern Ireland for everyone's benefit. He was almost portraying the Border Poll as a vote in favour of partnership and shared problem solving north and south, with sovereignty very much a background issue.

It was hard to oppose the "common sense" aspects of these projects. If only Jeffrey Donaldson and Michelle O'Neill had been able to work together as well! Some unionists who had supported the boycott of the devolved institutions were bemoaning the fact that they had driven themselves into a corner from which they had yet to find an escape.

Apparently there had been some behind the scenes discussions with both the British and Irish governments to give some cover to the DUP to get back into devolved government. But no one seemed to be terribly interested in trying to address their concerns even when they watered down their initial seven demands. The political agenda had simply moved on to the Border Poll.

Promising to re-enter the Assembly and Executive if the Border Poll was defeated was a classic case of too little, too late. Why on earth could they not have found a way of doing so before a Border Poll was called, or at least before the two general elections took place? If the Union really was the best option for all, why on earth had they not made a greater effort to ensure that it did work for all?

The Tánaiste, minister for economic development, Industry and Commerce, Leo Varadkar seemed to be as conservative as many unionists on economic matters, favouring the private sector over government intervention, wherever possible. He could be a natural ally for addressing many of the concerns of unionist business and agricultural interests.

He clearly had the ear of Brussels and could be a powerful advocate on their behalf. Who, in unionism, had any significant influence outside Northern Ireland? Inviting over failed and discredited Tory politicians to speak at unionist rallies didn't count for much in the real world.

Agriculture was a miniscule part of the total UK economy, and few farmers vote Labour anyway. The Starmer government's decision to dramatically reduce farmer support payments way below EU levels meant northern farmers faced extinction. At least English farmers were competing with Australian, New Zealand, and Latin American farmers who faced considerable additional transportation costs. But Northern Ireland farmers were competing with southern farmers just down the road who derived most of their income from EU subsidies. The money they got for selling their produce to the market was just a bonus.

Some northern farmers were already talking about selling up their farms. There seemed to be a lot of money pouring in from the south buying up any land and property that came on the market. It was the only thing keeping land and property prices any way stable.

Unionists speculated darkly that there was a conspiracy to take over Northern Ireland by stealth. That all the southern people buying up farms and houses were really only doing so to stuff the electoral register.

There certainly were a few suspicious cases of 11 voters suddenly being registered to vote from one address. But when I interviewed people highlighted as having moved up from the south, it was the stark differences in house prices and the ability to work from home that greatly influenced their decisions. If anything, they were concerned at the welcome they would receive from their unionist neighbours.

There were some isolated cases of intimidation reported and people being told "you are not wanted here". I spoke to some, but they were holding their heads down and anxious not to talk or be publicised in the media.

Off the record they said that most had welcomed them and that their children were getting on well in local schools. The politics of the situation did not seem a major concern for them other than as a negative factor they had to be careful about. Even if registered, they were not sure they would vote. The border seemed to mean very little to them, except that it could complicate who you paid your income and property taxes to and where you qualified for health benefits.

I was beginning to get very comfortable in my new role, driving up and down the country interviewing people who were either political candidates or businessmen and farmers who had come to my attention via local news reports. I always introduced myself as a reporter from the Tribune and that seemed to be a good enough reason for them to talk to me.

I never felt in any danger even though there had been sporadic reports of violent incidents. All seemed anxious to get my take on how events were unfolding both in Britain and Ireland. I always said that the news from Britain wasn't good and that the polls in Northern Ireland were too close to call, and that it all depended on who actually voted on the day.

It came as a complete shock to me when I heard that Sheila had been assaulted and injured and that two men had been seriously injured in an incident on a loyalist estate not far from where I lived. I was in Enniskillen at the time but hurried back to the Royal Victoria Hospital where the injured had been taken.

Claiming to be Sheila's brother, I blagged my way into her ward. I was not proud of myself but was genuinely very upset and concerned. I was embarrassed to see her surrounded by her family and said I would come back to see her later. She seemed very surprised but not too displeased to see me and motioned for me to stay.

I kept as quiet and unobtrusive as I could. I gathered that her injuries were not too serious, but that she was being kept in for a few days for observation to ensure everything was alright. She was very concerned for her two friends who had been driving a car keeping an eye on her and who had been set upon before they could get away. Most of her injuries had been incurred trying to protect them from a mob who were beating and kicking them. Some of the people whom she had been canvassing eventually came to their aid.

Sean had suffered head injuries that were initially described as "life threatening" but had since been re-described as "life altering, but stable". Both had suffered quite a few broken bones, but Ciaran's condition was now being described as comfortable.

I had completely forgotten that I was supposed to be a reporter taking notes and preparing to write a story. I stayed at her bedside for a couple of hours even after most of her family had left and missed my deadline for filing a story. It didn't seem to matter. This was personal. This was real. This was no longer me playing a newspaper game.

I was therefore surprised when Sheila asked me what I was going to write. I said I wasn't planning on writing anything, and she said I should. She said I should write about all the decent people on the estate she had been talking to, some of whom had come to their aid. She even offered to give me some notes she had been keeping of previous canvassing tours.

I later managed blag my way to see Ciaran (a posh accent helps) and he looked anything but comfortable. Absolutely devastated would be a more accurate description. Sean was still in intensive care.

With some trepidation I followed up on Sheila's notes and interviewed a few locals for my story on the incident. The atmosphere seemed to have changed a lot since her general election canvass.

Before, she had been received with benign amusement as a young woman on a fool's errand, and with no hope of success. Now the atmosphere was deadly serious. People were arguing with her and challenging her on many points she had made without being challenged in the past. She wasn't sure she could still deliver on the 2,000 votes from her constituency she had promised Sinn Féin head office.

I tried to reassure her that there were still the 22,000 people who had voted for Naomi Long. "Those are nearly all Pro-union voters in East Belfast" They are the people who want to make Northern Ireland work better as part of the union and think she would be good at making this happen. We'd be lucky to get 20 percent of those".

It was hard to argue with her hardheaded realism. She did however get flowers sent to her by the local Church of Ireland Rector who sympathised with her and her companions and said in the note that many of his parishioners were shocked at what had happened.

I chatted with a few people I knew in my local in Ballyhackamore and also wandered up to Knock to chat to a few more of a more middle class persuasion. All condemned the incident without reservation although a few said she had no right to be there. I did a long story on the incident which was featured on the main politics page of the Tribune. It was not as if it was the only or even the most serious incident during the campaign. It was just that it was the one I knew about most, and which seemed to encapsulate a lot of the problems of Northern Ireland.

Apparently, Naomi Long came to see Sheila in her home a few days later. Political pros tend to have a lot of respect for each other even if they are in opposing parties. Naomi was horrified at what had happened and recalled quite a few scary incidents that had happened to her. She was fortunate that, being a much more prominent politician, she generally now had a couple of undercover PSNI minders whenever she was out and about. It wouldn't do Britain's international reputation any good if it could not safeguard the lives of its parliamentarians.

Naomi was also apoplectic at how the Border Poll campaign was unfolding. Instinctively she supported the Union but had to remain studiously neutral in public. But the British government was making it very hard for her to maintain that neutrality. She described the Starmer government as uninterested, and the new Secretary of State, Peter Kyle as useless.

> "He's more interested in gay rights and international business issues. He's completely washed his hands of any responsibility to make the case for the Union."

By way of contrast, the Irish government was:

> "really on the ball and doing a great job of addressing every concern as it was raised and seemed genuinely interested in developing a north south partnership rather than a one-sided takeover".

Naomi was also quite taken with Micheál Martin's calm and statesmanlike approach and the level of resources the Irish government was throwing at the campaign. She had promised to make a recommendation to the Northern Ireland people before the poll and was coming under increasing pressure to do so sooner rather than later. Majority opinion in the party seemed to be leaning toward a pro-Ireland vote but there would be a major split when she did make her recommendation. The knives were still in their sheaths but would come out as soon as she did so.

She didn't give Sheila any indication of which way she would go with her recommendation, but Sheila got the distinct impression she was leaning towards the pro-Ireland position. Naomi had said this matter had to be resolved, one way or the other, sooner or later, and a pro-Ireland vote was the only way of doing that. A narrow pro-union vote would only tee things up for another referendum in seven years' time, and she couldn't bear to live through that.

I had been in on a group interview with Naomi only a week before and she had been far less forthcoming than that, maintaining Alliance's formal position of neutrality on the vote, pending further discussions with both the British and Irish governments. The interview was so anodyne, the Tribune hadn't even published my report, despite Naomi being recognised as the pivotal figure in the campaign. "Whatever you say, say nothing" was my editor's acerbic put down of my piece. I could almost hear it being pierced by his metaphorical spike.

I was half tempted to re-write the report based on what Naomi has said to Sheila at their private meeting but realised that would break my relationship with both. Some things were simply more important than a journalistic scoop, and Sheila had trusted me with the details of their private meeting knowing I was a journalist. I had to respect that relationship.

My editor never got to hear of that other meeting. He would have told me to use anonymous sources. But the point is Sheila, and perhaps Naomi, would have known where it came from, and it would have destroyed their trust in me and in each other.

Sinn Féin kept an incredibly low public profile throughout the campaign. Perhaps they had lost some self-confidence having failed to make it into government in the south. Perhaps they felt their presence would be counterproductive.

As usual, their message discipline was extraordinary. They were all in favour of the people of Northern Ireland having their say on their own future, and they would accept the result, whichever way it went. If any pro-union voters were motivated by a desire to give Sinn Féin a bloody nose, they would have been hard put to find a nose to punch. Nearly all of the running was made by the Irish government, with the SDLP playing a bit part support role.

Reports indicated that Sinn Féin were very active on the ground. Sheila confirmed there seemed to be no end of money to pay specially selected and trained "volunteers" to spread the message that a united Ireland was the only way to go, including in areas well outside Sinn Féin heartlands. There was also a huge voter registration effort and offers to organise lifts to the polls on the day for the aged and infirm.

Many of the volunteers were impeccably dressed in suits and could have been mistaken for Mormon missionaries. The always canvassed in male and female pairs and had a prompt card of well phrased replies to "Frequently Asked Questions" and a general briefing on all the advantages of a united Ireland for farmers, businesses, jobs, pensions, the standard of living and having more control than being subservient to a remote government in Westminster.

Sheila gave me a copy of each, and they were impressively well written and produced. Apparently, volunteers had to more or less learn them off by heart if they wanted the job. I tried picking holes in the documents, and while they omitted many details, the points made seemed solid enough.

Two weeks before the vote, the Alliance Party held a party conference, and, following a heated debate on the outcome of discussions with the two governments, decided, by a roughly two thirds majority, to come down on the side of the Irish government having made the better offer. The unionist parties were dismissive saying they always knew Alliance was "a closet pan-nationalist party and that Naomi had been bought off by the promise of a cabinet seat in Dublin."

It was an understandable jibe, but the cause of unionism was lost, even if only by a small margin, by that declaration. The Alliance decision was the signal for many undecided and relatively uninformed voters to get off the fence. It also gave cover to many middle class voters anxious not to upset their unionist neighbours.

The Border Poll was carried by 51.3% to 48.7%, much tighter than the last opinion polls had predicted when undecided voters were excluded from the calculation. Clearly not all undecideds had come down on the side of a united Ireland, and there may even have been some shy Catholic Unionist supporters who hadn't revealed their preference to the pollsters.

Any number of things might have given the unionist cause the extra 1 or 2% they needed to carry the poll: Had the UK government been more pro-active in the campaign, the Irish government less engaged, had Varadkar and Starmer not come to a deal which addressed some of the concerns about citizenship, identity, minority rights, funding, and a continued British government consultative role through the East West bodies of the Good Friday Agreement. Had the devolved institutions worked better, or had unionism been better at making their case "to the middle ground". Had Brexit not happened or had the British economy not been in such difficulty.

It was all a complete mess from a unionist perspective. There were so many "what might have beens" and the inquest and recriminations went on for quite some time. In retrospect, there were so many lost opportunities to do things differently, and probably very much better. But technically and legally, 50% +1 was all that was required, and the result was irreversible.

That didn't prevent some unionists from trying...

Sovereignty would have to be transferred within three months of an Irish referendum ratifying the Varadkar Starmer deal. But the real process of re-unification had only just begun. A formal legal change doesn't automatically change things on the ground, or at least not immediately. It certainly doesn't change the hearts and minds of many on the losing side.

In sport, once the full time whistle has been blown, the match is over, and former adversaries can embrace each other and clap each other off the pitch. I had to do it through gritted teeth on the rugby pitch, manys a time, particularly if the opposition had played dirty, or didn't deserve to win.

You can have all the recriminations that you want, but I never saw the result of a rugby match changed by arguing in the pub afterwards.

I have seen the odd brawl break out between opposing players who had had a few too many drinks. Sometimes the winning players can really rub it in. But it was usually in response to some individual animosity or ancient grudge, and the senior players and coaches put a stop to it soon enough.

If you didn't have that discipline, you were found out soon enough. Opposition teams would deliberately target and goad you, in the hope of getting you riled up and sent off. They never quite succeeded with me, but I have seen many a winnable match lost because one of our team lost the head and got on the wrong side of the referee. There was little point in arguing afterwards that he had been provoked. The point is, he had lost your team the match.

Unfortunately, the real world doesn't always operate like that. There is no selection process whereby players lacking the required discipline can be weeded out. There will always be a few head cases and psychopaths around.

What is inexcusable is when political leaders give them the licence to do their worst, either through dog whistles or weasel words, false sympathy for victims or lack of condemnation afterwards.

It wasn't long before violent incidents multiplied, usually targeted at the most innocent and the most vulnerable. I was really worried for Sheila. She lived close to a loyalist estate and was well known in the area. I should also have been worried for myself, but having never experienced any out and out hostility, never thought of myself as a potential target...

For the vast majority of unionists, the match was over, even if they were angry and disappointed at having lost. For a few it just signalled the beginning of a new and different game. One in which they felt they could set the rules. Their establishment had failed them. It was time for them to change the direction of travel.

The republicans could not be let win.

10. Kidnapped

Early one morning I woke up to the sound of my door being broken down. Before I had come to my senses and figured out what was happening, several men wearing balaclavas were into my room and carrying me out, semi naked, into a waiting car. I had a gun pressed to my head and was told to keep my head down and eyes closed. A blindfold was tied, very tightly, over my eyes, and a large gag stuffed into and over my mouth. Ear plugs were even shoved rather forcibly into my ears.

I had trouble breathing and might have suffocated had I had a heavy cold and blocked nose.

I tried to imagine it was all just a dream. Or a nightmare more like. Even though I was cold I could feel the sweat draining my body. It was July, and still I was shivering uncontrollably. I could feel every bump in the road, every gear change, some sharp cornering, heavy acceleration, and the muffled sound of people cursing.

After what seemed like an eternity I was shouted at, pulled out of the car, and dragged into what felt like a shed, because it was no warmer than the crisp July morning air. There was a vague farmyard smell about the place. Manure maybe, or slurry. I had this incredible urge to urinate and defecate, but was put sitting on a hard chair, and told to keep quiet. My earplugs and gag were removed. That, in itself, was an incredible relief. I had been hyperventilating and afraid I would suffocate.

My entreaties to go to a lavatory were denied. My bare feet were freezing on a cold stone floor. I was told to shut the f*ck up and keep quiet. The pain in my gut was unbearable.

In silent anger I decided I would do my own dirty protest and let go. Why hold onto the decencies of life when I was being treated like this? I shat and pissed all over the place. This provoked some hilarity amongst my guards. "He's shitting himself!" they laughed.

Somehow this put me a little at ease. Not only had I relieved myself, but I felt I got to know some of my captors a little more by the sound of their laughter. I felt that by letting go, I was actually getting back some control. This meeting was going to be on my terms.

An older more senior sounding voice said menacingly: "We're going to make you eat and drink all that stuff later!" "But first I need some details: Name, rank and serial number!"

I noted the mock military tone and phrase but said nothing. Someone gave me an almighty whack across the head. Knocking me and my chair over. Burly hands picked me up and put me back sitting. "NAME, RANK, and SERIAL NUMBER!" in a tone that brooked no argument.

"I'm a reporter for the Tribune. You can read my stuff there any day of the week."

"NAME!" I was half expecting another broadside across the bows.

"Jeremy Watson" I replied.

"WHO ARE YOU WORKING FOR?"

"The Tribune", I repeated, "you know the..." – and I was knocked off my chair again by another heavy blow from the other side.

"WE KNOW YOU ARE WORKING FOR THE SECURITY SERVICES; WE WANT TO KNOW WHICH ONE!"

"I was in the army cadets at school, but that was as far as it went for me and military service".

"WHICH COUNTRY?"

By that stage I was very confused. They didn't even know what country I was from?

"England, of course! I only lived in Dublin for a year, when I was posted there as a features writer and then a political reporter.""

"SO THAT WAS WHEN THEY TURNED YOU?"

"Who turned me into what? I've been doing the same job since I left college, as a sports reporter and then a political reporter" - omitting to mention my little stint in climate change.

"AND YOU EXPECT US TO BELIEVE THAT?"

"All you have to do is google my name on the Tribune website. You will see I have had a couple of hundred stories published there."

"WE KNOW THAT IS YOUR COVER JOB. WHAT WE REALLY WANT TO KNOW IS WHO ELSE YOU HAVE BEEN WORKING FOR, AND WHAT INFORMATION YOU HAVE BEEN PASSING ON."

"Well, frankly, I'll work for whoever pays me, but so far, the Tribune has been the only outfit that has offered me a job, and they don't even publish half the stories I send them."

"AHA! SO, YOU HAVE BEEN SENDING THEM A LOT OF ADDITIONAL INFORMATION!"

"Absolutely. As any reporter will tell you, most of the stuff we write gets cut by the Editors. If you want to see all the stuff I've written, you only have to look at my laptop. I'll give you the password if you want. There's nothing else there except stuff my editor thought was too boring for our readership."

"AND THE DETAILS OF EVERYONE YOU'VE SPOKEN TO?"

"Well yes, my email address book is there as well. But to be honest you can usually tell who I've been talking to from the stories themselves. There's nothing very secret in there. I haven't had much contact with the security services beyond the odd press conference. I'm not a crime reporter."

"YOU BROKE THAT STORY ABOUT SHEILA BUTLER!"

"Well yes, she is one of the people I interviewed."

"AND YOU SPOKE TO THE POLICE ABOUT HER STOOGES GETTING BEATEN UP?"

"Well not really. They gave a press conference and issued a couple of statements I used for my story. But I haven't really followed up on their investigation. I presume it was the local UVF that did it, but I don't think anyone has been arrested for it."

"AND FOR GOOD REASON! IT WAS THE ORDINARY DECENT FOLK OF ULSTER PROTECTING THEIR BIRTHRIGHT!"

"I'm sure she'll feel better for knowing that…"

Whack! I was on the floor again…

"SHE NEEDED TO BE TAUGHT A LESSON. AND LET THAT ALSO BE A LESSON TO YOU!"

"I think I get the message. You don't want me reporting from Northern Ireland?"

"WE WANT YOU TO BE REPORTING THE TRUTH! NOT THAT SINN FÉIN SHITE"

"I'd be very happy to do an interview with you. In fact, I've been looking to get an interview with all the loyalist paramilitary organisation leaders for some time. They don't seem to want to talk to me."

"That's because you've been peddling all that Sinn Féin and Free State propaganda" he said in a noticeably lower tone of voice. No longer was it the commanding, booming, almost shouting voice.

"Well, I can't report on interviews that haven't happened. If you give me a chance to get cleaned up, I'd be happy to do an interview with you now".

"WELL, YOU HAD BETTER REPORT ON IT TRUTHFULLY!"

I'll be happy to send you a copy of my report, but I can't promise my editors will publish it if it doesn't contain real news."

"WE'LL NEED YOUR EDITORS NAMES AND ADDRESSES AS WELL!"

"Their names and email addresses are all on the Tribune website. I can't give you their home addresses because I've never been to their homes. I don't know them personally all that well. I rarely even meet them".

---ooOoo---

And with that, the interrogation was over. I was hosed down with cold water from what seemed like a garden hose. There was no towel and only some rough clothes to wear. My feet were still freezing, and I could barely stand, never mind walk. I had to be helped over to the hose.

After some discussion I was brought, still blind folded, to what must have been a nearby house, given a cup of tea, and a pencil and paper. At least it was a bit warmer. My hands were so cold I could barely write. I can't remember when I last conducted an interview without my phone recorder and laptop.

My blindfold and earplugs were removed and as my eyes slowly readjusted to the bright light, I could see the outline of three men in balaclavas with the sunlight pouring into my eyes from a window behind them. There were some trees swaying in the wind outside, but I couldn't make out what type. Oak maybe, or beech.

I scribbled down what I could, asking questions when I couldn't make out the rather strong Belfast accent. It was mostly about how the people of Ulster had been betrayed by English perfidy. The government had manipulated the Border Poll to get the result they wanted. MI5 had stuffed the ballot boxes. Lots of people were registered to vote who no one had ever heard of before. People moved up from down south just so they could vote to take over Ulster. They wanted to chase protestants out so they could buy up all the land and houses on the cheap.

But it wasn't going to happen. True Ulstermen would stand their round. They would create no-go areas all over the place where no Taig or Free Stater would dare to enter. Sure, hadn't they taught that Butler woman and her henchmen a lesson. No Shinner (Sinn Féin party member) was going to get a foothold in East Belfast. They had warned people not to vote for outsiders and interlopers. Sure, wasn't she from West Belfast herself. And as for you English, you had better mind your manners. We fought in two world wars for you, and this is the thanks we get...

He went on and on for quite a while, but you get the drift. I decided not to challenge any of the points made. It would only have extended the "interview." I was desperate to get out of the place.

Apparently, the plan was to hold me until my report had actually been printed in the paper. I was to be held hostage to my editor. But when it came time for me to start typing out my report, my laptop was nowhere to be found. Surely, they had searched my apartment and taken my laptop and phone?

I remembered I had taken the laptop to bed with me to do some late editing and browsing work. I probably shoved it under a pillow as I was nodding off to sleep. There was some discussion in an adjoining room. Somebody appeared to zoom off in a car.

I was told to write it out long hand. That way my editor would know it was from me. I told them my editor had probably never seen my handwriting, and it was a long time since I had seen it! My hands had warmed up by this stage and I started writing in my near illegible scraw, asking a few more questions for clarification as I went along.

After what seemed like an age the car returned. There was still no laptop. More muffled conversations in an adjoining room. I was told that they would be watching me and there would be trouble if my report, containing all their statements, wasn't published in full. I was more than happy to say I would comply.

I was blindfolded, stuffed, gagged, and ear plugged again and dragged into a car, dumped by the side of a minor road in some remote rural area, and eventually managed to flag down a passing motorist, a woman.

She must have been alarmed at seeing such a dishevelled, badly dressed person at the side of the road, but stopped anyway and lowered the passenger side window to ask what I wanted.

I said I had been abducted and needed to get to a police station right away.

She said, *"hop in, I'll take you, I'm heading that direction anyway,"* almost as if this was an everyday occurrence for her.

I apologised for my appearance and the fact that I probably didn't smell too good, saying I had been dragged through a farmyard. *"You look decent enough to me"* was all she said. Perhaps my slightly posh English accent put her at ease.

"Are you sure you don't need to go to a hospital?"

Perhaps later, I'm alright really. I just need to talk to the police."

"Who are you anyway?".

"I'm just a press reporter. Jeremy Watson".

She hadn't heard of me. So much for my newfound fame...

"They wanted me to write some more positive stories about them."

"Who? The UVF?"

"I presume so. They didn't give me any names. Said they were speaking for the 'plain people of Ulster."

"Gangsters, more like. They're very active around here. Beat up some poor innocent farmer near here some years back. He was supposed to be keeping some drugs buried for them. Turned out his dogs sniffed them out, ripped open the packaging, and the rain destroyed them. The poor dogs died. He was more heartbroken by losing his dogs than by the beating he received. By the way I'm Elizabeth Bowen, I run the local pharmacy. I thought I might have seen you before."

I couldn't remember her, but I had been to the local Boots several times before.

Instead of just dropping me off at the police station, she parked the car and helped me in. My feet were still all pins and needles. I thanked her profusely and said I would be sure to drop into her pharmacy to see her. Some Paracetamol probably wouldn't go amiss!

I thought I might have some difficulty explaining to the police who I really was, hardly dressed, and with no ID. Instead, alarm bells seemed to go off straight away. Someone took my picture on their phone, and a lot of phone calls were made. I was asked was I hurt, and an ambulance was called, even though I had replied, "just a bit." I was asked to tell my story and said I had notes of my interview and would be typing out a full report as soon as I could find my laptop. My captors didn't seem to have it.

"I think we can help you there," the senior police officer said.

What I didn't know was that my abduction had been seen and reported by a passerby. The police quickly figured out who I was from an examination of my apartment, easily identifiable by its broken front door. My neighbours had also heard the commotion and confirmed my identity.

My phone and laptop had been recovered and they had rung some recently dialled numbers. One was my editor who quickly raised the media alarm. Reporters were despatched to Belfast and BBC NI informed. They had heard nothing at that stage but were quickly onto police headquarters looking for details.

By the time I was released, a few hours after my abduction, there was a full scale manhunt in action, and local police stations were on high alert. Months later I learned that there may have been a police informer in, or close to the gang that had abducted me. There was some suggestion that the police might even have known of my planned abduction in advance. I don't know whether that is just a conspiracy theory.

What I do know is that genetic residues had been found on the clothes, paper, and pencil I had been given and at the site where I had been interrogated. The police seemed to have found that isolated farmhouse quickly enough. Whoever was supposed to clean the place up hadn't done a particularly good job. Four people were convicted for my abduction largely based on that genetic evidence. Someone hadn't washed up after their cups of tea.

Following a relatively brief conversation with the police the ambulance arrived, and I was given a thorough going over at the hospital even though a bit of facial bruising and a possible slightly fractured cheekbone was my only obvious injury. I may have been in shock however, because I barely recall the medical conversations, and my feet and face hurt like hell. I was admitted for observation overnight.

After a warm shower, some clean bedwear, some Paracetamol and some food, I was suddenly feeling fine again, and embarrassed at all the fuss.

My laptop had been retained for forensic examination. I told the police my captors had never found it and that it contained privileged journalistic information. Could I have it back please? "Later", was as good as I got. But the police officer gave me another ancient model to type up my report. I was told I would have to let them clear it before I could submit a report for publication. Some details might have to be redacted "for operational reasons." It didn't have a modem or internet connectivity.

Matt Casey did publish my report including the statements from my captors I was supposed to have included. He also published a lot of stories about my abduction by other reporters.

I was embarrassed to have, once again, become *the* story. Matt didn't seem to mind, this time around. I even got a "Get well soon" card signed by all the political staff, including my old nemesis, Bill Featherstonhaugh.

Sheila Butler visited me in hospital that evening with a big bunch of flowers. I felt embarrassed because I really wasn't that injured. Nothing like the injuries she and her two minders had suffered. I was reminded I had forgotten to bring flowers the night I had visited her in Hospital. I really did lack all the social graces!

She said it must have been an awful ordeal, especially not knowing whether I would be alive at the end of it. I really hadn't thought of it that way. It dawned on me, that I had never really been all *that* afraid. There was a part of me which struggled to take the whole thing seriously.

The whole episode had obviously been designed to scare the bejasus out of me (as they say around these parts), but that very fact made me feel less scared. If they had wanted to kill or torture me, they would have just gotten on with it. But my interrogator had just wanted to talk with me. To get his point of view across. I doubt they really thought I was working for the security services, or if I did, that I had much useful information to give them.

A few blows to the side of the head and a stern interrogation tone allowed them to feel they were in control and giving me a hard time - and me to do what I do best - talk myself into my own comfort zone, interviewing people about what bothered them.

The fact I had never shown any hostility towards my captors had disarmed them. I was genuinely interested in what they had to say. A pity they couldn't just have rung me and offered to give me an interview...

Sheila seemed to think I was some sort of hero for having gone through the ordeal and reported on it so dispassionately afterwards. Personally, I felt that the media had just bigged it up because it was one of their own that was threatened. The media closed ranks behind me. It played to their sense of self-importance. Many people, including Sheila and her minders, had suffered far worse.

I never had too much trouble getting my stuff published after that. I was even a regular contributor on radio and TV on all manner of programmes, including rugby. The initial plan had been to locate me in Belfast just for the duration of the Border Poll campaign. Now Matt Casey told me I could stay as long as I wanted, but that he understood if I wanted to leave. I said why ever would I want to leave? I was falling in love with the place, warts and all.

I was even asked to cover the Dublin brief. Cutbacks meant the Tribune couldn't afford to have two reporters based on the island. Ireland had been gradually sinking down the global and British news agenda after the Border Poll. It was case closed on Ireland and Northern Ireland as far as many of the media were concerned.

Little did they know...

11.   The Irish Referendum Campaign

The weeks and months following the Border Poll just got steadily worse from a law enforcement point of view. The marching season had begun and there were numerous huge bonfires. Rioting on the fringes became worse and worse even when there was no immediate or obvious provocation. There were lots of abductions and beatings and a few killings which made my little episode look very small beer indeed. The police were getting more and more demoralised. They simply didn't have the resources to cope.

But Northern Ireland was in a sort of constitutional vacuum. Britain was in the process of withdrawing, but Ireland wasn't yet ready to take over. It needed to go through the process of passing a constitutional amendment to ratify the Transfer of Sovereignty and Cooperation Agreement TOSCA (the Varadkar/ Starmer deal) and give effect to its legal powers in Northern Ireland. But this was poorly understood in Northern Ireland where many seemed to think that the Border poll had rendered all that automatic.

Everyone was expecting the Irish government to declare some sort of state of emergency and to send in reinforcements, but that was the last thing the government wanted to do. It did not want to send in its own police or army where they would just be acting as target practice for loyalist paramilitaries. I had become more successful at getting interviews with loyalist leaders and, reading between the lines, their strategy seemed to be to lure southern security personnel in, and then give it to them with both barrels. The problem was there was no sign of them coming.

Instead, what seemed to be happening was a high level of cooperation between the PSNI, The rump Royal Irish Regiment, and MI5 which was rumoured to have lots of informers in the ranks of the loyalist paramilitaries and very extensive files on their leaders. Most of these files were now being made available to the PSNI and the Irish Department of Justice. Every now and then there would be a highly coordinated swoop on a group of paramilitary leaders and considerable evidence seemed to be available to convict them of mainly drug related offenses.

But the violence kept metastasising and involving younger elements unknown to the security forces. Sooner or later, it was felt, a government crackdown had to follow. Calls for law and order where most pronounced from middle class unionist circles whose businesses were suffering most. For what seemed an unconscionable period, to most observers, the government refused to crack down, choosing instead to direct increased funds to community, sporting, family support and drug treatment related services, even before the formal transfer of sovereignty.

It was in this context that the referendum in the south to give effect to the Northern Border Poll and ratify the TOSCA was carried out. People explained a lot of the violence in the north as being fomented by loyalist paramilitary groups hoping to convince southern voters that the whole re-unification thing was a very bad idea and would lead to a whole new world of pain and trouble for southern voters.

Apparently, there were quite a few attempts at major terrorist atrocities in Dublin and other key locations throughout the south thwarted by the authorities, presumably based on very good intelligence. A few attacks succeeded, killing 17 people in total, but no major, single "game changing" atrocity succeeded in having the desired effect.

The vast majority of voters in the south were unfazed by these attacks and there seemed to be a general optimism that these attacks would die out once the referendum was carried, the political situation became less tense, and the general turmoil in the North died down.

People generally were more concerned by the economic effects of re-unification and whether government projections of long term economic growth which would more than cancel out the phased loss of Barnett subvention payments over a 15 year period were realistic.

Experts pointed out that it was impossible to predict economic developments over a 15 year period, but that if past historic trends were any guide, the target of 3% GDP growth per annum for the island as a whole was more than achievable. This would be more than sufficient to cover the loss of Barnett payments and enable modest improvements in average living standards, north and south. There were also some hoped for synergies in combining and integrating public services, north and south, especially in border areas, leading to improved public services for all.

Towards the end of the referendum campaign, there were a couple of high profile investment decisions by US corporates in Donegal and Armagh which appeared to give substance to government claims that re-unification made Ireland a more attractive investment location, not less.

It later emerged that Brussels had relaxed some of its "State-aid rules" to enable the IDA to win those investment decisions in the wake of fierce competition from Israel and Romania. It was rumoured that the Romanian government was not best pleased and that efforts were under way to find some quid pro quo to give to the Romanian government.

There was quite a lot of controversy about the Northern Ireland Assembly and Executive continuing to operate and that this would give the 6 counties an unfair advantage when it came to focusing national political attention on the particular priorities of the region. Cynics pointed out that these institutions had often been in abeyance under UK sovereignty, so why would (say) the DUP be any more disposed to operate them under Irish Sovereignty?

The TOSCA provided for a complete review of the Good Friday Agreement and its institutions in 15 years' time in any case, and any ongoing problems could be addressed then. Most northern nationalists expressed the hope that the last vestiges of "British colonial rule" could be finally eradicated at that stage.

There were also some background concerns that the sheer effort required to harmonise and integrate northern and southern public services and policy decisions would suck all the oxygen out of the political room and leave some areas, notably in the west and midlands, relatively neglected.

The naysayers pointed to the TOSCA requirement to give the UK a continued say regarding the north through the east west institutions of the Good Friday Agreement and the likelihood that Ireland would end up joining the Commonwealth. Irish sovereignty was being infringed. Supporters of the TOSCA pointed out that the Good Friday Agreement contained no sunset clause and that the TOSCA at least provided for a comprehensive review of the Good Friday Agreement at the end of the 15 year transition period.

There was a lot of controversy about the TOSCA's provision for a new mutual defence treaty between Britain and Ireland as infringing on Ireland's neutrality, and conflicting with our responsibilities towards the EU. The governments had published a draft text which focused mainly on cooperation on maritime patrol, air space protection, intelligence sharing, cybersecurity and "mutual cooperation at times of civil emergency". Supporters pointed out that much of this was happening anyway and had not led to undue problems in the past. The European Court of Justice (ECJ) also later ruled that it did not conflict with Ireland's obligations under EU Treaties.

There was no great controversy about changing the Irish National Anthem although there wasn't wide agreement on what should replace it. Suggestions included Danny Boy, the Mountains of Mourne, and Ireland's call. Others called for the composition of an entirely new anthem.

Changing the flag was more controversial but critics generally didn't object to the inclusion of the emblems of the four provinces, including the Red Hand of Ulster, in the middle white section of the flag. It would make the otherwise rather plain flag more unique and interesting.

Supporters of that idea pointed out that the Irish Tricolour of green, white, and orange was easily confused with the Ivory Coast tricolour of orange, white, and green and wasn't all that different from the Indian and Niger flags which were also orange, white, and green, albeit with horizontal stripes.

However, overall, there was general agreement that all these changes were a small price to pay for ending the historic problem of Partition and that they could be reviewed at the end of the 15 year transition period in any case. There was a tremendous sense of the completion of the national project, that some concessions to unionist sensitivities were necessary, and that the overall package provided a reasonable basis for the whole country to move forward.

I was reporting quite a lot from Dublin as well now and got a good sense of how the campaign was progressing by frequent trips throughout the country. I was often asked to speak at local events to "give the English perspective" which was mostly that it was now up to all of Ireland, north and south to chart its own way forward.

I said that there was no great desire in Britain to interfere in that process generally and that the publication of the draft TOSCA had made no great waves in British public opinion.

Scots' nationalists had made great play of how it could be a template for a future Scotland, England, and Wales Treaty and the only organised opposition came from Tories objecting to the continuance of (albeit reducing) Barnett subventions and die hard Brexiteer extremists who condemned "Starmer's break-up of the UK" and the dilution of British sovereignty through the East West consultative bodies.

I pointed out that these bodies worked both ways and provided an avenue for Ireland to influence UK thinking on matters of mutual concern. They could even provide a bridge for better EU UK relations going forward, a major pre-occupation of the Starmer regime.

Overall, the British people just wished the new Ireland well and hoped it would mark the end of a long history of enmity and conflict between the two historic neighbours, to be replaced by an even longer period of friendship and mutual cooperation.

---ooOoo---

The PSNI had suggested I move out of my Ballyhackamore apartment as my address was now too well-known amongst "undesirable elements" and I decided to move to Armagh. I decided I had had enough of "unscheduled" interviews and didn't want to be answerable to paramilitaries. I didn't want my focus to shift entirely to Dublin and it was important to keep in touch with Northern sensitivities. Sheila asked was it okay for us to stay in touch and I said she was always welcome to stay in my spare room.

The Irish referendum was passed by a resounding 83% of the population and the formal signing and ratification of the TOSCA was formally completed soon afterwards. DUP MPs in Westminster protested loudly during the debate on the ratification of the TOSCA, but it was opposed by only 28 MPs. Most of the Conservative Party abstained despite the fact that it was a Conservative minister who had called the Border Poll and the terms of the Treaty had been largely worked out by Irish and British civil servants acting under the supervision and authority of Conservative Ministers.

There was widespread and sincere international praise for the achievement of this historic entente between Britain and Ireland. Micheál Martin called an all-Ireland general election soon afterwards to elect northern deputies to the Dáil and capitalise on the general feelgood mood in the country.

European Elections were also announced for the Northern Ireland constituency to the European Parliament following the ratification of Northern Ireland joining the EU as part of Ireland by the European Council and Parliament.

All the DUP MPs lost their Commons seats on the ratification of the Treaty, but all were ennobled to the House of Lords by the Labour government. None chose to stand in their constituencies in the subsequent first all-Ireland general election.

In what became known as "The Flight of the Arlenes" some prominent unionists, including former DUP leader Arlene Foster announced that they were leaving Northern Ireland to live on the mainland. There were fears that this could lead to a widespread exodus of unionists from Ulster.

In the event, very few followed her lead. Most unionists had deep roots in the province and were committed to living there through ties to family and friends, their careers, and their involvement in local communities. It didn't prevent some loudly announcing their departure, only to return quietly sometime later.

Individual circumstances varied, and international migration is a normal part of modern life, but there was no large movement of people out of Northern Ireland, and no pressure for them to do so. Arlene Foster would be spending most of her time in London attending the House of Lord's in any case. There, she, and her DUP colleagues kept up a constant refrain criticising the Irish government for all manner of misdeeds. No one paid much attention.

One northern judge, speaking at the sentencing of some young people for "riotous assembly," allowed himself to be provoked by their constant taunting of him as a Lundy doing the Irish state's dirty work for them. He told them there was nothing stopping them leaving the country if they didn't want to live in Ireland and preferred to live in Britain instead.

His comments were widely condemned as not representing official policy. People had a right to live in Ireland even if they felt they were British and wanted much closer links between Ireland and Britain. Just as there had to be "equality of esteem" for the Irish identity in a British ruled Northern Ireland, the Good Friday Agreement ensured that those who felt British and wanted closer links to Britain had a right to express their opinions under Irish sovereignty. The judge should have confined his remarks to the facts of the case and his judgement was overturned on appeal.

There were many ostentatious displays of "Britishness" in the lead up to the general election, the third in Northern Ireland within a year. Critics complained that the Irish government was "trying to beat people over the head with democracy" in the hope of exhausting opposition to the new dispensation.

However, the government had no choice but to call elections in Northern Ireland to replace their Westminster MPs with representatives to the Dáil and to provide Northern Ireland with representation in the European Parliament. The Irish Constitution, as amended by the TOSCA, did not provide for separate regional elections to the Dáil. It had to be a full all-Ireland election even if the previous general elections had been held only 7 months previously.

It would be interesting to see how the enactment of Irish sovereignty over the whole island would affect political attitudes and party voting patterns, north and south. Would the government parties in the south reap the awards for having achieved Irish re-unification, or would they be finally overtaken by Sinn Féin, the only large truly all Ireland political party in Ireland?

Would unionist parties be totally demoralised, and disengaged from the new political process? Would new or smaller parties like the Greens come to the fore, with politics no longer quite so obsessively dominated by the sovereignty question, allowing other issues to come to greater prominence? Would Alliance become the natural ruling party in the north?

Did the old civil war parties, Fine Gael, and Fianna Fáil, still have any relevance in the new political dispensation? Micheál Martin and Leo Varadkar were beginning to look rather long in tooth. Would the Irish electorate look to a new generation of leaders to move the country forward?

It is an old political truism that elections are not for rewarding what you have done in the past, but for deciding what the electorate want done in the future.

Whither Ireland now?

12.   The First All-Ireland Elections

The existing 18 Northen Ireland parliamentary constituencies were retained to facilitate the immediate holding of the election but increased from one to four seats when compared to the Westminster elections (and reduced from 5 to 4 seats when compared to the Northern Ireland Assembly elections).

The Transfer of Sovereignty and Cooperation Agreement (TOSCA) provided for the same 72 members elected to serve in the Dáil to serve in the Northern Ireland Assembly, resulting in a 252 member Dáil and a broadly consistent ratio of seats per head of population throughout the country.

The plan was for the northern representatives to sit in Dublin three weeks out of four with the fourth week based in Stormont. The remaining 180 seat Dáil could conduct some local and committee work during that fourth week but was primarily intended to be in recess for that week, with members focusing on their constituency work. There was provision for the government to call full Dáil sessions during the fourth week "in the event of a national emergency".

The TOSCA also provided for the abolition of the Seanad after the 15 year transition period and thus blunted criticism that the country was being overpopulated with politicians! In the meantime, the Taoiseach's 11 nominees to the Seanad were to be allocated to eminent persons resident in Ulster and primarily from a unionist background, although that was not formally codified in law. The phrase used was that the Taoiseach's nominations were to be used primarily to boost representation of "minority communities" which was generally understood to refer to Protestants (and Travellers).

The first all-Ireland elections were called for November 2025 and were fought with considerable enthusiasm by nationalist parties despite the danger of "election overload", there having been an election as recently as March and referendums in June in the North and September in the south, all keenly contested.

The TUV refused to take part in the elections on the basis that the formation of the new state was illegitimate. Their request to the British Supreme Court for an injunction to prevent the holding of the elections was refused on the grounds that the UK Supreme Court had no further jurisdiction in Ireland, save for the operation of the East West Good Friday Agreement.

The DUP did put up candidates but campaigned on an abstentionist ticket on the grounds that "the rights of the British people in Ireland had been grossly violated". Nationalists never complained about this as Sinn Féin had also pursued an abstentionist policy in Westminster for over a century. (Some commentators suggested nationalists were just as happy not to have to deal with DUP politicians in the Dáil).

The UUP also campaigned and said they would only take up their seats as opposition members to engage in "constructive opposition and hold the government to account to the British people of Ireland." They later changed their name to the "British Ireland Party" (BIP) and said they would campaign for greater links between Britain and Ireland, the maintenance of British standards in Ireland, and the protection of the British identity in Ireland. They also put up candidates in the border counties of Ulster formerly not contained within Northern Ireland to "give a voice to the British people who had been abandoned to the Free state."

The Alliance Party took a full part in the election, and some suggested they would be natural allies of Fine Gael. Both Micheál Martin and Leo Varadkar were invited to speak at an Alliance conference and Naomi Long accepted invitations to speak at Fine Gael and Fianna Fáil conferences. (No politically significant unionist accepted an invitation to speak at either of those conferences, although there were several speakers from a unionist background).

The SDLP campaigned in the election under its own banner despite suggestions it would soon formally merge with Fianna Fáil. It styled itself as the voice of the centre left in Ulster and claimed it was the only major moderate left party in Ulster.

Sinn Féin declared themselves to be the true inheritors of the new Ireland arguing that Fianna Fáil and Fine Gael had compromised the new nation, even if only for a transitionary period. Sounding like it was campaigning to lead the opposition despite being by far the largest party, they said there would ensure there was no resiling on Ireland's full independence and that all transitionary measures contained in the TOSCA would definitively end in 2040.

Sinn Féin's claim to be the only true all Ireland party was challenged by the Greens who warned that the challenges of global warming and biodiversity loss respected no boundaries or borders. There were real hopes it could make the breakthrough into a mainstream major party in Ireland, and it made a point of running a candidate in every constituency regardless of whether they had much chance of being elected.

Despite rumours that both Fianna Fáil and Fine Gael would run candidates in all northern constituencies, they only put in token efforts with relatively unknown candidates and limited funding in a few northern constituencies. At very short notice, and seemingly as an afterthought, Fine Gael managed to find two well-known Ulster celebrity personalities to stand on their behalf., including a former Ulster and Irish International rugby player, Trevor Ringland. Leo Varadkar did some campaigning on their behalf, but the candidates stood more like Independents, using the Fine Gael label as a badge of convenience to promote "Ulster concerns."

The Irish Labour Party and the Social Democrats agreed a joint platform and a common slate of candidates to provide a "broad left alternative to the dominant conservative parties." There was some talk of a merger, but the policy and personality differences remained too great.

As usual there was a plethora of Independent and minor party candidates mostly focused on local issues seeking to capitalise on a widespread feeling that the "Northern Ireland Issue" had sucked all of the oxygen out of the political room, and that more rural areas in the rest of Ireland were being neglected.

Aontú campaigned on the basis of the New Ireland becoming too secular and too liberal and that there needed to be a return to more traditional values. Some of their candidates even received informal endorsements from DUP personalities at a local level.

Party	NI Assembly	Dail (Excl. NI)	Total Ireland
Sinn Féin	20	60	80
Fine Gael	2	42	44
Fianna Fail	n/a	40	40
DUP	18	n/a	18
UUP	6	0	6
Alliance	16	0	16
Greens	2	6	8
SDLP	6	n/a	6
SDP/Lab	0	15	15
Left Alliance	2	6	8
Aontú	0	2	2
Independents	0	9	9
TOTAL	72	180	252

The election results came out much as opinion polls had predicted with Sinn Féin by far the largest party but well short of an overall majority with 80 seats, including 20 in Northern Ireland, where it maintained its position as the largest party.

Fine Gael (thanks to a surprise win by their two candidates in Ulster) came out marginally ahead as "the best of the rest" with 44 seats and with Fianna Fáil (40) close behind. Combined with the SDLP (6), the Greens (8) the Alliance Party (16), and some independents, they had just about enough support to form a majority government, but only because the DUP members elected did not take up their seats.

Micheál Martin and Leo Varadkar again agreed to rotate the offices of Taoiseach and Tánaiste between them with Micheál Martin having the first two and a half year term as Taoiseach.

The DUP did reasonably well, winning 18 seats, but not as well as they had hoped not having competing TUV candidates to contend with. It appeared that turnout amongst TUV supporters was low, in line with the party policy of considering the new state to be illegitimate.

There were ongoing rumours that the DUP might adopt "guerrilla tactics" and ambush the government, defeating its measures by turning up unexpectedly just for crunch votes. But the DUP stuck to their abstentionist policy and expressed a complete lack of interest in Dáil politics, but surprisingly turned up to take their seats in the Northern Ireland Assembly. Why had they not done so under British sovereignty was the common refrain.

That worked for about 6 months but collapsed when Sinn Féin declared it would boycott the Northern Ireland Assembly until such time as the DUP took up their seats in the Dáil (and help defeat the government). That stand-off continued for years leading to charges that the DUP was "enabling the southern government to undermine Ulster's British heritage unhindered," while giving Northern Ireland no ability to resist through the Assembly. The issue was never resolved and the devolved institutions in Northern Ireland remained moribund, to the satisfaction of most nationalists who preferred direct rule from Dublin.

Alliance did extremely well, winning 16 seats, almost in line with the DUP, and promised to become "the voice of Ulster" in the Dáil and the Assembly. The UUP were greatly disappointed with their result, winning only 6 of the 72 assembly seats, and none south of the old border. Many wondered what was the point of a party that had lost its ancient fiefdom of Northern Ireland through sectarianism, incompetence, and mismanagement.

The SDLP were disappointed with their 6 seats, having campaigned mainly on local issues and warning that rule from Dublin could be almost as remote as Westminster. The Northern Ireland Greens won 2 seats, not as well as they had hoped given the urgency of climate change issues and the reduced prominence of the constitutional question.

The Left SDP/Labour alliance did moderately well, winning 15 seats, all outside Northern Ireland, but the hard left were disappointed with their result (2 seats in Northern Ireland and 6 in the south) given that they had predicted a seismic shift from sectarian and tribal politics throughout Ireland to a class based Left Right political system. They disputed Sinn Féin's claim to be a left party and declared their opposition to nationalism in all its forms, whether unionist or nationalist, British, or Irish.

To my great surprise Sheila managed to scrape into the last and fourth seat in East Belfast on transfers which seemed to come from all over the place. Alliance and the DUP secured the first three seats easily, but Sheila became the first Sinn Féin representative for the area despite having been behind the UUP candidate on first preferences. Political analysts were left scratching their heads as to how she seemed to have gotten so many transfers from Unionist candidates, particularly when the second DUP candidate was eliminated.

I was down in Dublin covering the overall election results but couldn't get up to Belfast fast enough to congratulate her. She said she had been inundated with messages of support from right across the political spectrum and that her core Sinn Féin first preference vote hadn't risen much above 3,000. I was so happy for her. She was a dedicated and truly professional politician with an eye and ear for local issues and concerns and an incredibly hard worker on the ground particularly through (non-sectarian) women's groups and local community groups.

She hadn't received much support from Sinn Féin HQ who preferred to focus on "winnable seats". Even they hadn't seen her victory coming. She was particularly pleased to have been accompanied throughout her campaign by Sean and Ciaran, her two "minders" who had been so badly injured during the Border Poll campaign. They greeted me enthusiastically as a fellow sufferer of sectarian violence.

I was again embarrassed. In no way were my minor injuries comparable to theirs but I was very glad to see both had made a good recovery. I surmised that I had suffered less because of my English accent and ability to talk smoothly with my captors. I later managed to interview one of the men convicted for my abduction (my interrogator) in prison and he agreed that might have been a factor. They had been genuinely shocked by my defecating all over the place and feared I might snuff it because of some medical condition unknown to them.

The intention had only been to scare me into leaving Ireland or to get me to moderate my tone in their favour. He accepted that the escapade had back-fired rather badly and bemoaned the incompetence of his men to even find my laptop. The police were all over the place when they returned to my apartment to recover it. (My phone was to be left in place in case the police could trace my whereabouts through it). He expressed surprise my defecating and urinating all over the place hadn't been reported in the media. I said I had friends in low places...

Sheila was particularly shocked by Fine Gael managing to win two seats in North and South Down with their celebrity candidate in South Down "never having done a day's work in politics" and it showed, in her opinion, how middle class people can just breeze into top jobs without even trying, while working class people have to work their socks off. I explained that Trever Ringland had done a lot of work for reconciliation and was a well-known rugby player. "Not in my area" was her only response, saying that unionists still blamed him for splitting the vote in 2010 and allowing Naomi Long to get in for the first time. "No wonder he stood in North Down this time around!"

I suggested that the Fine Gael candidates had no chance of re-election if they didn't put in the hard yards in their constituencies now. Their election had been a bit of a flash in the pan because of the novelty of a southern partitionist party putting up candidates in the north. Some conservative nationalists might have welcomed the opportunity to vote for a southern conservative party without compromising their nationalist beliefs. Besides, their election had been at the expense of the DUP or more likely Alliance, as Sinn Féin was hardly likely to have won those seats anyway.

"Yes", she agreed. "Those are middle class seats. Class differences are beginning to over-ride religious or national concerns. People want stability and prosperity and seem to think Fine Gael can deliver that, for the middle classes at least. It was priceless seeing the shock on the faces of the DUP candidates who had run an entirely negative campaign. People are tired of all the negativity and want to have some hope for a better future, regardless of which side of the fence they come from".

It had been a seismic election result.

Sinn Féin had felt sure they would win an overall majority and were devastated when they didn't. Fine Gael, Fianna Fail, Alliance, and the Greens had done better than expected, and the SDLP and Labour/SDP had survived. The DUP and the UUP (soon to become the BIP) were disappointed with the turnout of their supporters but had made little effort to garner support beyond their base. TUV supporters hadn't seemed to come out for DUP candidates as expected. The "Left Alternative" had made little progress despite their common all Ireland platform.

Aontú doubled their seats to 2 and their vote to 4% and seemed to be capturing a wave of nostalgic support for a simpler, more religious, and traditional time. They may even have picked up a few disillusioned DUP lower preference votes from people who shared their social conservatism. They may have only won a couple of seats but were contenders in several more constituencies. Analysts wondered whether this presaged a bit of a backlash against the "brave new Ireland with its focus on secularism, integrated education, and "disrespect for tradition and religion".

In terms of the government and its agenda, it was full steam ahead for progressing the growth of both economies and integrating schools and public services. There was a lot of internal opposition to rapid change within the educational establishments and in both civil services. Sinn Féin formed a strong and energetic opposition highlighting any government failings. They were always in favour of the general principles of integration and transformation, but frequently opposed concrete proposals on the grounds of lack of consultation or sensitivity to local concerns. Analysts noted that they had also always been very vocal on the housing issue, while opposing many planning applications for social and affordable housing.

Naomi Long became a well-liked and regarded Justice Minister, even if violent incidents increased on her watch. This was regarded as almost inevitable by most observers. Stephen Farry became a successful Minister for European Affairs who managed the re-integration of Northern Ireland into the EU and was especially popular amongst northern farmers for ensuring they got their CAP payments backdated to the time of the Border Poll, even if the formal incorporation of Northern Ireland into the EU didn't happen until the ratification of TOSCA following the Irish referendum. Minister for Education, Colm Eastwood, was less popular, and often caught in the crossfire between vested interests trying to protect their positions. In fairness, it was an almost impossible brief.

But generally, there was a welcome for the novelty of having northern ministers in cabinet. It would not have happened in Westminster. If anything, there was concern in southern political circles that their often rather mediocre, parochial, and complacent politicians were being shown up by battle hardened northern warriors attuned to the ideological battles of the day and acutely sensitive to local rivalries.

Sheila was more than a little exercised by the need to pump resources into disadvantaged areas, her constituency being one of the worst affected. It was to take a considerable number of years before many young loyalists were weaned from drugs and gangs. Anti-social behaviour was widespread, especially in loyalist areas, even if the capability to commit major terrorist atrocities appeared to have been lost with the arrest and conviction of so many senior paramilitaries.

It was going to be a long haul to lift some areas out of the sinkholes they had slipped into. No better person than Sheila to progress that agenda, I thought. She seemed to be very successful at extracting funds from the relevant departments and I sometimes helped her to draft project and funding proposals.

I was lost in admiration for her persistence and so pleased she now had a voice in the Dáil. I would be reporting on her every utterance regardless of whether my editors, back at the Tribune, thought they were newsworthy or not! England seemed so very far away from me now...

13.   Disappointment

The European Elections were held at the same time as the general election in Northern Ireland, and, not surprisingly, resulted in one seat each for Sinn Féin, the DUP and Alliance, with the DUP saying they would take their seat in Europe (while abstaining in Dublin), in order to highlight the plight of Northern Ireland farmers who had yet to receive their Common Agricultural Policy (CAP) payments at that stage.

Jim Allister, who campaigned on an abstentionist ticket to highlight the "EU's anti-British policies and complicity in the United Ireland conspiracy," got just 6% of the vote, most of which transferred to help elect the DUP candidate.

What caused major surprise and anger within Fianna Fáil was Micheál Martin's decision to offer Jeffrey Donaldson the Irish nomination for the EU Commission. It was Fianna Fáil's turn to nominate the Commissioner to replace Fine Gael's popular Commissioner, Mairead McGuinness, and there was also some general disappointment that she had not been renominated. The major anger came from within Fianna Fáil ranks, however, as it was felt that the plum job should have gone to one of their own. The position carried a €275,000 salary and more than made up for the loss of Donaldson's Westminster Salary.

Donaldson faced a stiff vetting process in the European Parliament with many members noting that he was a successor to the notorious Ian Paisley who had disrupted many a European Parliament session, not least a speech by Pope John Paul II. The irony of a "Britisher" who was a member of the House of Lords and who had supported the hardest form of Brexit becoming a European Commissioner was not lost on anyone . There were also dark mutterings that he would act as a Trojan Horse for Britain within the Commission. Sir Keir Starmer's fulsome welcome for the nomination did not lesson those concerns.

In the end Donaldson survived a sometimes intemperate grilling by the European Parliament's vetting committees and was nominated to the post by the European Council. He was, however, disappointed in his bid to secure the prestigious Agriculture Portfolio and had to be satisfied with a more marginal brief responsible for Digital Media, Online Commerce and Cybersecurity.

This prompted more outrage from Fianna Fáil back benchers who pointed out that previous Irish Commissioners had secured major portfolios as Vice President of the Commission (Patrick Hillery), Commissioner for Agriculture and Rural Development (Ray MacSharry), Competition (Peter Sutherland), Health and Consumer Protection (David Byrne), Social Affairs (Pádraig Flynn), Internal Market and Services (Charlie McCreevy), Trade (Phil Hogan), and Banking and Finance (Mairead McGuinness).

In the end there was a minor backbench heave against the leadership of Micheál Martin which didn't succeed but may have contributed to his later decision to retire from public office immediately after his two and a half year stint as Taoiseach was over.

The heave led to something of a power vacuum in Fianna Fáil until Michael McGrath took over as party leader while Martin was still in office. This freed him to devote his energies entirely to doing his job as Taoiseach. There was fulsome praise for Martin's career in politics from most parties - not including the Left Alliance, the DUP, and the TUV — when he eventually retired.

Jeffrey Donaldson's departure to Brussels did not lead to any moderation of the DUP's abstentionist policies under new DUP leader Gavin Robinson, a fact that was frequently criticised by his constituency colleague (and my friend) Síle De Buitléar (SF). She pointed out that the DUP was happy to take the Dublin government's "dime" but not actually prepared to do any of the hard work of government.

(I must confess I had previously been spelling her name in the anglicised form of Sheila Butler, as that was the way it had appeared on the ballot paper and in many of the media reports I was following. She had never pointed out my rather embarrassing error).

I was based in Armagh now but spending much of my time in Dublin following political events and the odd rugby match. I was doing a lot of milage and, given the quality of the roads, could understand the need for the large infrastructural investments the government were proposing. There were increasing tensions between the Greens and the other government parties as the Greens were adamant that the expansion of the rail network should be prioritised over more road improvements or motorway building.

In the end I reverted to living in Belfast as it was much easier to get to Dublin from there, and I could cover Ulster rugby matches as well. Síle had bought her first house now that she could get a mortgage based on her Dáil salary. She offered me a room if I would help out with the mortgage payments, and I was happy to agree. We had been getting on extremely well and I had begun to help her write some of her Dáil speeches and grant applications.

She was focusing very much on getting increased funding for community facilities especially for the more disadvantaged parts of her constituency, which happened to be mainly loyalist areas. She was surprised at the degree to which she was pushing open doors given the fact that she was a Sinn Féin TD opposing a largely conservative government. Any halfway decently thought through and presented proposals seemed to be getting government approval. In time, this was to lead to some resentment from her West Belfast Sinn Féin colleagues who didn't seem to be having as much success with their funding applications.

On one memorable occasion she was confronted by some Sinn Féin colleagues complaining about a rather large grant she had obtained for a sports and entertainment centre for Ballyhackamore. They shut up when she responded "Well, did you apply for the grant?" It reminded me of the old joke about the Christian praying to God and complaining he hadn't ever won a lottery. God responded, "Well did you ever meet me half-way and even buy a ticket?"

Síle had a constant police bodyguard when she was out and about in the constituency but felt increasingly confident that she didn't need it. Even loyalist stalwarts seemed to appreciate her efforts on behalf of their communities. Drug problems were endemic in the area, and she was able to get funding for a comprehensive range of holistic drug treatment, methadone, needle exchange, counselling, family support, prison links support, community employment, restorative justice, gardening and community sports and art projects.

I have to say I was alarmed when she also got involved in some domestic violence cases and on more than one occasion physically disarmed a husband who had been threatening his wife with a gun. I suggested some cases were best left to the PSNI and social work services, but she said the former would simply exacerbate the situation and the latter were overwhelmed with work and could not respond to crisis situations in a timely manner. It was not the work I had envisaged a member of Parliament to be doing and her protection detail were even more alarmed when they found out.

But she was getting frustrated with her parliamentary duties. Sinn Féin were in opposition and could only verbalise problems and complain at government inaction. She would far rather have taken the initiative and dealt with the problems herself. The party leadership said they were very pleased with her work but some of her colleagues were much more disparaging. They said her primary responsibility was to look after "her own community."

As a very new TD she did not expect to be appointed to an opposition spokesperson role but was surprised at some of the people who were appointed. They did not appear to her to have an awful lot positive to contribute to anything and were most comfortable when they could find an angle to criticise the government. She wasn't into playing "media games" and was critical of my tendency to cover the activities of "important people" rather than the plight of many ordinary people in very dysfunctional family and community situations.

I did my best to write stories about the latter, but it wasn't necessarily my strong point and Matt Casey wasn't publishing much of my stuff on local issues. "We are a national paper covering Ireland as a foreign policy issue now. One or two stories about the difficulties people were experiencing in the new Ireland was ok, but my real job was to cover national politics (and rugby)".

I found myself getting more and more removed from the national political scene in Britain. If former Tory leadership contender, Michael Howard, was said to have "something of the night about him," Sir Keir Starmer could be said to light up a stage only by getting off it... British politics seemed incredibly boring to me now.

By comparison, there seemed to be a real edge to Irish politics, especially at the local level. People actually believed that politics should be able to solve their problems, whereas in Britain, people seemed to have given up on politics altogether. I found much of England to be really depressing on the few occasions I got back to visit my family or to attend meetings at head office. Nothing much seemed to change, whereas in Belfast, and in Ireland more generally, transformation was in the air.

Not that you would have guessed it from the arguments still raging between Sinn Féin and unionist politicians, most of whom were still fighting old battles and engaging in competitive abstentionism against each other. Sinn Féin refused to allow the Northern Ireland Assembly and Executive to function until unionists ceased to abstain from the Dáil, and that wasn't happening any time soon. "OK, so its Direct rule from Dublin, if that's what you want" said Sinn Féin spokespersons, mirroring unionists' jibes of yesteryear.

"I wish they would all just grow up and stop playing playground games" was Síle's attitude privately. "There are so many real people suffering with real problems, and these games aren't helping anyone". I sensed she was getting disillusioned with the party leadership, and that they didn't seem to be overly well disposed towards her.

A lot of arcane policy and tactical disputes seemed to be raging in the background, but the main problem was that Sinn Féin weren't leading the Government and thus weren't in power despite being the largest party in the country. I sensed some sort of internal party bust-up seemed to be on the way, and I didn't want Síle to be caught in the crossfire. She never really told me much about what was going on in internal party meetings, beyond noting that the policy agenda wasn't really being set by the Parliamentary party, even though it now had 85 members, 80 in the Dáil and 5 in the Seanad.

But the much bigger problem was that the PSNI and Gardai weren't having much success in quelling violence and anti-social behaviour generally. There were still a lot of fights and riots between gangs from mostly republican and loyalist estates. Some young people were getting killed, and a lot injured. Sinn Féin were looking for a crack-down on all anti-social behaviour, but the government, led by Justice and policing Minister, Naomi Long, were adopting a softly, softly, approach. Síle De Buitléar felt that the government didn't care so long as it was only working class communities who were mostly affected.

Discussions on Commonwealth membership, anthems, flags, and emblems didn't seem to be making much progress either, chiefly for lack of unionist involvement. The government just seemed to hope the problem would go away. To her credit, Naomi Long insisted they tackle the issue, as provided for in the transition plan of the TOSCA.

Ireland did join the Commonwealth, but it turned out to be a bit of a damp squib, other than a few (mainly northern) athletes taking part in the Commonwealth Games. It helped that King Charles was a longtime supporter of Ireland, having visited all 32 counties on multiple visits over many years. But unionists didn't seem to care overmuch. Most were simply not engaging with the new state, any more than they absolutely had to, and didn't regard Commonwealth membership as giving them much of what they had lost back. It didn't help that some nationalists accused them of sulking.

I tried to cover as much of the "public services transformation process" as I could, but it was seriously boring stuff, more marketing hype than real. Civil servants from both sides of the old border didn't seem to have much appetite for radical change. An easy life more like. I think I got one article on the topic published by the Tribune in a very inconspicuous part of the paper. It didn't make for riveting reading. I began to wonder whether I should try to get a job with an Irish newspaper instead, but they seemed very cliquish and inward looking, for the most part.

Every now and then there was a big story when another attempted bombing in Dublin failed. The Irish government still seemed to have pretty good intelligence on Belfast paramilitaries. But it was the little stuff that wore people down: local youths going on the rampage trying to destroy as much "enemy property" as possible. It just seemed like a computer game for some of them when they were finally hauled before the courts. I found I was rapidly losing my liberal spots and becoming something of a "law and order" enthusiast. This stuff had to be stopped. It was making ordinary people's lives miserable.

My new right wing instincts didn't extend to condoning heavy handed policing, and there was plenty of that to report. But somehow the Tribune wasn't interested. Matt Casey was having difficulty getting my stories published. His boss was telling him Northern Ireland wasn't a big story anymore. An occasional background feature article would suffice. One day he asked me would I like to return to England and become Parliamentary correspondent for the Tribune. It would be a big promotion. I couldn't think of anything worse.

Ireland, and particularly Northern Ireland seemed to me to be where the action was, not so much at a parliamentary or national governmental level, but at the local level on the ground. A huge transformation in local inter-community relations was required, and we were only at the beginnings of that process.

Many people saw a united Ireland as a constitutional, legal, and diplomatic construct. They saw it as being about Treaties and Constitutions and legislation and party politics. I was beginning to see it more and more as being about the hearts and minds of people, and how they related to one another at work and in local communities. People Like Síle De Buitléar were doing very good work, but it was mostly within separate loyalist and nationalist estates. Something had to be done to bring those estates together, and that would mean confronting the loyalist and republican power structures that depended on keeping them apart.

I started doing interviews with and stories about local paramilitary and community leaders, challenging them on why they were keeping local rivalries on the boil. But it was not what the Tribune wanted from me. I would have to find myself a new job...

14. My political career move

Síle was getting pissed off at my constant carping at what loyalist and republican leaders were doing on the ground to keep communities divided. Why didn't I stand for election and do something about it, she almost taunted. "Yea right, I would get about three votes, and I'm not even sure I would get yours. Ireland didn't fight for hundreds of years to be free from British rule only to elect an Englishman into office. And besides, who would I run for, and who would have me?"

She laughed. "You could always run for the protestant vote of all those ex-unionists who are fed up with abstentionism and just want to get on with their lives and make the best of whatever Ireland has to offer." "Isn't that what the Alliance Party is there for?" I countered. "Well yes, but most of them are just closet unionists who yearn for the old days but realise they have to work with Dublin now. They would far rather stick to just working within a Northern Ireland context, if that were still possible. Why don't you go the whole hog, and join an Irish political party like Sinn Féin, or even Fianna Fáil or Fine Gael?"

"Well, you are never going to get unionists or ex-unionist protestant voters to vote for Sinn Féin in any numbers. Fianna Fáil and Fine Gael are too right wing for me, but the Greens and the social democrats are just too marginal and will never deal with the core issue of a divided society in Northern Ireland." "I have" she countered. "There must have been at least 4,000 first and lower preference protestant votes in my pile, there simply aren't enough nationalist voters here to elect me."

"Yea but you're special! I simply couldn't do the sort of work you do. Spending hours and hours listening to people's problems and sorting out their family and neighbour disputes". She agreed, "Yes, you're much better at stirring things up than calming people down. You'd have a war on in no time!"

"I can't help it if I like to tear people's assumptions apart. Somebody has to tell them things can't go on like this, with the different working class communities still more or less at each other's throats. But an Englishman is the last person who can tell them that." "You'd be surprised", she said. "People will listen to an outsider when they won't listen to their own. What you have to figure out is what's in it for you. People won't believe you if you tell them you are doing it entirely for their benefit."

"So why are you doing all this crap for loyalists who'd probably shoot you If they got half a chance. What's in it for you?" I was becoming argumentative. "Because they did shoot and kill my grandfather and my granduncle, and my grandfather made my father promise, as he lay dying, that he would love and do everything he could for those who had done such harm to him. When my father was dying of cancer, he passed that request on to me."

I broke down in tears. I had known her now for over a year, and we had never discussed our family situations. My own English reserve had prevented me from discussing my family, and I would have felt I was being very intrusive asking her about hers. I knew her mother lived in West Belfast but had never heard her speak of her father. I was so embarrassed at my own ignorance. How could I not have known? I was supposed to be an ace reporter. But we had really only ever talked shop. I started to apologise...

> "Oh, shut up. It's none of your business. You were right not to ask. Anyway, this was never supposed to happen. Sinn Féin asked me to stand in East Belfast in the last British general election because they had no one else and didn't have a chance to win a seat anyway. But they wanted someone to fly the flag and bring up their overall percentage vote for the Border Poll. When that worked out so well, they asked me to stand in the Irish general election as well. I didn't really want to but had nothing better to do and nothing to lose. I still can't believe I won. It was a fluke, and it won't happen again, and then I'll be out on my ear. But at least I will have kept my promise to my dad. No one bar my mum and sister know about this, so you're not to tell anyone!"

I didn't know what to say. I babbled. Somewhere deep inside me burned the fire of the abuse I had suffered at the hands of my own dad. My public school education had taught me to bury that anger, shame, and disgust very deeply. I became a smart ass to compensate for not really being able to relate to people closely. I used people to get their stories for the paper. I didn't really make friends even if I pretended to be their friend. And now, suddenly, she had opened me up like a can of worms.

I didn't know whether to laugh or cry, but somehow, I felt an incredible relief. We talked for a long time. A few glasses of wine helped and then we kind of fell asleep in each other's arms. Crying bitterly. When we came to, it was morning.

---oo0oo---

My whole world seemed to change after that. I am not overly given to sentiment, emotion, or romance. But I think I had fallen in love. I trusted her implicitly and Síle seemed to trust me. I still couldn't believe I had done nothing to research her family background, but my time in Northern Ireland had been relatively short, and I was laser focused on gathering the information I needed for my next story. All else was an irrelevant distraction.

That was, of course, until the focus of my stories started to change. I was less and less interested in the big picture stuff – whatever Dublin or Downing Street were up to. The minutiae of new EU Directives bored me to tears. Even the stupendous legal and administrative changes that were starting to take shape in Northern Ireland seemed to me less important than what was happening in ordinary people's lives.

Was their standard of living going up? Was there an improvement in their quality of life? How were they being affected by anti-social behaviour? Were public services improving?

Regardless of the popular good will extended to the new government in most of the island, problems started to mount on all fronts. Many in the north started to complain that law and order was better under the old British regime. Behaviour which wouldn't be tolerated in the south was permitted to proliferate, unchecked, in the north.

It led to northerners complaining that they were being treated as second class citizens, expected to endure crime levels that would never be permitted in the south. Some southerners, on the other hand, complained the reverse: that Northern Ireland was getting disproportionate political attention and public expenditure, and it was they who were being disadvantaged.

Something had to happen, and somebody had to take control. The government appointed a northerner as a new hardline overall police chief, with a brief to do "whatever it takes to reduce crime to pre-re-unification levels, if not below." Despite rumours of low morale, early police actions were extremely well targeted, ruthless, and effective, but inevitably some relatively innocent people got caught in the crossfire, threatening a popular backlash.

Other complaints were that "the benefits of re-unification" were too slow to materialise. The government seemed to be taking an ultra-cautious approach to integration and harmonisation of services. Northerners were still not getting the same benefits as southerners, and vice versa. It didn't matter that the

TOSCA gave the government 15 years to complete the transition to full integration. What was the excuse for it not happening NOW?

A number of social science studies claimed there was no reduction in polarisation, division, or the alienation of young people from society or the political system as a whole. There were many calls for huge increases in community funding and yet a great deal of scepticism as to how effective it was. Some claimed existing funding was merely funding more middle class social worker and bureaucratic posts, and not reaching those who needed it most. Others claimed much of the funding was being funnelled off by paramilitary groups.

More comprehensive Restorative Justice services were set up giving offenders the legal right to opt for a restorative sanction as opposed to more traditional fines and imprisonment. Many felt this was just mollycoddling ne'er do wells, giving them the soft option of a light touch sanction. But many of these offenders ended up doing great community work, and in some cases ended up getting professional qualifications through adult education programmes.

Gangs with paramilitary trappings continued to be very active, often terrorising local communities. Attempts by the Orange Order and others to harness youthful energy into organised bands and disciplined marches seemed to have very limited success, attracting only those less inclined to anti-social behaviour in the first place. Government funding for such bands proved to be very controversial.

But Síle kept giving me examples of local community initiatives that were extremely successful, often across community lines. I did as many stories on them as I could, but very few were being published by the Tribune. Britain was truly disengaging from almost everything to do with Ireland.

Matt Casey even suggested I could submit them to local papers instead – provided the Tribune had first refusal. That was fine, but I wondered how long it might take for him to go further and suggest I might wish to seek full time employment elsewhere...

Quite a few of my stories got published in the Irish news, in particular, but I was disappointed the Belfast Newsletter or Telegraph didn't publish more, especially seeing many of them related to East Belfast. It seemed good news about the new dispensation wasn't welcome in unionist circles.

Any stories I did about middle class areas tended to have a better chance of publication. Apparently, that was where the market and the advertising revenue was. They were more interested in reports of rioting and anti-social behaviour elsewhere.

I was beginning to feel increasingly useless. My own paper was only publishing the occasional report, and then usually about something that was centred on Dublin. I couldn't see any clear opportunities in the Irish papers, many of which were downsizing their reporting staff and using semi-retired eminences for opinion columns.

I was getting more traction for my rugby reportage, and while I enjoyed doing it, it didn't seem to be adding a lot to the sum total of human wellbeing. When Irish rugby fortunes took a downward turn, the Tribune even stopped publishing all of my reports except those involving English, Welsh or Scottish clubs or international matches.

In the very brief period of time since my arrival from Britain up to the first all-Ireland general election, I had become quite a prominent journalist, often featured on radio or TV. Now nobody seemed to care very much whatever I might have had to say – either in Britain or Ireland. I considered writing a book on all my experiences, but as you can see from this tome, that project took a long time to come to fruition.

I needed a new career.

Síle was sympathetic, but there wasn't a lot she could do. She had used up her expense allowance to employ local advisors and organisers from the loyalist community. That, too, didn't go down too well with some in Sinn Féin. She seemed a long way from securing a front bench opposition spokesperson role and potential minister in any Sinn Féin government – Sinn Féin had 85 TDs and Senators to accommodate. Few seemed to be as active as her in loyalist communities, however. Her detailed knowledge of community development issues would have been invaluable to inform national debate, but opposition back benchers got few opportunities to speak.

It seemed obvious, to me, that her "face didn't fit" for some in the Sinn Féin leadership, but she just shrugged when I raised the topic. It felt like I wasn't the only misfit in the room, when we got to have a chat after dinner after a long day's work – for her. I was finding it harder and harder to find stories my editors would publish and felt I was swanning around, doing inconsequential stories that often didn't get published. Once again, I felt I was hamming it. But I really didn't know what to do next.

A conversation with a Green party activist changed all that. We were chatting about policy issues generally and I happened to mention I had had a rather short lived stint as the Tribune's Climate Change correspondent. His eyes lit up! "We could badly do with someone like you to run for us. There are some constituencies where we can't even find a party member willing to run in a local election!

I quickly explained I had moved on to a politics brief because I found some of the Climate Science jargon in scientific journals difficult to follow. "You and just about everyone else!" He exclaimed. "What we need is people who can put the key issues into plain English. A lot of people's eyes just glaze over when you start talking about accelerated ice flow melts and others feel there is not a lot we can do about it anyway, what with the Chinese building more coal fired power stations..."

"The Chinese are also putting in more sustainable energy generation capacity than anybody else and more electrified train lines than the rest of the world put together" – I countered. "Precisely, but not many people know that, and that is precisely what we should be doing. We need someone who can write readable policy documents that people can understand and relate to. Let me talk to head office about this!"

I was happy enough to go along with this. An interview with Green Party leader Eamonn Ryan wouldn't go amiss. Perhaps the Tribune would even print it, as there had been a lot of talk of building more connectors between British and Irish power grids and making better use of our combined wind and solar resources. Electricity power distribution and management was one of the few areas that was being managed on an all-Ireland basis even before the Border Poll, and the Transfer of Sovereignty and Cooperation Agreement had explicitly mentioned it as a key area for British Irish cooperation in the future.

A week later I was asked to go down to Dublin for a meeting with the Green "leadership team". The team was led by Senator Pippa Hackett, Minister of State at the Department of Agriculture, Food, and the Marine with responsibility for Land Use and Biodiversity. She was not the party leader but attended cabinet as a non-voting member. We had a very good discussion on Ireland's environmental and energy policies with particular reference to the opportunities for cooperation with Britain. The energy department under

Eamonn Ryan had become quite frustrated at the slow pace of progress on the integrated international electricity grid.

I may have oversold the extent of my contacts with environmental and sustainable energy experts in the UK, but she seemed intrigued by the possibility of using me to push things along. I sent my report of the meeting to my old Environment Editor, Professor Meeken, as well as Matt Casey, and she got back immediately to me saying that the lack of progress on that aspect of the TOSCA was an absolute disgrace. The Starmer government seemed to be obsessed with economic growth and debt reduction and didn't appear to appreciate the degree to which sustainable energy integration across Europe could make a major contribution to both.

She published my report – significantly improved by her – very prominently on the environmental page of the Tribune with a link on the front page of the paper. Green Party HQ in Dublin seemed to be very impressed by my ability to summarise the issues involved and get them featured in a major daily in Britain. The final version of the report had been very critical of British government inaction. I was asked to come down to Dublin for a second meeting, and this time with Party Leader Eamonn Ryan.

We had a long and rather expansive meeting, covering a variety of topics – agricultural emissions, problems with storm damage to offshore turbines in the Atlantic, local resistance to onshore wind farms, delays in the housing retrofit schemes, the costs of rail extensions and electrification, problems with the electric car charge points roll-out, and the lack of baseload capacity in the Irish electricity generation system. But his particular bugbear was the lack of willingness, on the British side to invest heavily in interconnector capacity so that imbalances in supply and demand in both Britain and Ireland could be smoothed out, as much as possible. "Everything is short term with them, low hanging fruit, but no strategic vision."

I explained that the Starmer government was obsessed with keeping borrowing down – they had been badly burned by borrowing at variable rates, and even now were still paying 2-3 percent more on government borrowings than Ireland. That made a lot of infrastructural projects, with their very high upfront capital costs, very marginal from a return on capital point of view. Any further rise in interest rates, and the marginal increased income derived from electricity generation and distribution would be insufficient to cover the interest costs.

"Yes, yes, we know all that, but we have even offered to pay for the projects – on condition we own the assets - and still they are dragging their feet," he replied. "I think Briton is still getting used to the reality of not always being in the driving seat, especially when it comes to smaller countries like Ireland," I suggested. That seemed to strike a chord. At the end of the meeting, he said "I know you are a journalist and have to stay officially neutral, but I understand you might be interested in joining us, and perhaps standing as a candidate in the next election?

"I think that might be a bridge too far. At present I am living in East Belfast, and there isn't a Green seat there. In fact, there is hardly a Green seat anywhere in Northern Ireland, and probably won't be for quite a while. I think a more realistic option might be for me to act as a Ministerial advisor, focused on improving British Irish cooperation."

> "And would you give up your job as a journalist? That seems quite a useful platform to be working off..."

"We could see how it goes. You could give me exclusives on Irish government policy announcements, I could try to get access to your British counterparts and get a handle on their thinking, and together we might be able to work through some of the frustrations you are currently experiencing. Often, it's the way policy or project proposals are put, which helps to get them through the civil service and political approval processes. I suspect there has been an element of people talking past each other. Losing Northern Ireland is still an open wound for some in the service."

That seemed to clinch the deal.

Having an Englishman as an informal go between might be able to grease a few wheels. As well as being the Tribune Irish Correspondent and occasional Sports reporter, I once again added environmental stories to my brief. Prof. Meekan seemed terribly pleased with some of the very well informed reports I was sending back from Ireland, and opened doors for me to see the relevant ministers in London. I may have omitted to mention that a lot of the data and analysis I was presenting had been largely prepared by Irish civil servants and their expert advisers.

Starmer government ministers, on the other hand, seemed obsessed with keeping the press on-side. Prof. Meekan had a considerable reputation on environmental matters, and a Tribune editorial criticising the government's performance on environmental matters would not go down well in Downing Street.

Doors were opening for me everywhere I went, and even though I say so myself, British Irish cooperation on energy and environmental matters seemed to get better and better from that point. I was also able to charge the Irish government some "consultancy fees" for time spent at meetings and briefing them on British concerns. It all made for a very cosy relationship.

Some might even regard some of my work as spying. I prefer to characterise it as mutually beneficial diplomacy. Whenever asked, I was always happy to discuss where my information was coming from, within the bounds of journalistic privilege and confidentiality. Most of it ended up on the pages of the Tribune in any case, which blended nicely with the Tribune's attempts to position itself as an environmentally aware newspaper. Once again, I felt secure in my job.

Not so much for Síle, unfortunately. Unionists had obviously targeted her seat as one they had to win at the next election. They still couldn't believe they had lost it last time out. So much so, that they had rather taken it for granted that it was a unionist seat and hadn't made any great effort to get their vote out. They would not make the same mistake next time around. The Sinn Féin label hung like an albatross around her neck, making it impossible for many unionists, particularly from middle class areas, to work with her. I suggested she might be better off as an independent. She wouldn't hear of it. Something to do with her loyalty to her father, I suspected.

15.   A brave new world

In some ways politics in Northern Ireland was becoming increasingly normalised, if by that you mean the normal humdrum business of back room deals, trying to improve public services, and getting investment for your area. There was still plenty of crime and anti-social behaviour, but it seemed to fade into background noise that you barely noticed. Not only was my paper not printing stories about it anymore, but I was losing interest in writing about it.

I was getting fully engrossed in my new role as (background) advisor to the Irish government on British Irish environmental cooperation. Our work was highlighted in a report to the Dáil by Environment Minister Eamonn Ryan and repeatedly referenced by An Taoiseach, Micheál Martin, as a good example of British Irish cooperation working in practice.

I was becoming increasingly intrigued by the possibility of Belfast shipyard becoming a hub for the construction and maintenance of floating offshore wind turbines. Somebody had to do it, so why not a port close to many of the proposed windfarm locations with a history and tradition of ship building. I wrote a couple of speeches for Síle about it. I even spoke to a couple of companies who were thinking of investing in such a project.

Government support, within EU state aid guidelines, was certainly forthcoming. Eamonn Ryan was excited about it. But nothing seemed to come of the tentative enquiries. I got the impression that these companies, or their executives, didn't want to become embroiled in what they saw as a difficult political and social scene in Belfast. The official reason was that the Far East was much cheaper for steel fabrication and ship building even if you factored in transport costs. I never saw a spreadsheet which justified that assertion. The IDA were certainly frustrated by the lack of progress.

Improving employment prospects for Belfast youth was certainly seen as key to reducing anti-social behaviour. If anyone had a realistic business proposition, the government was all over it, with civil servants practically writing the grant application for you. Government ministers were coming up for even the most trivial new jobs announcements. Síle had to stand back, with gritted teeth, as yet another minister took credit for the launching of a project she had championed.

I spoke to Eamonn Ryan about it on one of our frequent trips to London. The government was so keen to be seen to reach out to unionists, they were forgetting the nationalist and other communities in Belfast. Resentment against Dublin was building up amongst nationalists who were comparing Dublin rule with London rule. I mentioned Síle was getting a lot of grief from Sinn Féin representative in West Belfast because she seemed to be getting far more cash for East Belfast. What he said surprised me.

> "We could do with a few more Síle's in the Green party. She is one of their most impressive performers in the Dáil when she gets a chance to speak – which isn't often because she's not a frontbencher. But she seems to know a lot more about community outreach programmes than most of them".

I said I knew her quite well and could set up a meeting if he wished. He said that would be great, but I wasn't sure if he was just fobbing me off. To my surprise Síle was asked to a meeting about community employment in Dublin shortly afterwards. Pippa Hackett met her and seemed very interested in all her ideas, some of which had been slow to get traction in Belfast.

Pippa Hackett also mentioned they were looking for a candidate to run in East Belfast. Would she be interested? Síle seemed shocked at the suggestion she would consider switching party. She immediately suspected I had put Pippa up to it and gave me a bit of a roasting for interfering with her business. If the word got out she was talking to the wrong people, she could be finished in Sinn Féin.

I felt like saying that that was one more reason she should consider leaving Sinn Féin but held my peace. She seemed to have gotten on very well with Pippa, however, and several projects they discussed made good progress afterwards. She complained that the Greens were a middle class party whose concerns were far removed from the back streets of East Belfast. I replied that I thought I knew someone who could change that...

I covered the Sinn Féin Ard Féis as a political reporter. There was a lot of anger directed at the government for the slow pace of integration and the alleged over reliance on the private sector to "lift all boats." There had to be direct government investment in places like West Belfast and disadvantaged rural areas. I was sorry Síle didn't get a speaking slot. She was getting all the money the community could handle for projects in East Belfast. That obviously wasn't the message the leadership wanted to hear.

I asked her why West Belfast wasn't getting more resources pumped into it. She was scathing. Apart from Féile An Phobail, and a few other existing projects, no one was actively championing many new projects. It's as if they didn't want the competition. The Casement Park redevelopment was being driven entirely by the GAA. The Sinn Féin TDs for the area were so sure of their seats, they didn't have to do any work. They just swanned around making speeches at commemorations. They did one for my granddad and grand uncle and didn't even know what they were talking about.

"Surely they asked you to do the keynote speech?" I asked innocently. "Oh no, I would be too emotional. We would have to focus on the political project. That was before the Border Poll." I could see she was close to tears. We hugged. "He was your grandfather, not theirs. They had no right to appropriate him for their political cause," I tried to sympathise.

> *"That's only the half of it. He had become disillusioned with the armed struggle. He was trying to put an end to it long before Gerry Adams. That was before the British army sniper got him. I*

always wondered whether the British Army wanted the armed struggle to go on, because dealing with violence through greater violence is what they are comfortable with. Who gave the order to target my father? It was well known he was trying to put a stop to it."

And she burst out in tears.

We embraced for a long time. I was so angry. But there was nothing I could say.

The next time I was in Dublin, I asked for a meeting with the Minister for Justice, Naomi Long. She knew I was working closely with Eamonn Ryan. She assumed it was about making sure all the Garda car fleet went electric on schedule. She was a bit taken aback when I asked could she find out who gave the order to shoot Síle's grandfather, and why. She knew I was a friend of Síle. She didn't know how close we had become. She asked:

> *"You know I know Síle quite well?"* - I do.

> *"And you know I would do anything to help her?"* – I do.

> *"And you know the British security services won't open their files to anyone?"* – I do.

> *"So why do you think I can help?"*

"Well, I know from my work with Eamonn that there's a lot of give and take between British and Irish Ministers. People helping each other out with publicity, covering over problems, things like that..."

> *"Yes, but the security services are a whole different world, things are kept very tight".*

"Yes, I know. But there is also a lot of intelligence sharing going on. We give them stuff. They give us stuff. All's fair in love and war, and we're still trying to move away from the war..."

"Leave it with me, I'll see what I can do. They do owe me a favour or two, but this sort of stuff... its usually totally off limits, no one wants to go back to those days."

"Tell you what, I'm a reporter. You don't want to be talking to me about this sort of stuff. If you do find out something, talk to Síle. I know you are friends. And she really needs to know."

Naomi came good on the police car electrification programme.

Some weeks later Síle came back from her week in Dublin looking quite pale. She wanted to talk to me. Apparently, the order to target her father had come from an intelligence officer who was handling several IRA informants.

Apparently one of the informants told him that Síle's grandfather had been interfering with attempts to broker a cease fire and that he needed to be eliminated. It was only afterwards that the intelligence officer learned that the opposite was the case.

The informant was now a powerful Sinn Féin backroom figure who called the shots on a lot of tactical decisions. Síle felt that might explain some of the problems she was having with head office. She was devastated. They were always going on about "unreliable elements" in the party, but she had never realised she might be regarded as one.

She confronted Sinn Féin leader Mary Lou MacDonald with the information and said she was resigning from the party. Mary Lou said she knew nothing of all this, and offered to investigate, but it was too late. Once Síle had made up her mind, there was no turning her. "I actually believe Mary Lou was sincere about knowing nothing and being willing to investigate" she said. But Mary Lou doesn't run that side of the show.

Síle announced she would be standing as an independent at the next election soon afterwards. Many doors which had been tightly closed to her seemed to open ever so slightly afterwards. The Greens never put pressure on her to join, but made it clear she would be welcome. They weren't sure they could find another candidate to run in East Belfast in any case.

In the end she accepted their invitation to join and run on their behalf. They needed someone who could organise a branch of the party in East Belfast. The Greens there were totally disorganised, run by a few elderly gentlemen who organised garden and hill walks. It was time they developed a proper electoral machine. Síle managed to bring most of her personal supporters with her. A few were initially aghast but were eventually won over. I don't know if she ever told them her true reason for leaving Sinn Féin. It was not a policy dispute as was reported in the press.

In no time she was organising party meetings and information seminars all over the constituency, even in loyalist estates. She exposed the myth that working class people aren't interested in environmental, biodiversity and climate change issues. Quite a few expressed relief that she had left Sinn Féin. They had always admired her work but couldn't bring themselves to support Sinn Féin. She told them she understood why.

The Greens were delighted to have another TD in Northern Ireland. Three is a lot better than two. One was thinking of retiring and was relieved that the party had new talent coming through to take his place. Her community work was much admired, and she felt appreciated for the first time.

When I asked her to marry me, she practically jumped on top of me. It was a spur of the moment decision by me. I hadn't even organised a ring. She forgave me that, and many other things.

It was the beginning of a whole new world for me.

Síle encountered quite a lot of hostility from Sinn Féin activists from then on in. Some said they always knew she was an unreliable sort. Had it been me I would have outed the senior party figure who had fingered her grandfather. I now understood why Sunak had said, at our private meeting in Chequers which now seemed many years ago, that he wasn't worried about having to deal with a Sinn Féin government. That they had enough information on all their senior figures to keep them in line.

After our engagement became public, I was also targeted. It was suggested I was the "English agent who had turned Síle!" The idea that the British government had agents running around trying to turn Sinn Féin TDs into Green TDs seemed so ridiculous to me I actually burst out laughing when someone accused me of it. "We have ways of dealing with your sort" he said rather ominously.

When I told Síle about it afterwards, she laughed and said not to worry about it. She knew the guy in question, and he was "all mouth." She'd have a word with his mother, and she would sort him out! I had to laugh at the thought of a Sinn Féin hard man being brought to heel by his mother.

It did make me a little wary of who I spoke to and who was walking behind me on the street, but I never had a problem after that. I accompanied Síle to quite a lot of functions in the area and so became quite well known to all and sundry. Quite a few thanked me for making "an honest woman of her," while others cursed me for "taking her off the market." She was, apparently, a much admired woman by many in the locality, right across party lines.

I had got to know her as an accomplished politician. I was only really beginning to see her as a woman. And a woman of considerable beauty at that.

I can be a bit slow sometimes.

16. Our Wedding

Some relationships start out well and turn sour. Some start badly and get better. I was one of the very lucky ones. Our relationship started well, and just got better and better. Of course, we had rows, but they were generally about politics. When it came to the really important things in life, like how to deal with the aftermath of the Russian invasion of Ukraine, I felt I was the expert, and insisted on having my way. She dealt with all the little things in life like where to live, what car to buy, and how to organise our wedding.

I was utterly shocked to discover that, despite her rage at the Catholic Church, she wanted a church wedding. One of the many other little contradictions in Irish life I found difficult to understand. Apparently, a wedding is not so much for the benefit of the people getting married, but for their families and friends to get to know each other and form a larger joint community surrounding both partners. I knew very little about her family and had shared even less about mine. Some very complex and sensitive negotiations followed.

Having been involved in covering high politics for some time, I thought this would be a breeze. It turned out I seemed to lose the negotiation every time. Her mother seemed to be calling most of the shots. I had barely gotten to know her, meeting at a funeral, another almost unique Irish institution. She was the sort of woman who would put the fear of God into anyone, and, it turned out, that included her local Parish Priest in the Ardoyne, a Catholic working class estate in West Belfast, and a Sinn Féin stronghold.

Well, that rules out inviting any of my loyalist friends and acquaintances I had been keeping up contact with, I thought. But would Greens even be welcome? "Divil the bit of it" was her dismissive response. They'll all come if you invite them. They'll have no choice. We can have the reception up in Knock in that posh place to make them feel more comfortable. The Stormont Hotel was not my idea of a politically neutral or discreetly low profile venue. I had in mind a low key small family gathering. They seemed to think that 200 guests was a minimum requirement, and that was only their side of the family!

I doubted I could find 200 friends and family who would be bothered to come. I would have to delve back into my student and rugby days to make up that number, and I hadn't kept in touch with some of them in years! In the end we settled for 150 from her side, and I felt I could rustle up 50 from mine. Any English wedding I had ever been at had barely had 50 guests. Funerals could be even smaller. I was therefore shocked to find the best part of 1,000 mourners at her granny's sisters' funeral. "Gran will be very upset her sister won't be at our wedding," Síle said. "We should have organised it sooner."

Yea right! I should organise my love life to suit Gran's sister I thought. The look she gave me was enough to indicate clearly that a response wasn't required... Oh God! I felt I was already hurtling along a totally unfamiliar track at breakneck speed, and that was with a wedding date still six months away! I was already being asked what I would be wearing, and discretely being shown pictures of toffs in Ascot suits and tails. That was the very last thing I would be wearing. I couldn't think of anything worse. It brought back bad memories of all that Public School dress uniform and other crap I had spent years unlearning. No one from my school days was going to be on my guest list. I had gone under deep cover from all that the moment I left school and wasn't ready to re-surface. I hadn't seen them in many years anyway.

I said, to general shock and consternation, that I would probably be able to find an old, frayed jeans on the day. I just know there was a conspiracy afoot to subvert all of that. Some mornings I subconsciously checked my wardrobe half expecting half my wardrobe to have ben mysteriously brought to the "cleaners", never to be seen again. It's not that I didn't have a decent suit or two. I needed them for work when accompanying government ministers or for some TV interview. But I was greeted with some scorn when I said they would do fine. I thought I had set out quite a strong negotiating position when I had mentioned the frayed Jeans. A good business suit, perhaps even a new one, should have been greeted with much relief as a very reasonable compromise and a major concession on my behalf.

Not a bit of it! I was virtually marched into Louis Copeland's, a specialist tailor in Dublin, only to discover that "wedding wear" was a genre all of its own. I thought that sort of thing only happened in Four weddings and a Funeral. Anyway, I had maintained an air of studious indifference, and couldn't be seen to care overmuch now, one way or the other. But I was adamant I wasn't going to be dressed up as an English Toff. It was bad enough being English with a posh accent in Ballyhackamore or the Ardoyne. I wasn't going to dress the part as well. There would be no cravat, and I seriously didn't like having to wear a tie.

The sales assistant was very understanding. "Would sir like a winged collar, they can be very comfortable, especially on a hot or humid day!" I was sweating already. But I was also saving my trump card until last. I happened to mention to Eamonn Ryan, while on another trip to London, that I was getting married in July, and the women were already fussing over what I should wear. "Well of course you'll be wearing a sustainable suit!" he said. I didn't know there was such a thing. So, I replied to the sales assistant, "It doesn't matter as long as everything is sustainable, I'm marrying a Green TD after all!"

I was waiting for the stumped look on their faces. Not a bit of it. "Excellent choice sir, we have a range over here." Now I was truly hoist on my own petard. I succumbed meekly from that point on. I had hoped that whatever clothes I bought would be useful for other occasions as well. I wasn't sure that there would be too many occasions where I would need an ecofriendly organic cotton suit and dress shirt with silk tie, vegan leather belt, and re-cycled pet bottle shoes, responsibly sourced, and made in factories with ethical codes of conduct. But I was feeling more virtuous already! I was also going to have to ask the Tribune for a raise...

The big day arrived. I had sent out invitations to immediate family and relations, some distant cousins I had rarely met and a range of friends from my college and rugby days in England and Ireland, plus almost every politician I had regular dealings with. I thought that if 25% of them arrived, it would be a good turnout.

It turns out that everyone in Ireland seems to like a good day out. The Parish church in the Ardoyne was packed. I hardly recognised anyone. It seems half the parish came to have a good look at the Bride and Groom, most not invited to the reception. There were cameras and smartphones everywhere, and I swear what looked like a TV camera.

I had thought all the politicians I had invited would turn up only at the reception, if at all. But there they were, working the waiting crowd, as if they were meeting long lost friends. Sinn Féin had turned out in force, led by Michelle O'Neill. It seems that being a local trumped a political change of allegiance. But so too did Naomi Long, Eamonn Ryan, Neale Richmond, and Pippa Hacket. A virtual coalition of government ministers. It seems that no opportunity to build north south relationships was to be missed. No wonder the TV cameras were there.

But what really shocked me was the number of loyalists from East Belfast who had made the trip across town to a Catholic church in enemy territory. They were warmly greeted and seemed to know a lot of the Sinn Féin politicos. Gavin Robinson (DUP leader) met me at the door. His religious principles wouldn't allow him to enter, but he wished me well and said he would see me at the reception. He wouldn't be boycotting the Stormont Hotel!

Síle finally arrived looking absolutely gorgeous. I felt I had won the Lotto and then some. The ceremony was much as the rehearsal had said. The homily was mercifully brief and to the point. We were to have children and lots of them, apparently. I wasn't asked to foreswear my religion or my identity. My family had all arrived suitably attired. My mother looked ever so well, and even my father seemed well behaved. They had not approved of my match of course, but relented somewhat when they heard she was a member of parliament. They also knew their approval wasn't required.

But as usual, Síle had charmed them all when they met for the first time some months before the wedding. I think my mum secretly approved. My father couldn't bring himself to approve anything I had ever done. Apparently, I had "let the side down" which was unforgiveable in his view. It didn't help that I didn't seem to know which side I was supposed to be on, or even understand why there had to be sides in the first place. His army service had never taken him to Northern Ireland, thank God, or else he would have known he was surrounded by Shinners.

Or perhaps he did know. I learned afterwards that he had taken advice from the security services and insisted on having a security detail. I never noticed them until the hotel. Apparently, he had been in a similar situation "in the colonies" and knew that the main thing was to look imperious and imposing. He could do that very well. I never did know precisely what he did in the army, except that it involved intelligence work.

I was shocked to find out later that the Shinners knew of him. Apparently, they had also kept a close eye on me when I first arrived, although the political situation was far less tense by then. In fact, they saw my reporting as evidence that the "British establishment" was ready to let go of Northern Ireland. I had never thought of myself as representing the "British establishment." In fact, my student days had been one long rebellion against what I saw as a snobby class system. My abduction by the UVF had increased my street cred enormously. Apparently, I was supposed to high tail it back to England after that, and I was respected for having stayed the course. The war was long over, as was the political struggle. We could all be friends now.

The reception also went off very well. Everyone was well oiled and in excellent form. Síle was charming everyone and greeting them as long lost friends. I was amazed at her ability to remember names and faces of hundreds of people. (I was shocked to discover that the reception was actually for 300 people). I had been dreading the speeches. I had asked my editor, Matt Casey to be my best man as he had stuck by me through thick and thin when I really needed him at the start of my career.

If his speech in praise of me was any guide, I was in line for a Pulitzer prize for journalism. There were unconcealed guffaws when I was described as having had a huge influence on improving Anglo-Irish relations. I had a quick look over at a loyalist table and they were pointing cocked hands at me as if they were carrying handguns! Apparently, I had a way of getting under people's skin which was ultimately for the benefit of all. I'm not sure everyone in the room agreed.

This made me all the more determined that my speech would be uncontroversial. There would be no dodgy jokes or acerbic asides. There were too many loyalists and republicans in the room with drink taken to take any risks. I started with the usual list of thanks for all the people who had made long journeys to be here. My family, my college and rugby friends, my journalistic colleagues. The politicians I had harassed and hounded at press conferences. Peter Kyle had made the trip over even though he was a busy Culture Secretary in the Starmer cabinet and no longer had any responsibilities in Northern Ireland – beyond attendance at a very occasional British-Irish Intergovernmental Conference.

I noted we almost had a quorum for a British-Irish Intergovernmental Conference, but that there were to be no discussions on the restoration of the devolved Stormont institutions tonight! But most of all I just wanted to extend my heartfelt thanks to Síle's family for welcoming me into their family. I felt that my family circle of friends had just been extended manyfold in one day. I really meant that.

Just as Matt was about to bring the formalities to a close, as I thought, my dad stood up to speak. I was horrified. The thought of him speaking at my wedding had never occurred to me. It wasn't on the agenda. He spoke of how proud he was of me making my way through academia and rugby to a career in journalism. How I had never shied away from difficult assignments and saying difficult things that needed to be said. (I had no idea he ever read my stuff). He was proud that the "historic enmity between Britain and Ireland was over" and that his family had played a very small role in that.

He said he very much enjoyed meeting our guests at the wedding, many of whom he only knew through government intelligence files... You could hear a pin drop. But he was so happy that the bad days were over and that those files could be consigned to history. He finished to scattered applause. I think there were a few people in shock. I certainly was. If people were worried I was a British agent, they had almost heard it from the horse's mouth now. There was no point in telling them I had been estranged from my father since my school days.

Síle handed me a glass of champaign and said, "drink this". I gulped it down in one go. My father was looking over at me. I think I saw love in his eyes for the first time in a long time. He was almost in tears, as I was. I went over and gave him a hug. He just said, "well done!" I didn't know what to say, except "Thanks Dad" in what I hoped was a sincere way.

But the drama wasn't quite yet over. Late in the evening it was time for Síle and me to take our ceremonial leave. Stopping by every table, saying a few words of thanks, listening to a few comments, and moving on. I felt like a politician working the crowd, until we stopped at a Republican table. There, to my shock, was the man who had fingered Síle's grandfather for execution. I had no idea he had been invited. Síle looked him in the eye and said she forgave him for what he had done to her grandfather.

There was a very uncomfortable shuffle around the table. Most, no doubt, had no idea what she was talking about. But he knew, you could tell it in his eyes. He stood up, embraced her, and apologised. "If I could only undo what I did" he whispered in her ear, thanked her for her forgiveness, and left the room.

People on adjoining tables had gone quiet. The music might even have stopped, or else I could no longer hear. We continued on our round as if nothing had happened. Naomi greeted us on our way out the door, her security detail close behind. We hugged and thanked her for coming and for all her help and disappeared into the cool night air. Our car was waiting. We were both exhausted, but it had been a great day.

17. The Ukraine War

In all this time the war in Ukraine was still raging. Much of the east of the country had been devastated. It had been bombed so much there were bombs destroying the remnants of old bombs. Mines were everywhere close to the front lines. The human toll had been devastating.

Russia was also suffering badly, but there was no sign of Putin being overthrown. It was long past devising any face saving plan which would allow Putin to claim victory and then allow the occupied territories determine their own future by way of a UN supervised referendum. Hardly any civilians were still living in most of the captured areas in any case.

Ukraine had set its face against any "land for peace deal". Whatever the rights and wrongs of the origins of the war, this one was going to be fought until one side or the other conceded defeat. Neither government, nor indeed, nomenklatura could hope to survive such a concession. For Ukraine it was a matter of survival as an independent state. For Russia it was a matter of survival of the ruling class, the neo-imperial dream, and Russia's pretensions to be a world power.

Many in the West complained that a stalemate was just what the arms industry wanted. Arms sales were booming. New more effective and expensive weapons were being tested in live fire situations. What was less well known was that Northern Ireland was at the forefront of the advanced arms industry, manufacturing some of the most sophisticated missile systems, and more recently drone swarm systems. Many of these were now playing an important part in the Ukraine war enabling Ukraine to counter Russia's air, manpower and hardware superiority.

The drone systems were ostensibly for civilian use – personal transportation for a new age. But they were supposed to be only at the development stage, and yet to be licenced for personal transport. Industry insiders who would speak - and they were few and far between

– couldn't understand why an expensive product, not yet available for sale, was being manufactured in such industrial quantities, far beyond the needs of a normal R&D programme. I investigated as much as I could, but was meeting closed doors everywhere I went, even in those government circles where doors were open for me for anything else.

Gradually rumours emerged from the Ukraine that the drones were being manufactured in Northern Ireland in skeleton form, and then being shipped to France and weaponized and equipped with the latest navigation, jamming resistance, and collision avoidance software. Ireland was shipping a lot of civilian aid to the Ukraine in line with our policy of neutrality. (I say "our" because, following my marriage, I was granted Irish citizenship through an accelerated naturalisation process). I managed to blag my way onto a convoy delivering aid to Kiev and surrounding cities.

When I got to Kharkiv I filed my reports and took a couple of weeks off. Using my press pass and some Euros and Ukrainian hryvnias I made my way to the battlefront and saw the drones in action. They were a sight to behold. Large enough to carry a passenger, which was their civilian design intention, they were instead fitted with machine guns, anti-tank bombs, and a lot of sensors and communication equipment.

But what was extraordinary was that they moved in swarms rather like bees with the software, geo-location and anti-collision sensors ensuring they didn't collide with each other. When attacked by an enemy missile, they simply parted like a bee swarm to allow the missile pass through, all the while firing at the missile on approach and departure. The software was sophisticated and fast enough to prevent them firing on each other as each drone was aware of the locations of the other drones.

They were so agile that they could change position, both horizontally and vertically so quickly and at the last moment, that no conventional missile could alter course rapidly enough to actually strike them. Conventional collision avoidance software had been upgraded to avoid missile strikes. Only the larger missiles with proximity fuses packed enough power to destroy them, and Russia was running out of those.

Besides, it was a good bargain if Russia had to use a large missile to destroy a couple of drones.

Their electric motors emitted so little heat that even sensitive heat seeking missiles found it difficult to target them, and optical systems found it hard to target them at night. The only effective way to down them was by conventional machine gun fire which, again, was difficult to do at night.

They carried infrared sensors which could detect human body heat, and which allowed them to accurately target and shoot all humans in their sphere of operations at night, to a range of up to 300 metres. They could carry bombs big enough to drop onto, and destroy a tank, truck, tanker, artillery unit or missile launcher, again targeted either through infrared or optical sensors.

A remote human operator with a laptop or smartphone could define the sphere of operations (to avoid friendly fire incidents) and prioritise targets. They had a range of up to 300 miles which meant they had basically laid waste to an area up to 150 miles beyond the front line. The really revolutionary aspect of their physical design was that their aluminium bodies were simultaneously the rigid frame of the craft and the aluminium based battery power source. This improved their range and power to weight ratio considerably.

They were directed to an area by satellite reconnaissance and proceeded to kill or destroy everything in sight, or which emitted a heat signal. Computers systems "remembered" the areas devastated to ensure no wasteful flights or munitions usage.

Of course, losses were still high, but the rate of manufacture seemed to be able to keep up with the rate of destruction. They had basically neutralised all ground and sea based Russian military activity within 150 miles of the front line, and any Russian forces within that zone were unable to be re-supplied and were gradually being picked off.

The beauty of the system, from a Ukrainian point of view, was that they didn't have to invade and hold onto heavily mined and fortified enemy held territory at all. All they needed were a few "spearheads" where they could locate, recharge, and rearm the drones to complete several missions in one night. Recharging took place mainly during the day using solar panels where diesel generators were unavailable. There were even rumours that elite units had located several spearheads deep into Russian territory so they could target airfields, military installations, energy infrastructure and industrial factories in Russian territory well behind the front line.

The satellite based intelligence and targeting systems was so accurate and effective that wasteful and politically counterproductive attacks on civilian infrastructure could be avoided, although "dual use" infrastructure such as bridges, railway lines, electricity substations, gas pipelines, and fuel depots were increasingly targeted. Basically, nothing could move anywhere near the Ukrainian border anymore.

The remaining Russian garrisons on Ukrainian territory were being starved into submission, their supply lines blocked, and their equipment destroyed. Ukraine was actually taking its time recovering its territory to allow the mine sweepers do their work. There was no point in risking soldiers' lives when holding territory conferred no military advantage. Virtually no Ukrainian civilians were still living there anymore anyway.

Russia's war effort was basically being reduced to medium and long range air and missile strikes. Even their long range artillery installations were being destroyed. It would be some time before the general public would know that the invasion had failed, but those near the front lines knew the tide had turned.

I was arrested by the Ukrainian military authorities shortly after arriving near the front line, and my phone and laptop seized. But not before I had sent off a couple of reports to Matt Casey who was busy and having difficulty finding corroborating sources without telling the defence authorities what he knew. He published my reports anyway having had difficulty contacting me for a couple of days. Apparently, they caused a major stir in Britain, France, and Ireland.

Ukrainian military intelligence was busy trying to find out how much I knew, but basically gave up having read my reports in the Tribune. They were amazed I had gotten so close to several frontline units, who gave me the information for my reports. I had not been authorised to be anywhere near the front line, but I refused to reveal who I had been speaking to. (In fact, it was mostly front line ground troops thrilled at their successes with the new technology. Some had surprisingly good English or directed me to someone who did. I avoided officers who might have ordered my immediate arrest or removal).

I actually enjoyed my time being interrogated by military intelligence. It became a game of cat and mouse where I was able to deduce the importance of certain issues by their persistence in asking about them. They seemed rather alarmed when I asked had the drones been manufactured in Northern Ireland. Ireland is a neutral state and doesn't provide us with weaponry was their standard response which seemed to have been learned off a script.

It wasn't that I was the first reporter to find out all this. But previous reports had been mostly successfully suppressed. Not even Matt had known I was heading for the front line. I wondered if I would have been ordered home, had any of the higher ups in the Tribune known. The British Ministry of defence had been very active issuing DSMA (do not publish) advisory notices recently.

But it was the Irish government that was truly alarmed. The Mutual Defence Treaty with Britain had been controversial enough, with Sinn Féin objecting to it as compromising our neutrality. But the idea that lethal assault weapons were being shipped from Ireland to Ukraine, albeit via a weaponizing process in France, was political dynamite.

The Russian ambassador was not slow to go public. He had been telling the Irish authorities about this for months, he said, and they had always denied any involvement in weapons exports. (The TOSCA had specifically exempted Northern Ireland arms manufacturers from restrictions on their exports to Britain, NATO, or the EU). It later emerged the weaponization and export to Ukraine had been authorized by the French government.

That did not prevent an almighty political row breaking out in Ireland. The Russian Ambassador had hinted that Ireland was now a legitimate target in the war. Security around northern Ireland defence manufacturing sites was greatly increased. The Irish government pointed out that the drones were in the process of being licensed for civilian use, and then anyone (not subject to sanctions) would be able to buy them for personal transport purposes. They could not control what the French government chose to do with pre-licensed developmental models which had been part of the research and development effort.

The opposition focused on who knew what, when, and what they did about it. It would be a clear breach of Ireland's policy of neutrality if the government knew the drones were being weaponized and forwarded to Ukraine.

Some government friendly commentators noted that Ireland had also informally supported the British war effort during WWII while maintaining a formal policy of neutrality. Irish citizens were allowed to join the British army, British airmen lost over Ireland were repatriated, while Germans were not, and weather reports and other intelligence was forwarded to assist in D-Day and Allied sea operations.

The Government ordered a halt to any new export orders pending an investigation as to what they were being used for, but apparently there were by now enough on order and within the supply chain to keep Ukraine supplied with replacements at current loss rates for at least a year. In the view of many military analysts, Russia had already effectively lost the war, although this fact was not yet generally appreciated.

The big geopolitical concern was that the prospect of a humiliating defeat would force Putin to resort to using tactical nuclear weapons. President Kamala Harris made it clear that would elicit a nuclear response from the USA.

The carrot being offered to Putin was that his occupation of Crimea could be internationally recognised. The US had pointedly refused to give Ukraine any satellite intelligence on the peninsula, Ukrainian attacks there had been limited to isolated kamikaze drone attacks of limited effectiveness, restricted as they were to static targets which did not require active satellite navigation facilities and remote control communications support.

It was probably a complete coincidence, but my reports were published just as there was a huge increase in western reportage that Russia had effectively lost the war. There was huge anxiety that Putin would resort to tactical nuclear weapons and as to whether President Harris would have the "bottle" to respond effectively.

She was in a relatively weak position, having ascended to the Presidency only on the illness and later death of President Biden. The US military were known to regard her with a certain amount of contempt. Would she be forced to over-react and start an all-out nuclear war if Putin broke the nuclear taboo?

Some suggested she was pursuing a ""madwoman strategy." Nixon's administration had used a "madman strategy" to make the leaders of hostile Communist Bloc nations think he was irrational and volatile. It was used to incentivise those leaders to avoid provoking the United States, fearing an unpredictable and perhaps nuclear American response.

There were reports from "informed sources" that the US would go all out for a full nuclear first strike which would effectively destroy Russia's entire nuclear arsenal in the event of Russia employing tactical nuclear weapons in Ukraine. The worry was that while the US had the capability to destroy all of Russia's static nuclear launch sites, there were still enough difficult to track down submarine and mobile launchers to ensure enough nuclear weapons could be launched to destroy major western cities.

Or would Putin go all out and get his retaliation in first?

Not since the Cuban Missile Crisis had the world been in such jeopardy, and then too, America had had a young and inexperienced President. It was feared that Harris was a chess novice playing a grandmaster.

In the end it turned out Putin's strategic capabilities had been grossly over-estimated. Many Russian ICBM's (Inter-Continental Ballistic Missiles) had been used to deliver conventional payloads to Ukraine, such had been the depletion of their cruise missiles and conventional bomber stocks. Others were of very old manufacture and uncertain reliability. Corruption and lack of maintenance had reduced his operational nuclear weapons stockpile to a small fraction of their former capability.

It was a battle Putin couldn't win, and he knew it. He did a deal with President Harris, completely over the heads of the Ukraine government, NATO, and the EU. Russia's Sovereignty over Crimea would be officially recognised. Russian forces would withdraw to pre-war boundaries and UN supervised referenda would be held in occupied territories to determine whether the inhabitants (those that had survived or could be repatriated) wished to be part of Russia or Ukraine.

All prisoners would be exchanged and repatriated. There would be no war crime tribunals or reparations. Each country would bear its own costs and losses. Western sanctions would end. Ukraine would not be allowed to join NATO but could join the EU as long as it did not take part in its defence programmes.

President Zelenskyy was furious. Russia had given nothing that it hadn't already lost on the battlefield. Ukraine had lost Crimea, many lives, and an enormous amount of civilian infrastructure without any prospect of compensation.

Outside observers noted that Ukraine would have lost everything without western military, economic, and diplomatic support. President Harris was entitled to call a halt as the Ukraine war effort could not succeed without US support. The war had done enough damage to all sides and simply couldn't be allowed go on. The risk of nuclear war was too great. It was time to turn a new page.

UN peacekeepers were supposed to man the Russian Ukraine border to prevent any further hostilities and to manage the flow of prisoners and refugees. In practice Ukraine erected a second border outside the UN zone checking the identities of all refugees and refusing entry to any who could not find a sponsor within Ukraine.

They claimed to do this because there was nowhere in the Russian invaded zones still suitable for civilian habitation without extensive Ukrainian support which it couldn't currently resource. Independent observers noted that it also prevented many Russian speakers, with strong ties to Russia rather than Ukraine, returning to vote in the UN referendums.

Not surprisingly, all the previously Russian occupied zones voted heavily to remain in Ukraine and Russia gained no territory beyond Crimea which it had occupied prior to the war in any case.

The costs of Ukrainian re-construction were enormous and were beyond the manpower of the Ukraine and the resources of the EU to finance for many years and are still ongoing as I write this in 2040. The Ukraine became a full member of the EU and rejected any restraints on its involvement in EU defence programmes on the grounds that it had not been party to the Harris Putin deal. EU Russia relations remained strained, and trade never recovered to pre-war levels. Putin retired soon afterwards to his Dacha in Sochi on the Black Sea coast.

The Irish government and many Irish construction and other companies played quite a significant role in Ukrainian re-construction. Many Ukrainian refugees stayed in Ireland for many years and made a major contribution to the Irish economy and society. There was a gradual drift back to Ukraine as circumstances there improved, as had happened with Polish immigrants many years before.

There were some isolated instances of racist abuse of refugees in particular areas but attempts to politicise the immigration issue by the

Irish Freedom Party fell on deaf ears and it never had any success in getting any representatives elected to Dáil Eireann. The situation in Hungary, Romania and Bulgaria was more fraught as they struggled to raise the living standards of their own people in the face of the considerable costs of Ukrainian reconstruction.

Some anti-EU politicians in the north also sought to politicise the issue of EU aid to Ukraine saying those costs could have been avoided had Northern Ireland remained in the UK outside the EU. It was not a widely adopted political position and Síle was scathing about those who begrudged Ukraine the opportunity to become a modern European state through the co-financed reconstruction and modernisation of its infrastructure. Ireland had benefited from EU membership in like manner many years before and many Irish firms benefited from being able to do business in Ukraine now.

The irony of Ukraine's success in the war having been significantly aided by "neutral" Ireland was lost on no one. The government investigation into drone exports to Ukraine via France found that "no one in political authority" knew that these drones were being weaponized in France and re-exported to Ukraine.

Until my reports that is, which were referenced in the enquiry's report. It noted that the government took decisive action to end the export of drones when this fact became known. It never adequately addressed the question of who, outside "those in political authority" knew what was going on, saying it was beyond its terms of reference.

The general assumption was that everyone who needed to know, knew. Everyone who didn't want to know, didn't. And thus, an ongoing staple of Irish public life was maintained. Irish "neutrality" was kept intact by the political system. It was the Private sector in Northern Ireland wot dunnit.

18.   Ambassador Filatov

I thought my breaking of the drone exports story would damage the close working relationship on British Irish energy cooperation I had with Eamonn Ryan. But he seemed quite philosophical about it all. The Greens had always supported neutrality and disarmament and "it was bound to come out sooner or later, and it was better coming from an Irish rather than a foreign source". I liked the way I was now considered an Irish source, even though I was working for a British newspaper.

He said he hadn't known about the Drones, but that Belfast built Thames missile systems were widely distributed to NATO and some were also being used in Ukraine. There was nothing that could be done about it under the terms of the TOSCA, and it would all die over once Sinn Féin had made whatever hay they could from the situation.

People were just glad the war seemed to be over, and perhaps secretly pleased Ireland had made a contribution to ending it. Russia and the Russian Ambassador Filatov weren't exactly popular in Ireland, and Ryan enjoyed linking Sinn Féin to Filatov's intemperate statements in his Dáil speeches.

Síle wasn't quite so comfortable with this, but let it pass. "The usual political games. We all do it sometimes." Some People Before Profit TDs accused me of one sided anti-Russian reporting. I replied that my reports didn't claim to be anything other than reports from the Ukrainian side of the front line. If I had been able to get to the Russian side of the front line, I could have reported from their perspective.

Shortly afterwards I was invited by Ambassador Filatov for a chat in the Russian embassy.

I was subjected to a long monologue about how the West had provoked the "special operation" by supporting an anti-Russian Coup, the 2014 Maidan Revolution. It had also reneged on promises that the Ukraine would not be allowed to join NATO until the "special operation" put a stop to that. That the West had allowed the Ukrainian regime to make war on Russian speakers in its eastern provinces and had been conducting an anti-Russian propaganda war ever since.

I make no claims to be an expert of Russo-Ukrainian history or recent relations, but I had written a piece back in April 2022 when I was still a sports reporter for the Wolverhampton Echo, shortly after the invasion, which was re-published by the Irish Independent at the time. I drew the Ambassador's attention to it:

"Government should summon ambassador Yuri Filatov to explain Moscow's 'denazification' policies.

> *"Ria Novosti, a pro-Russian government state-controlled media outlet, recently published an article entitled What should Russia do with Ukraine?*
>
> *It was written by Timofey Sergeytsev, an influential commentator who has worked on the presidential campaigns of Mikhail Prokhorov in Russia and Viktor Yanukovych in Ukraine.*
>
> *In it he states that "the special operation revealed that not only the political leadership in Ukraine is Nazi, but also the majority of the population. All Ukrainians who have taken up arms must be eliminated – because they are responsible for the genocide of the Russian people".*
>
> *He clarifies this by stating: "Denazification means de-Ukrainianisation. Ukrainians are an artificial anti-Russian construct.*
>
> *"They should no longer have a national identity.*
>
> *"Denazification of Ukraine also means its inevitable de-Europeanisation."*
>
> *He argues that "Ukraine's political elite must be eliminated as it cannot be re-educated".*

"Ordinary Ukrainians must experience all the horrors of war and absorb the experience as a historical lesson and atonement for their guilt," he states.

He then lists the tasks which must be undertaken by Russia, including:

- *the liquidation of Ukrainian armed forces and all supporting infrastructure.*
- *the formation of an anti-Nazi (read pro-Russian) government.*
- *the installation of a Russian information space.*
- *a mass investigation programme into Ukrainian war crimes and support for the Nazi regime.*
- *forced labour, imprisonment, and death sentences for all accomplices of the "Nazi regime".*
- *and the creation of permanent denazification bodies.*

Mr Sergeytsev places the conflict in the context of the eradication of US subjugation and western totalitarianism and their ungrateful treatment of Russia after all that Russia has done for the West by way of providing alternatives to capitalism.

Given that Russian president Vladimir Putin has also spoken about the need to denazify Ukraine, and has also claimed that Ukraine is not a real country, perhaps the Government here might like to summon ambassador Yuri Filatov to explain whether this represents official Russian government policy?"

I asked him, "As far as I am aware, Mr. Ambassador, the Irish government never did summon you to explain either Mr Sergeytsev or President Putin's comments". Ambassador Filatov replied:

No, they did not. Do we summon the Irish ambassador in Moscow every time RTE or some Journalist makes some remarks defamatory to Russia? No, we do not. Your Ambassador would have to be in our Foreign Ministry every day of the week. You would accuse us of interfering in press freedom if we did.

And as for President Putin, he is only expressing our long held belief that Ukraine is Russian and should be part of Russia. I believe the British felt that Ireland should be part of the UK for a very long time as well!

"Ah yes" But the British learned the error of their ways and eventually gave the people of Northern Ireland the right to join Ireland. And that was long before there was a majority of people in Northern Ireland wishing to leave the UK. Russia seems intent on learning the hard way that Ukraine doesn't wish to be part of Russia!

"Ukraine would be part of Russia now if it wasn't for the interference of the United States and NATO. What right has the United States to determine how we should relate to our neighbours!"

"But it wasn't just the USA, was it? Your invasion violated the UN Charter and was condemned worldwide. Even here in Ireland there was widespread condemnation – with the exception of two MEPs, Mick Wallace, and Claire Day - who were subsequently rejected by the people in the in the 2024 European Elections. And your relationship with Ireland has been anything but friendly. I draw your attention to a second article published in May 2022 in which I wrote the following:"

What more provocation do we need before we break off diplomatic relations with Russia?

The Irish Government expelled four out of 30 registered Russian diplomats in Ireland, allegedly for meeting dissident republican and loyalist paramilitaries in an attempt to stoke tensions here and in Northern Ireland.

In response, Russia expelled two of our six embassy staff in Moscow – one third of our full complement, which is equivalent to us expelling 10 of their diplomats here.

Russia has also been seeking to develop its four-acre site on Orwell Road as an intelligence-gathering hub for western Europe while doing nothing to prevent the activities of Russian-based hackers inserting ransomware software on our health service's systems, costing us millions, and putting lives at risk.

The Russian invasion of Ukraine will cost us billions of euro in aid and refugee hospitality costs, not to mention the Irish-owned aircraft worth billions that Russia has effectively stolen by re-registering them as Russian. Irish lessor Avolon has already lost €173 million this year after it could not get back aircraft leased to Russian airlines.

Now the most popular state-owned television channel, Russia-1, has broadcast mocked-up clips of nuclear weapons destroying Ireland in a report introduced by Dmitry Kiselyov, a close associate of Russian president Vladimir Putin.

What more provocation do we need before we finally break off diplomatic relations with this odious regime and expel the Russian ambassador who now claims to speak for Ukrainians and has been encouraging pro-Russian demonstrations here?

Surely the time has come to advise all remaining Irish nationals to leave Russia immediately and shut down our embassy there completely?

In the meantime, we can use their ample grounds in Orwell Road to house Ukrainian refugees and, if necessary, sell them off to fund our relief efforts.

"Is not the reality," Mr. Ambassador, "that President Putin has been plotting the elimination of most of the leadership and armed forces of

Ukraine all along, together with its liquidation as an independent state and incorporation into a greater Russia by force, whether it wanted to or not?

You have never accepted that an independent Ukraine should be allowed to exist, and you have also acted as a hostile actor towards Ireland, in total breach of your diplomatic status. Why should you and all your staff not be expelled from Ireland?"

Ambassador Filatov replied:

> *"Well, that is entirely a matter for the Irish Government, and they have had the good sense not to agree with you. It is important, even in times of war, that diplomatic channels remain open. I believe you kept both the German and British embassies here open during WWII.*
>
> *But your articles are examples of the sort of anti-Russian propaganda that the West has been propagating. All we sought to do in Ukraine was to protect the rights of Russians living there, as the British government is trying to do for British citizens living here under the TOSCA which your government signed.*
>
> *All you have done in your articles is to take some remarks by a journalist and by a TV show out of context. In reality Russia wants to have friendly relations with Ireland despite attempts by journalists like you to stir things up.*

I replied: "The remarks I quoted were published by a Russian State media organisation and Broadcast on Russian state TV. Putin himself has stated that Ukraine is not a real country and has become just a western satellite. You threatened nuclear war. Your staff have tried to promote violence in Ireland and allowed Russian hackers to compromise our health care systems. On what basis can you claim to want good relations with Ireland, Europe, or the Ukraine?"

The ambassador replied:

Ukraine is a difficult case. It allowed itself to come under the control of Nazi elements hostile to Russia. We had to protect our people there. Some things might have been said, in the heat of battle, which ought not to have been said. Those articles and programmes were part of our propaganda effort to make everyone realise the seriousness of the situation. We thought Zelenskyy might come to his senses and negotiate a peace deal. Any serious politician would have done so. But he wasn't interested. He wanted war. But we have a peace agreement now, and the time has come to reset relations on a more normal trajectory."

So, we should just forget the fact that hundreds of thousands have been killed, a quarter of the Ukraine destroyed, many war crimes have been committed, and, by the way, *Zelenskyy* is a democratically elected President who also happens to be a Jew. Your claims in relation to Ukraine being a Nazi led country have zero credibility."

"That is your opinion. We know from his actions against Russians living in Ukraine that Zelenskyy is no better than a Nazi. That is why we have had no dealings with him to the end. Presidents Putin and Harris have now signed a peace agreement over his head which settles all these matters. Do you want peace or not? You have just been trying to stir things up again. Nobody wants the war to continue. I am giving you my time now to convince you that it is time to move things on to a peaceful trajectory. You don't seem to want that."

"I would like to see war criminals punished, reparations paid, and Ambassadors who engage in unfriendly acts against Ireland expelled. Is that too much to expect?"

It is if you want peace. Russia would never accede to the sort of measures you suggest. We are a great power and will not let ourselves be humiliated like that. And by the way war crimes and acts of mass destruction against civilians and their infrastructure have been committed against Russia as well, and you yourselves don't have clean hand on that, having exported all those drones knowing what they were going to be used for. I protested many times to your Foreign Ministry. Your Foreign Minister would not even meet with me!"

"All of which goes to show what happens if you engage in hostile acts against Ireland. I still think you should have been expelled!"

And with that, the meeting was over. The Tribune published my report as its front page news. It must have been a quiet news day in Britain. The headline read:

"Russian Ambassador threatens war if attempts are made to humiliate Russia".

I felt the headline, composed by some editor, was way over the top. The Ambassador clearly wanted to normalise relations and move on with a peace deal having been signed. When I asked Matt Casey about it, he said that it may have been a bit sensationalist, but that with Russia, there is always some kind of background threat if they don't get their way. Without their ability to threaten nuclear war, they would have gotten nothing. He continued:

"And by the way, neither Britain, Ireland nor the EU are signatories to that deal. I wouldn't be surprised if the International Criminal Court pursued war crimes charges regardless of the deal. They have been investigating war crimes all along and it wouldn't be fair if they prosecuted only Ukrainian perpetrators. The USA doesn't get to ride roughshod over all of Europe and tell us who we can and can't trade with. Kamala Harris created a very bad precedent signing a deal over our heads and allowing war criminals go free ."

In Kamala Harris' defence, I countered: "I suppose she thought avoiding a nuclear war and ending the current conflict was worth it. She would have been risking nuclear bombs falling on her cities for a war fought on our behalf. There was very little in this war for the USA bar a lot of military expenditure which was eating up their defence budget and threatening the social and healthcare programmes she is committed to. The war was getting increasingly unpopular in the USA, and she had no chance of re-election if she didn't end it.

Besides, She can't force us to trade with Russia or allow their war criminals to roam free. The Russian economy is a basket case and their military have been exposed as a busted flush. Their nuclear capability has been much degraded and their dreams of remaining a world power are down the toilet. Putin has been put out to grass in Sochi and I don't think they will be invading anywhere else any time soon."

On that, we could agree.

Whether by total coincidence or otherwise. Ambassador Filatov was recalled soon afterwards to be replaced by a much more conciliatory figure; a woman journalist not associated with the Russian war effort. She was an environmentalist known for her reporting on climate change issues.

It was extremely unusual for a Russian Ambassador to be selected from outside the Foreign Ministry or security services. I like to think my articles might have had some influence on that, although I was never invited to the Russian embassy again. It would have been interesting to ask her the question!

19. Economic and social transformation

Work proceeded apace on broadening and deepening British Irish cooperation on sustainable energy production and distribution. Eamonn Ryan managed to get some very ambitious schemes approved by the Cabinet. The most ambitious being Ireland taking a full part in developing a European wide ultra-high voltage electricity supergrid (EUHVSG).

The idea was relatively simple. Wind is intermittent and solar panels rely on daylight if not out and out sunshine. What do you do when the wind doesn't blow and winter nights close in?

The largest windless areas are in the middle of anti-cyclones where the windless area can be up to several hundred kilometres across. Within this area very little wind energy can be captured although solar radiation may be high as anti-cyclones tend to generate good weather with very little cloud coverage. But at night, in an anti-cyclone, there may be no energy available for capture at all. Wave and tidal energy make a relatively small contribution to the sustainable energy mix and are also lower when there is no wind.

The solution is to have an energy grid that covers a very wide area so that it is always windy in some parts of the system. The wider the area, the more wind energy is available for capture somewhere in the system as a whole. The further the east west spread of the grid, the greater the number of daylight hours available for energy capture as sun rises earlier in the east and sets later in the west.

So, the concept of a EUHVSG is to connect solar and windfarms throughout the continent. The higher the voltage the less the transmission losses of electricity transmitted over long distances.

Over subsequent years, the system also connected to highly efficient Saharan solar farms, and Arctic wind farms in Iceland, the Faroe Islands, the Hebrides, and northern Scandinavia. Windfarms didn't have to be on the doorstep of highly populated areas interfering with their scenic amenities.

Ireland being a windy place on the western edge of the continent, could play a key role in the entire system. Additional undersea power cables would be required to Britain and France, but also to Spain, Iceland, and the Faroe Isles.

The initial capital cost of the wind and solar farms combined with the transmission lines would be high. But the cost of electricity production after that would be very low, limited to the maintenance costs of the system.

Ireland's very high budget surpluses and low cost of sovereign borrowing also made it much easier to fund the initial very high capital costs and meant that the Irish Sovereign Wealth Fund was at the forefront of these developments, providing long term steady returns to fund Ireland's increasing pensions bill.

Among the additional benefits would be the ability to tap into French and British baseload nuclear power or Norwegian Hydro when demand exceeded sustainable supply. However, the experience of Germany was that wind and solar alone can provide almost all the baseload power previously supplied by all the nuclear stations they had closed down.

Gas fired "peaker plants" were used to generate additional power at short notice when peak demand exceeded supply – generally around dinner time in most countries. But the experience of most countries, even with very limited inter-national interconnector lines, was that gas fired peaker plants were required less and less, for shorter and shorter periods of the day – reducing the consumption of expensive and greenhouse gas emitting gas year on year.

Oil, Coal, and lignite power stations were also gradually becoming redundant, as more and more of total electricity demand was met from renewable sources. Europe was becoming much less dependent on imported oil and gas, reducing its strategic vulnerability, and improving its standard of living as the money spent on imports could be spent on domestically produced goods.

This was partly because improvements in battery technology, and the widespread distribution of Batteries in rapidly expanding electric vehicle fleets meant more and more electricity could be stored at times of peak production and used when demand exceeded supply.

Smart metering and household demand management systems meant consumers could control their electricity consumption to use most when supply was plentiful. Wholesale and consumer electricity pricing incentivised usage when supply exceeded demand.

All of this was happening anyway but was greatly accelerated and improved through the construction of the Supergrid. Eamonn Ryan was on the case. Political barriers between national electricity producers had to be overcome. Huge finance was required to enhance both national grids and the connections between them.

Vested interests in the oil, gas and coal businesses with their powerful political lobbies and disinformation campaigns had to be overcome. Political prejudice and ignorance had to be addressed. And this was where my communication skills were to be harnessed.

What was the significance of all this to the unification of Ireland? You might well ask. Well, in some ways not a lot, and in other ways a great deal indeed.

The "not a lot" refers to the fact that Ireland had a unified grid management system before political re-unification was ever on the horizon. The whole point of the European Supergrid concept was that it crossed many national boundaries. Unification wasn't necessary for this to happen, although the existence of EU wide energy security and energy management policies were a great help. However, Brexit didn't prevent Britain from being part of the process itself, even if much of it was led from Brussels.

The "a great deal indeed" refers to the fact that Ireland's active, early, and extensive involvement in the Supergrid was to lead to very considerable economic benefits, firstly by reducing our huge oil and gas importation bills, and later through the considerable income generated by our net electricity exports. It was one of the big reasons why the tapering off of the Barnett subvention wasn't resulting in any reduction in average living standards across Ireland. Indeed, the Irish economy continued to grow faster than was required to offset the reduction in subvention payments by the UK, and part of that success story was the development of Ireland sustainable energy sector.

Rishi Sunak, now often known by the anagram of his name, Irish Sunak, said as much at a global investors conference his investment company was hosting in Dublin. "Invest in sustainable energy, Invest in Ireland" was the theme of the conference. Hardheaded investors saw huge potential in the Ireland energy economy and its integration into a European wide grid. It was also the one area where Brexit wasn't having a negative effect on combined British/EU projects.

I had the pleasure of asking him a question at the press conference launching the event.

"Mr Sunak, the last time I had the pleasure of meeting you was following a press briefing in Chequers where you broached the subject of possibly calling a Border Poll in Northern Ireland. You said you regretted that decision in an interview soon after you left 10 Downing Street. Is that still your position? The all-Ireland economy seems to have done rather well afterwards as evidenced by your holding an investment conference here extolling its benefits!"

"I'm glad you asked me that!" he smiled.

> *"Yes, indeed, the Irish economy has done extremely well since re-unification, which is why we are extolling the opportunities it presents at this conference. My concerns about calling the Border Poll were more political in nature. I was afraid we were setting a cat among the pigeons. But I have to say the Irish*

government has handled the transition extremely well. We were expecting far more violence from the paramilitaries."

"So why did you not do more to disarm the paramilitaries before you jumped ship?"

"I would have to take issue with your characterisation of us as jumping ship. We had an obligation, under the GFA, to call a Border Poll when a vote for a united Ireland seemed likely, and as you know, that judgement call ultimately proved to be correct, albeit by a small margin."

But many unionists felt utterly betrayed and have still not fully reconciled themselves to being governed from Dublin. Do you not feel a responsibility towards them?

Absolutely, and hence we have the TOSCA guaranteeing their rights, and we have investment conferences like this bringing improved benefits to all. Most unionists have done very well out of re-unification."

"I think they would find it hard to accept that", I interjected.

"Oh, give it time. 5 years is a very short time in the history of a nation."

And then the conversation moved on to investment and sustainable energy matters.

What was undeniable, even for unionists, was that the "costs of re-unification," such a huge issue at the time of the Border Poll, had rapidly disappeared from the political landscape as a major concern. Government finances remained relatively sound, the Debt/GDP ratio continued an erratic decline, and average living standards were steadily improving despite the declining subvention.

But there were a lot of other factors behind this economic success as well.

The IDA successfully sold a united Ireland as offering the potential of a larger workforce, reduced pressure on the total housing infrastructure, and improved utilisation and integration of healthcare and educational services. It continued its brilliant track record of identifying emerging Information and Communications Technology (ICT), Pharmaceutical and Medical Technology (MedTech) companies and getting them to locate their European operations in Ireland. It built on Belfast's emerging expertise in cybersecurity and web services development. The northern defence and aerospace industry diversified into manufacturing drones for commercial applications.

Many depressed areas of Belfast and larger towns and cities were rejuvenated, and gentrified, to a degree, as workers in new industries moved in. This, naturally, led to some resentment and friction with traditional working class communities, but their children, too, were beginning to benefit from better job opportunities. These new workers and their families were largely ignorant of ancient sectarian grievances and blurred previously well-defined community boundaries.

One major success story was the development of an integrated healthcare information system.

Previously each hospital and many other clinics and healthcare providers operated their own, frequently unique information systems which recorded what tests and services a patient had received within their orbit. But there were no common data standards or integration between systems.

Patients moving from one health care provider to another often had to manually transfer whatever medical records they had from one provider to another – often with just their memories to go on...Test results were lost or had to be repeated. Diagnoses and treatments were delayed. Doctors had to make clinical judgement calls based on incomplete information. Costs skyrocketed as examinations and tests were duplicated. Staff became frustrated, disillusioned, and cynical or left to work abroad. Management layers multiplied to no discernible patient benefit. Best practices in systems in use elsewhere in the world were ignored.

A relatively young, and very bright doctor by the name of Victor Emerson had been elected as a member of Parliament on an abstentionist ticket for the DUP. He kept on writing articles for various papers very critical of the dysfunctionality of the health care systems, North and south. He had worked in both jurisdictions and had very little time for either.

I interviewed him for the Tribune, because most of his criticisms applied almost as much to the NHS in Britain as well. Matt Casey had recently been hospitalised and very much identified with many of the criticisms. A couple of follow up articles were also published. I was covering a medical conference in Belfast when I came across him again. He thanked me for highlighting the issues in the Tribune, but I had a challenge for him:

"How do you square your criticisms with how health systems are run in Ireland and Britain with your party's abstentionist policies in Ireland? Surely if you want things to improve, you have to engage with the powers that be?"

> *"I'm a relatively junior physician and politician. I can't change the political or healthcare system single handedly. That's why I write newspaper articles and deliver papers at conferences like this."*

"Fair enough, but couldn't you be much more effective as Minister for Health?"

> He laughed, *"in what universe do you think it would be possible for a junior DUP politician to become Minister for Health?"*

"Would you take the job if offered?"

> *"Of Course, but the DUP would expel me if I took it, and many of my friends and colleagues would turn against me."*

"So, which is more important to you, patient welfare or your political future?"

"You have me there. I would have to be true to my Hippocratic oath".

"Leave it with me" I said. Feeling very self-important. Perhaps all my high level contacts with ministers were going to my head.

I rang Eamonn Ryan on his private mobile phone — the first time I had used that privilege and relayed my conversation to him. To my surprise he didn't immediately pooh-pooh the idea. "Let me think about it and maybe raise it at our leaders meeting tomorrow — the regular meeting he had with Martin and Varadkar.

I didn't hear back for a few days. Síle said there was no chance the government would give up a plum cabinet position to a DUP member who wasn't even currently taking up his seat in parliament. But she was underestimating how desperate Varadkar and Martin were to try and bring the DUP and the wider unionist community into the fold. Sinn Féin were again ahead in the polls, and without at least some support from the unionist political community, it was unlikely that Fianna Fáil and Fine Gael would be leading the next government.

What almost everyone had missed was that the Irish Cabinet had been reduced from the maximum 19 members allowed under the TOSCA to 18 full cabinet posts after the last election, in order to keep the proportions of senior ministerial roles in line with TD numbers for each party in the government. Several Junior ministers sat in on cabinet, but there was, formally, one senior cabinet seat vacant. To have given that seat to any one of Fianna Fáil (6), Fine Gael (6), the Greens (2), Alliance(3) or the SDLP (1) would have unbalanced their proportionate representation.

The department of Health was colloquially known as "Angola" as it had been the graveyard of many an ambitious minister. Nothing ever seemed to change there, except the budget over-runs and patient treatment waiting lists, which always went in the wrong direction. Anyone with any political sense had gotten out of it as quickly as possible. The current incumbent wanted to retire at the next election in any case, and there wasn't exactly a long queue of ambitious politicians' keen on the role. A judicious reshuffle could lead to an ambitious junior Minster getting a different portfolio leaving the vacant cabinet seat available for a DUP member.

I got a phone call from Dr. Emerson.

> *"You b*stard, you called my bluff. How was I to know you had friends in such high places!"*

"They're not my friends, they're my clients, and I give them a hard time for not being more inclusive towards unionists".

> *"Yes, but there's no way the DUP won't expel and de-select me if I take the job. Besides, I'm a full time doctor, and abstentionism suits me just fine. I don't have to do a day's work for the extra salary."*

"Can I quote you on that?"

> *"Oh shit, I didn't say that. I suppose I'm hoist on my own petard. The Taoiseach asked me to put up or shut up. Either I took the job, or I had no credibility as a health service critic. I was being offered an opportunity to fix the health service, and if I had any integrity, I would take it."*

"So, you took it?" I couldn't conceal my surprise.

> *"Well forever long it lasts anyway. I'll be out on my ear at the next election."*

"Oh, I don't know about that. Northern Ireland is crying out for people who can improve public services for the better. You won't necessarily get the DUP vote. But you'll get almost everyone else's."

> *"That's if I can actually make things better. I've never run a large bureaucracy before".*

"For what it's worth, I can give you some advice and guidance on how to deal with civil servants. They're very risk averse, but quite happy to go along if someone else is carrying the can".

> *"We'll see. I can see a giant cluster f*ck coming on. I'm not the most diplomatic of people. As a clinician it's my way or you can go and see someone else – if you can afford it. It's easy to get my way."*

"Yes, and you also know what needs to be done to fix the health service. You just have to be prepared to bash heads together and to hell with the consequences. After all, if you fail, the failure is all yours. If you succeed everyone will claim the credit.

> *"I'll bear that in mind."*

And with that came another little private consultancy sideline for me as advisor to a second cabinet minister...

---ooOoo---

Public reaction to the appointment of a DUP health minister ranged from shock to amusement. This would really put it up to the DUP. Do you want to help people have better lives and health outcomes or do you not?

To be fair, the DUP didn't disappoint. They immediately expelled Dr. Emerson and declared they would run an official candidate against him if he stood at the next election. He had been bought off by the Dublin establishment, who would now be able to evade their responsibilities and put all the health service failings on him.

Well, they weren't having it. They had been quite happy to have a properly funded NHS style public health care service in Northern Ireland and all the problems were now being created by Dublin. They were not going to be caught holding that baby and Dr Emerson was out on his own, a sacrificial lamb on a fool's errand.

I did point out in my article on his appointment – which was greeted with some interest in England – that his Ministerial salary would barely match the medical salary he would now have to forego. That he had written long and eloquently on the problems of the health service and should be applauded for having the courage of his convictions and being prepared to have a go at fixing them.

There is nothing worse for a conscientious clinician than to be faced with patients he can do nothing for because they have been too long on the waiting list, and their condition has already deteriorated too far. There are some things that absolutely need to be fixed, and which should be above party politics.

The transfer of sovereignty from Britain to Ireland was barely relevant to all this. Limited health service cooperation north and south of the border had been happening under British sovereignty in any case. But there would have been little or no chance of a DUP member and working clinician in the North every getting a full ministerial cabinet position in Westminster. For the first time ever, a Minister from Northern Ireland would be driving the integration and transformation of the health service on the entire island.

And as it turned out, no better man than Dr. Emerson. He was utterly ruthless. He imposed European data standards and an integrated health care information system on all public health care providers in Ireland. In time, and with the patient's permission, a certified professional had access to all the relevant medical records on a patient's history file at the touch of his fingertips – and the relevant security key, supplied by the patient. Private services, if they wanted to benefit from public healthcare contracts had to adopt the same system.

There was to be no duplication of tests, no asking the patient the same questions over and over again, and the outcomes of previous consultations were available on electronic file, no matter where they had taken place. In time the system was even integrated with other European systems, so that a patient on holidays had the benefit of similar treatment abroad. Ireland became the lead site for many patient information systems projects for the EU as a whole and was the first to benefit from similar initiatives elsewhere within the EU.

Public health care service providers who failed to adopt the new systems on schedule were defunded, to the utter shock of almost everyone working in the health service. This had never happened before. Unjustifiable delays and budget over-runs had become utterly routine, with no one batting an eyelid. It only took just a few highly publicised service closures to bring everyone into line.

Dr. Emerson was deaf to all entreaties "to be reasonable". He had an Ulster "thranness" about him that insisted there had to be consequences for a failure to perform. Better patient outcomes were the only imperative, utterly non-negotiable. Dr. Emerson worked with the urgency of one who knew his days in political life were numbered.

And yet, surprisingly they weren't. Budget over-runs became a thing of the past. Patient waiting lists declined. Life expectancies improved. Survival rates from Cancer and other serious conditions went up. And strangely, people appreciated this, regardless of their political affiliations or national identities.

Dr. Emerson was spoken of as a potential Taoiseach, even though he didn't have a political party to support him. He himself declared he was just a physician, anxious to do the best for his patients. That was the over-riding responsibility of all healthcare professionals. He had no political ambitions beyond that.

He declared a moratorium on all non-frontline jobs in the health service. Every administrator had to have a plan to make him/herself redundant. Early retirement was only available as an option for those who succeeded. Any monies saved would be re-invested in more up to date equipment. Only services which succeeded in improving their service outputs to costs ratio were given additional funding to expand. Failure was no longer rewarded. Those who didn't drive the process of transformation forward were sidelined.

Many in Ulster, he argued, had developed a sense of "learned helplessness" when many of these processes had been managed from London. Dublin was less remote, and therefore more accountable, but still utterly chaotic. Not all these processes needed to be managed from Dublin. Belfast and some other regional cities took the lead role on specific projects, as Ireland did for the EU as a whole.

Coming from far behind some member states, in terms of the sophistication of its health information systems, Ireland, in conjunction with its global IT service providers took a lead role. Soon Irish developed systems were being implemented, in large part, in other member states, and they eventually became the EU mandated standard.

Meanwhile the DUP continued to complain about the erosion of "Britishness" on the island. Very few cared. What mattered was better health care, better health outcomes, better life expectancies, better job opportunities, a better quality of life and standard of living for the aged and the young.

The dinosaurs were no longer ruling the earth.

20. The normalisation of politics

Síle and I were very happy together but saw each other more often professionally than matrimonially. By that I mean she was down in Dublin three weeks in four for Dáil sessions and I was often down there on journalistic assignments or working for Ministers Ryan or Emerson. It was exciting being part of a political scene and yet detached enough to write about it. We were both working long hours and sometimes fell asleep at our desks.

Occasionally I might have to write a piece that was critical of Green party policies or actions, or Dr. Emerson's traumatising (for some) transformation of the Health Department. I would pay them the courtesy of giving them a look at the copy first. They might argue the toss about some of the points made but never requested me not to publish.

Sometimes my editors would save them any embarrassment by deciding my story wasn't newsworthy enough for publication, but I never withheld a story because it might anger them. I didn't feel my occasional consultancy role for them compromised my journalistic integrity in any way and in fact my journalism was much more well informed as a direct result. I could comment authoritatively on government policies or actions with little fear of having gotten my facts wrong.

Síle had found her switch to the Greens had opened many previously shut doors for her in Belfast but didn't make a whole lot of difference in Dublin. If anything, being a government back-bencher was more constraining than being an opposition back bencher, because any criticism of the government had to be very restrained. You were supposed to settle your differences with ministers behind closed doors.

Eamonn Ryan had promised her a junior ministerial role if the Greens did well enough in the next elections to become entitled to a larger quota of Ministers. He was anxious to give northern Greens a higher profile as an alternative to Alliance for voters who wanted to vote for non-tribal parties but who found Alliance too conservative. Síle had been busy transforming her local party branches in East Belfast into a younger, more working class and dynamic organisation.

There were plenty of policy disputes and lively debates and she often found herself being accused of being too conservative and in league with the Dublin Government. Younger protestants could be quite extreme in their views veering from radical right to radical left. Their one common denominator was that they were very critical of the "Dublin Government" and Síle's presence on the government back benches did not sit easily with them. Whereas Síle could have been sure of unionist hostility when she was a Sinn Féin TD, now she was getting it in the neck from both sides.

Had Stormont been up and running she could have used it as a platform to express more independent and local views without being obviously critical of her own government ministers. But there was no sign of the DUP ending their boycott of the Dáil, and therefore the Sinn Féin boycott of Stormont continued, giving Northern Ireland no distinct voice.

Alliance had been seriously spooked by the success of two Fine Gael candidates in North and South Down and had resolved to reclaim what they regarded as their territory. But relations between Síle and Naomi Long remained extremely cordial and they cooperated extremely well on a range of projects in East Belfast. The next election was shaping up to being quite a battle between Alliance, Síle, the British Irish Party and Sinn Féin for the last two seats, with Naomi and Gavin Robinson shoe-ins for the first two.

While Síle's contention that there wasn't a Sinn Féin seat in East Belfast was borne out by local polling, she was finding it extremely difficult carving out a sufficiently wide base of her own. If anything, the natural Green Party base in East Belfast was even smaller than the Sinn Féin one, and trying to straddle the divides between a number of middle class and working class areas and a generational divide as well as the sectarian divide was a most uncomfortable place to be.

I tried to console her that that was what politics was all about – bringing together people from different backgrounds and persuasions to work for some common goals. She said that was all very well in theory, but in practice each group felt they had an absolute right to pursue their ideology and saw no reason why they should accommodate anyone else's. They didn't see this so much as sectarian as their democratic right. It was hard to argue with that, but it meant that a lot of local community projects were being stymied by divisions within the community which some people seemed to enjoy pursuing.

Síle was reminded of Yeats's poem "The second coming:"

Things fall apart; the centre cannot hold;
Mere anarchy is loosed upon the world,
The blood-dimmed tide is loosed, and everywhere
The ceremony of innocence is drowned;
The best lack all conviction, while the worst
Are full of passionate intensity.

But it was like that in much of Europe as well. Young people were alienated from their national establishments and violent protests were not uncommon. In some ways Belfast, and to a lesser extent other parts of the north, were simply falling in line with broader international trends. The greying of European populations, where older retired people were becoming more and more numerous compared to the working age population was putting a great strain on government budgets and public services. Younger people could not necessarily look forward to the retirement ages and benefits their parents had enjoyed.

After one particularly exhausting week's work we fell into each other's arms on return to Belfast and resolved that something had to change. We were now both earning good money but didn't have the free time to enjoy it. Every night she had meetings and I sometimes had deadlines and it was all becoming such a grind. She said she didn't want to stand at the next election, but I persuaded her that it was for the electorate to decide whether they wanted her or not. All she could do was her best, and that included having more time off for us.

Paradoxically, for all the controversy created by Dr. Emerson's health system reforms, the government started doing a little better in the polls as the 2030 elections approached. The economy had continued doing reasonably well and there was close to full employment. There were still a lot of pockets of deprivation and disadvantage particularly in Belfast and some rural areas, but the sustained investment in social inclusion projects, part funded by the EU was beginning to have some cumulative effect.

One Government Minister put the overall strategy to me thus:

> *"We may not be making huge amounts of progress in any one policy or regional area, but when you add together the cumulative effects of hundreds of projects and initiatives, the total effect over a few years can be quite substantial. A lot of this is going on beneath the radar, and national journalists like yourself may not always see it. It doesn't make for big stories but can mean quite a lot to local people. It's only when you stand back and remember what things were like in 2024 that you realise what a positive quantum shift has taken place, for all the negative newspaper headlines".*

I certainly saw quite a lot of projects happening in East Belfast, but I wasn't seeing much of a moderating effect on local politics. The old sectarian divides might be lessoning, but the class and generational divides seemed to be becoming more intense. Whatever it was younger people wanted from the government, they certainly didn't seem to feel they were getting it. The picture seemed very confused. Society was in turmoil, and I had very little idea of how the 2030 elections would turn out.

Some foreign correspondents I met in Dublin were bemused.

> *"Ireland must be the only country in the world where, the better a government does, the more support it loses. Most countries*

we know would give a lot to have an economy going so well, public services slowly improving, and the sectarian divide in Northern Ireland becoming more blurred around the edges. And yet everybody seems to be unhappy!"

I replied "Part of the problem is that the same parties have been in power for so long, a lot of people just want a change. To give the other guys a chance. They feel they are being held to ransom by the DUP boycott and want to give them one in the eye by voting Sinn Féin. People are tired of the same old arguments."

Whatever the reasons, Sinn Féin won a resounding victory in the 2030 general election, and, thanks to the continued DUP policy of abstentionism, had an effective majority in the Dáil.

Matt Casey kept on urging me to write more stories about Sinn Féin coming to power justifying unionist concerns of a nationalist takeover. That the protections of the TOSCA would be removed and that there would be a unionist backlash and re-emergence of widespread violence.

But I couldn't see any of that happening. Sinn Féin had moderated their policies considerably and seemed to me to be genuine in wanting to govern for "all the people of Ireland," and that included people who claimed a British identity.

Dr. Emerson was re-elected as an independent, heading the poll, and Sinn Féin leader, Michelle O'Neill, promptly offered him a continuing stint as Minister for Health, despite the fact they had severely criticised him while they were in opposition. This enraged the DUP still further. Working with a Fianna Fáil, Fine Gael government was bad enough, but Sinn Féin? He might as well have signed up to join the IRA. Despite none to veiled threats against his wellbeing, he graciously accepted.

Síle wasn't quite so fortunate in East Belfast. Her first preference vote was just less than half a quota, and there weren't too many transfers going her way when the Sinn Féin candidate was eliminated. However, she picked up more transfers as the SDLP, British Irish Party and independent candidates were eliminated, and finally edged ahead of the second DUP candidate when Naomi's surplus was distributed. It had been a long night, and she had sweated blood for each of those transfers, sometimes begging for a 6th. preference, when a voter declared their first five were going to other candidates.

It turned out she was not alone. Green party candidates were in trouble all over the country and quite a few seats were lost, including those of party leader Eamonn Ryan and Minister of State Pippa Hackett. He seemed quite philosophical about it when I spoke to him. He had had a good run in office and had been thinking of retiring anyway. He would have liked to leave the party in better shape and expressed regret for all the good Green candidates who had lost or had failed to win seats. He expressed delight that Síle had made it through in the end. Would she be interested in the Leadership, he wondered? It was time the Greens had a leader from the north to counter act the appeal of Michelle O'Neill of Sinn Féin.

I told him he would have to ask her himself. She had been disappointed by her poor performance and wasn't too sure she had a future in politics.

> *"Oh, she has a future, alright, that's for sure. Not too many of our candidates have worked so hard to build up a base across sectarian, class and generational divides. Anyone who can survive in the bear pit that is East Belfast will find national politics a breeze."*

I wasn't too sure of his logic but left it to them to discuss. With only 6 TD's re-elected, the Greens weren't exactly spoiled for choice, and there seemed to be a general feeling that the next leader should come from the north. Síle wasn't too impressed with the other Green TD from South Belfast who was making noises about putting his name in the ring, so she allowed her name to go forward. To her surprise, she was elected without opposition. No one else seemed to want what some considered a poisoned chalice.

I told her the Greens had been unlucky to miss out in quite a few constituencies, and it wouldn't take much of a swing to double their seat count. A few years in office should reduce the allure of Sinn Féin as a party of opposition and reduce their appeal to the young and disaffected. Síle seemed more concerned with holding what was left of the Green party together. The adoption of a Green agenda by all the main parties had reduced the distinctiveness of their offering to the electorate.

Paradoxically, her election as leader of the Greens seemed to free her from all the stresses and strains, she had been feeling in trying to build her base in the East Belfast constituency. Party leaders weren't expected to be quite so active on the ground. East Belfast was unique in electing the Leaders of three parties – Alliance's Naomi Long, the DUP's Gavin Robinson, and now Síle De Butléir of the Greens. None of them would have too much time to spend in the constituency building up their base at her expense.

After the all night ordeal winning the last seat by the skin of her teeth, Síle had decided she would never put herself through all that again. She would do her job as best as she could, and then it was up to the electorate to decide who should represent them. If they wanted someone else, she was fine with that. She was done with begging for 6th. preference votes. From now on she was going to be a take it or leave it politician. Dr. Emerson hadn't done too badly cutting a swathe through multiple bureaucracies and upsetting everyone. It turns out that was just what the electorate wanted.

Reducing her commitment to constituency work coincided with my losing my part time gig as advisor to Eamon Ryan. We both would have a little more time on our hands. We decided to try for a baby and bought a house near Dublin to replace the flat we had been renting for her three weeks out of four stints in the Dáil. We would still spend our weekends in her house in Ballyhackamore and do some constituency work there while we were at it, but most of her work would be around the Dáil in Dublin from now on.

It turned out that being the leader of a relatively small party in Opposition was a relatively easy gig. There were plenty of things to criticise the new government for when you didn't have the risk of upsetting party colleagues or the responsibility of governing yourself. Sinn Féin in government was a gift that kept on giving. Hardly a week went by without some mistake or scandal for which they could be held accountable, even if it was a civil service blunder they hadn't caused themselves. Sinn Féin were finding out the hard way that opposition was a breeze compared to taking responsibility and governing.

As leader of an opposition party, Síle got plenty of opportunities to speak. She and Naomi often tag teamed the government, criticising them from different angles, so that no matter how the government responded, they were always vulnerable to an attack from a different position. I was working almost fulltime as an unpaid researcher and speech writer for Síle. I don't think the Tribune ever realised how much they were supporting a foreign power. The Barnett subvention, even if declining, was being supplemented by my salary!

All the while our family life was blossoming. Síle got pregnant and we were glad we had bought a house more suitable for a family in Skerries just north of Dublin. It took every last penny of our savings just for the deposit and we were now mortgaged to the hilt for two houses. Being pregnant also seemed to humanise her in the public eye. Gone was the hard-nosed ex-Sinn Féin community worker to be replaced by a more demure mother figure. It became easier for a lot of people to identify or empathise with her and the difficulty of combining a full time job with pregnancy and then motherhood.

It almost seemed that baby Ciara, when she emerged, was a matter of public interest if not public property. We tried to keep our family life as private as possible, but it didn't prevent people from all the time coming up to her asking how the baby was and was she managing ok. I thought it rather sweet myself. I did as much to help as I could but also decided we had to afford a regular cleaner once a week. I had never realised how much work minding a baby was!

The actual birth was a huge eye opener for me as well. We had insisted on a natural childbirth, and, as no birthing pool was available, this meant me supporting and holding Síle upright for much of the end labour process to let gravity do its work. My pain obviously didn't compare to hers, but my back almost felt it was broken towards the end. Rugby training had never been so hard!

But politics now, for both of us, had become the bread and butter of daily life. It seemed to have lost the hard edge of the mean streets of Belfast. Anti-social behaviour still happened, of course, but it was a matter for the police. I made Síle promise she would never again march into an abusing husband's house and take his gun away from him... That didn't come under the heading of "constituency work" for me.

Politics had almost become normal, complete with the normal, run of the mill scandals that pass for politics in a democracy...

21.   Scandal

The Sinn Féin government was in deep dodo. This was no ordinary scandal. A government minister, had, it seems, been caught with his hands in the till, benefiting from public contracts without declaring their interest. In another case planning permissions had been achieved where many had tried and failed before.

The first round of defence was complete denial.

When that became untenable, it was a case of "sure isn't everybody at it, the opposition didn't have clean hands either".

When asked to evidence that assertion they pointed at me.

"Sure, wasn't I taking payments from Eamonn Ryan's department while claiming to be an independent journalist for a foreign newspaper."

I quickly issued a statement to clarify. Yes, I had done some consultancy work for Minister Ryan for which I had been paid. But that was completely separate to my job as a journalist and didn't affect my copy one iota. If my employer had a problem with that that was a matter between them and me.

(I had discussed the matter with Matt Casey beforehand, and he had confirmed it didn't cause him a problem. He had been happy with my work and always found it to be well balanced with a critical distance from the previous government. He couldn't recall ever having to publish a correction or apology. No doubt my close working relationship with some in government contributed to my reports being well informed).

That didn't mollify the Sinn Féin government one iota. They had a target, and they were sticking to it. It was the best distraction they had from their own much greater misdeeds. There were calls for a judicial enquiry. The implication was that the previous Government had effectively been bribing me with public funds to give them favourable coverage. Anyone who could read could see I had frequently been critical of the previous government.

I was summoned before a Dáil Committee to explain my misdeeds. Previous "witnesses" before the Public Accounts committee had been subjected to some very aggressive questioning:

I explained there was nothing to explain. I had been contracted by the Department of Energy to produce publicity material for the European Ultra High Voltage SuperGrid (EUHVSG) project and coordinate cooperation between Britain and Ireland. With Britain no longer being a member of the EU, that included managing some sensitivities with our EU partners.

The EUHVSG project and particularly the EU/UK partnership within it was now being hailed as an outstanding success. I even gave them copies of publicity leaflets and Ireland/UK memorandums of understanding I had authored. When asked had I won the contract by public tender I answered that, as far as I was aware, the contracts were too small to require a tendering process under EU rules, but that was ultimately a matter for the Department.

> *"Did you declare a conflict of interest when writing on energy matters for the Tribune? "*

"I did, when writing about those memorandums of understanding and the cooperation they enabled and also had discussions on the matter with my editors. The Tribune is a private company. It is not unusual for journalists to take on other work as well, especially in these days of declining incomes for newspapers and journalists".

> *"But when writing on other matters the public was deceived into thinking you were an independent journalist when, really, you were working for the government."*

"I was and remain an independent journalist. Any work I do for others is entirely incidental. Any time there might be a risk of a conflict of interest, I declared it."

> *"And you expect us to believe that?"*

"I have no expectation of you whatsoever. I'm sure you will believe whatever you want to believe."

That didn't exactly lower the tension in the room. I felt I was being put on trial for unspecified offences with unknowable consequences. I knew they were trying to get at Síle through me. But I wasn't going to give them the satisfaction of involving her.

"And did the leader of the Green Party know of these arrangements?

"I keep no secrets from my wife, but she has the good sense to mind her own business".

"But she has benefited directly from the public funds you have received".

"As I have from her own salary."

"So, she is complicit in this abuse of public funds. This work could and should have been done by civil servants."

"There was no abuse. All payments were duly authorised by the department for work invoiced and done. If you want any more information on this, you will have to ask Departmental officials about this."

"We certainly will! But right now, we are trying to establish the degree of complicity by the leader of the Green Party in all this".

"The Leader of the Green party is not complicit in anything. She is my wife. And I will thank you for not prying into our private relationship".

"This is a matter of GREAT PUBLIC IMPORTANCE"

"This is a matter of you being a nosey busybody interfering in other people's private lives in order to try and distract attention from some really serious misdeeds by your own government Ministers!"

And general pandemonium broke out.

I just left the hearing, without requesting a by your leave from the chair. I was a private individual, and I wasn't going to allow my private life to become subject of a show trial without the benefit of a lawyer or even knowing what I was being charged with. This was a fishing expedition by government backbenchers on the committee trying to sully Síle or at least drag her into a public controversy with negative connotations. When mud starts flying around, it tends to stick to anyone in the vicinity.

---ooOoo---

General public reaction was mixed, but generally sympathetic. Some fellow journalists argued there should be some form of charter for the protection of citizen's rights when called before a Dáil Committee. At least you were entitled to a lawyer if you are hauled before the courts, and there were rules of evidence which had to be followed. A judge presided who was not a political partisan. At a Dáil Committee, you were at the mercy of grandstanding back-benchers anxious for TV exposure.

I was furious because I had allowed myself to be provoked. I had once again allowed myself to become the issue. Only now, I had become an embarrassment to my wife as well.

Síle would have none of it. Those Sinn Féin committee members are just bottom feeding, knuckle dragging, scum. They would do anything to smear innocent people in an attempt to distract from their own Minister's misdeeds. That was their intention today, and thanks to you they didn't succeed.

Síle said she would give it to the Government with both barrels in the Dáil tomorrow.

I said, "don't do that, that's just what they want, to provoke you, so that this nothing burger controversy drags on for another few days. Just be your usual self, all sweetness and light, as if nothing has happened. And dare them to bring up the controversy, attacking a private citizen in the Dáil…"

In the end, no one brought it up. There was no more percentage gain in highlighting the issue for the government. All Ministers hired special advisors with public funds, sometimes from their own families. This was small beer by comparison. I didn't dare mention I had also done lots of unpaid speech writing for the Leader of the Greens!

But what many appeared to have missed, was that I had also done some work under contract to the Department of Health for the current Minister, Dr. Emerson. I certainly wasn't going to bring it up, as it might only have embarrassed him. Sinn Féin weren't going to bring it up, because he was a Minister in their government, even if he wasn't a member of Sinn Féin.

But true to form Dr. Emerson brought it up himself in the Dáil during a Healthcare debate a few days later. He had asked the department to employ me to do specific tasks and they had done so through the normal procurement procedure for small jobs. I had done an excellent job, and he was happy it was money well spent. If the Taoiseach had a problem with that, he was happy to hand in his resignation.

That was the end of the matter.

Dr. Emerson's reforms had resulted in major improvements in health services, and he was the most popular minister in the government. Sinn Féin could ill afford to lose him. And besides, he was the living embodiment of "power sharing" in the government at a time when there was no power sharing in Stormont.

The controversy moved on the real and serious misdeeds of the two Sinn Féin Ministers who were eventually forced to resign. But not before serious damage had been done to the Government's popularity and reputation. Opinion polls recorded an acceleration in their decline in popularity, which had begun about six months after they had taken office. Many observers later regarded this scandal as the key turning point in the Government's fortunes, from which they never recovered.

I was later asked to do more work for the Department of health developing information leaflets for British and EU visitors unsure of their health care entitlements in Ireland. I declined on the grounds that I was too busy doing other work. It simply wasn't worth the potential hassle.

I did, however, continue to do a great deal of background research work and speech writing for Síle and some of her fellow TDs. A small parliamentary party of 6 TDs has very limited resources to provide informed critiques of government performance in many different policy areas.

I also spent quite a lot of time in Brussels researching their proposed new policy initiatives in the energy, transport, environment, agriculture, and health care sectors. For a time, I practically became the Tribune's Brussels correspondent as well, when their regular correspondent was on leave. Covering all of Ireland, Brussels, politics, sport, European Affairs, environment, and energy made for quite a full portfolio.

Matt Casey and my other editors seemed to appreciate the different perspectives I could bring to all these topics. Now coming from more of an Irish and a basically Europhile perspective was very different from the usual rants against all things Brussels that were still a staple for much of the British press.

Some had never forgiven Brussels and Ireland, for what they perceived as a hostile response to Brexit. There was a little "revenge porn" and Schadenfreude in the Irish media directed at England as well. I liked to think I could cover topics from both perspectives and add a little balance.

I was really torn as to whether I should now be supporting the Irish rather than the English rugby team, however. Many of my unionist contacts seemed to have no difficulty supporting Ireland against England, but England against everyone else. I compromised by supporting England in soccer and Ireland in rugby. I found that many loyalties in Ulster were becoming more confused as well.

My personal relationship with Síle flourished through childbirth and child minding. Far from taking away from our political and journalistic work it seemed to enrich our experiences and broaden our perspectives on life. Politics wasn't so much about the issues of today but building a better future for our children.

I was never the greatest at remembering anniversaries. I left it too late to organise a child minder for our anniversary and so ended up cooking what was to be a very special dinner. I decided to play it safe and go for a prawn/seafood cocktail starter and steak, onions, mushrooms, broccoli, and carrot for the main. Some craft ice cream and fresh fruit salad would have to do for dessert. The nice man at the wine shop recommended a prosecco for pre-dinner drinks and starter followed by a full bodied Côtes du Rhône for the main. Some Baileys with a coffee should finish things off nicely.

What could possibly go wrong? Well, quite a lot, actually.

Firstly, the steak was well done when she preferred it medium rare. Secondly the onions weren't so much caramelised as incinerated. The carrots ended up soggy rather than firm. I had also totally underestimated the time it would take to chop the fresh fruit and vegetables, and it all became rather frantic, rather than the calm, serene presentation I had in mind. I never quite got time to dress the table or even complete the place settings. A hastily lit candle had to do for atmosphere. I'd left the flowers a bit long without water and they hung about rather droopily.

She never batted an eyelid. It had all been wonderful, despite her having to get up twice during the meal to settle Ciara. My skills didn't quite extend to fulfil that particular task. The food looked a bit sorry by the time she got to eat it having been re-heated twice. But the wine helped. By the time we got to the Bailey's we were both in good form. We debated the state of the world and what the future would hold.

I was surprised to hear her say that she really hated the DUP. They had absolutely nothing positive to contribute to anything. Never had. Not under British sovereignty, nor now under Irish. They were always negative, always demanding , never satisfied. They were the perpetual contrary teenager.

I was surprised because she always seemed to have infinite patience dealing with constituents and listening to their problems at meetings. She was always positive, engaging, encouraging, helpful. And could see the bright side of almost anything.

I would have lost patience a long time ago. I often felt like saying "well if you think Britain is so great you should try living there! I have, and it's been going downhill ever since the Beetles and the 1966 World Cup". I never did of course, but my English reserve was often tested.

We discussed what would happen to the protestant community and the DUP in particular.

> "Oh, the protestants will be fine. They did very well in the south even when they were a small minority. It's the DUP that can't die out fast enough, as far as I'm concerned. They're holding everybody back, particularly their own supporters. Look at Dr. Emerson. He's doing a great job, and yet he needs an armed guard everywhere he goes. He's increasing everyone's life expectancy at the expense of his own".

I had quite a few DUP politicians on my contacts list, even if I rarely got to speak to them. At an individual level you couldn't meet nicer people, even if I was seen to be on the wrong side. What made them, collectively, so backward looking?

> "Quite a few of them or their families lost family members in the Troubles, and they have never resolved that grief. They see the IRA as having gotten away with murder, and now they see them running the government. They don't appreciate that we saw the B-Specials, the RUC and the UDR in exactly the same way. Just because you put on a uniform doesn't make you any less of a thug. In fact, it's worse, because it was all state sanctioned and assisted. They had the backing of the might of the British Empire. We were prosecuted by the Free Staters down south. "

"You're sounding like your old Sinn Féin self".

"The history doesn't change. It's just that we have chosen to move on. They never will. We'll have to wait until they all die off and a new generation takes over".

And what guarantee do we have that the younger generation will be any different?

They already are. None of the younger loyalists I meet are bothered about flags or their British identity. They'll fly whatever flags they want, support English soccer teams, watch the BBC or more likely TikTok or YouTube, and aren't really much different from their nationalist counterparts. The much greater number of integrated schools are also having an effect. The SDLP were really getting it in the neck for the slow pace of integrated schooling, but it's no better under Sinn Féin. If anything, Sinn Féin are happier with the status quo.

So, we just have to wait for DUP supporters to die out?

They were down to 25% support at the last election in Northern Ireland. That's 7% of the population of Ireland as a whole. If they slide down much further, they will just become another minor party and irrelevant distraction. In a lot of countries, parties with less than 5% support don't even get into parliament.

I didn't dare point out the Green's had got less than 7% as well. "So, we should just, basically forget about them?"

"You can't help those who don't want to be helped, and indeed who will hate you if you try."

But you got quite a few loyalist transfers, last time out?

"Yes, more than ever. But those weren't DUP voters in any case. The second DUP candidate was the last to be eliminated, so his votes were never transferred, but my team didn't see any lower preferences for me on his pile of ballot papers we looked at. They

are basically a lost cause. They hate Dr. Emerson more than anyone because he is proving the new Ireland can work for everyone. And if they hate Sinn Féin so much, why don't they enter the Dáil and vote them out. Sinn Féin only have an overall majority because they haven't taken their seats."

---ooOoo---

I decided I would revisit my list of loyalist contacts to see if there was any change in DUP thinking. One interviewee, a prominent leader in the DUP was particularly revealing.

After we got past the usual jibes of "I hear you're working for the Irish government as well as the Tribune these days" I said this story was for the Tribune. My editor wanted to know how loyalists were getting on in the new Ireland. Under guarantee of no attribution, he said:

> *"It's not so bad, truth be told, most would say, or some variation thereof. The thing is, it's not our country anymore. And the better the other side do the more it hurts us to have to admit that. I'll go to my grave never giving themmums credit for anything. They never gave us credit for anything anyway."*

What did you do that they should be giving you more credit for?

> *"Well, for a long time, they had a better standard of living here than they would have had in the Free State. And then, the first time the British had some problems they wanted to up sticks and leave. But we're not like that. For us it's the principle of the thing. My country right or wrong. And my country is British, not Irish. Now they tell us we should go back to Britain if we like it so much. But we belong here. This is our country as well, And we want it to be British. So, it doesn't really matter what they do. Our Britishness will never change."*

But who is asking you to change? Can't you be just as British now as you ever were? What makes you less British now?

> *"Well, for a start we're not running the show. They've taken over and left us with nothing".*

But you can still go to your church, play rugby or soccer or whatever you want, fly your flags, light your bonfires, play in your bands. How has any of that changed?

> *"All those things used to mean something. It meant we were in control. Now it means nothing. It's just nostalgia for the old times".*

So, what makes you think you were entitled to run the show. What's wrong with the opposition winning once in a while and showing us what they can do. And if they don't do it well you can vote them out. The DUP could vote Sinn Féin out tomorrow if they wanted to.

> *"Aye, that's the bait. But once you go in there you'll never get out. You'll become part of the system. You'll be absorbed by it".*

So, you want to remain separate and distinct? That's possible too. Nobody is forcing you to take part. I've never seen Sinn Féin complaining about your abstentionist policy. Because they did it in Westminster for over a century, and besides it suits them. It means they have a majority and can do what they like. Why would you let them get away with that?

> *"Because it shows up what they really are like, like those corruption scandals. They were just the tip of the iceberg you know".*

"So, expose them. Vote them out. Uncover all their wrongdoing. Dr. Emerson has exposed a lot of messing in the health service, and now everybody benefits".

> *"That's a sore one. He let the side down, and you should never do that".*

"He's taken the Hippocratic oath to help people get better. You wouldn't expect him to break his oath and just go along with the old system of longer and longer waiting lists".

"Why didn't he do that when Britain was sovereign. We didn't need to be in a united Ireland to fix the health service!"

"Precisely! Firstly, he wasn't long qualified as a doctor at that stage and was still learning his trade. Secondly, as he says himself, he would never have had a chance of becoming a health Minister with a real budget while Westminster ran the show. He has €40 Billion each year to spend now, and he gets to decide!"

"Only if he can get the Taoiseach and cabinet to agree. I hear he wanted to go much further in reforming the health service and they wouldn't let him".

"Well, he is pretty radical, and in a democracy, you have to bring people along. You can't just fire everyone who doesn't see things your way. He's gotten on further than we ever did under British sovereignty. Just think if there were a few more Dr. Emersons in the cabinet, representing the British Irish Party or the DUP. He doesn't have a party to back him up if there is a disagreement in cabinet. You could have more control over what goes on in Ireland than you ever had when Britain ruled the roost."

"Aye, that's possible. It's a hard one. We'd have to swallow our pride, and we can be pretty thrann when we want to be. It's probably easier to sit on the sidelines and jeer everyone else. But you won't catch me parlaying with the enemy. It's their country now, and up to them to sort it out."

So, which is **your** country?

"We don't have one anymore".

And what about your children?

"They'll make up their own minds. A lot of them are heading abroad".

And would you not prefer if they had better opportunities here?

"Of course! But it's no longer our job to make that happen."

So, you're just going to sit tight as the unionist community ages and diminishes and becomes less and less influential?

"If that's God's will, so be it. It used to be our promised land. He seems to have given it to themmums now. There's a real sense of betrayal in the protestant community. Many have lost their faith, which is worse than losing your identity. Most are just going through the motions now. Waiting to die".

That's a pretty gloomy outlook. You don't think that there are opportunities that unionism isn't grasping. The protestants in the south were a much smaller minority, and yet they never died out.

"Well, how true to their faith have they been? Most have made their deals with the devil."

Well, I can't judge people by their faith or lack of it. I also can't blame people for being bitter and resentful if someone belonging to them got murdered and the killer got off scot-free. But isn't Christianity also about forgiveness?

"For sinners who repent, yes. But I see no sign of repentance down south. Instead, they want to lord it over us".

What would that repentance look like for you. What would it take for you to be able to forgive them.

"Give us back our British heritage, allow us to be British again".

What's stopping you being British now?

"They can't stop us. That is our strength. That is how we resist their rule."

So, nothing changes. Sinn Féin stay in government with a majority given to them by the DUP. You guys stay negative, and don't contribute to anything. And everybody else is past caring. They just wait for you to die out.

"If that's God's will, we have to abide by it".

And you don't think God has any better options for you?

"Not that I can see".

OK. We've covered a lot of ground there. I'll send you a copy of my draft report and you can tell me if I got anything wrong. And please let me know if God ever does give you a better option!

---ooOoo---

We parted on good terms.

A few weeks later he made a speech calling on the DUP to end their boycott to help get rid of "this odious government".

Some months later, a motion to that effect was passed at the DUP's Annual conference. The DUP entered the Dáil, laid down a motion of no confidence in the government, and the government was defeated. New elections were called for October 2032. The DUP pledged to take their seats if elected.

22. Transforming the Environment

The 2032 general elections produced quite an interesting result. Sinn Féin remained by far the largest party. But lost 25 seats overall. The DUP consolidated its position in Ulster and came remarkably close to matching Sinn Féin in terms of seats. The other parties in the north were very disappointed with the results. Alliance treaded water. The TUV, British Irish Party and the SDLP were all but wiped out. Fine Gael gained a third seat, and the Greens increased their tally to 4 seats in the North.

Síle was delighted, all the more so as they also increased their seats from 4 to 11 in the south for a grand total of 15, putting them within touching distance of Fianna Fáil. Fine Gael became by far the second largest party and the Social Democrats did well.

Forming a government was going to be tricky because every party had campaigned on their own manifesto, and none campaigned on forming a coalition. Sinn Féin were still in the box seat but found no one willing to form a coalition with them. Fine Gael were considered too conservative by most of the other parties. The DUP were barely able to tolerate being in the Dáil at all, never mind forming part of a government. They were going to be a "constructive" opposition., protecting the interests of unionists.

In the end, after several failed attempts, and when a second election seemed imminent, Fine Gael, under new leader Helen McEntee, managed to cobble together a minority coalition with Fianna Fáil, Alliance, the Greens, and the SDP. They were still relying on the DUP or a lot of the minor parties and independents to abstain, and it didn't look like the new government could last long.

Síle played "hard to get" for as long as she could. Everyone seemed to assume the Greens would want to be part of the government so weren't offering much in the way of policy concessions. Síle insisted the Greens were a policy led party and wouldn't be joining any government unless the programme for government included their priorities. Some of the other parties seemed to view this somewhat askance. What were they on about, wasn't it all about getting as many plum jobs in government as possible?

In the end she got her way on both policy and jobs. The Greens would control Energy, transport, climate change, the environment, regional and local government (including the north and the Gaeltachts), and agriculture. Agriculture was the kicker because it was still one of the largest sources of greenhouse gas emissions in Ireland, and farmers were generally very hostile to the Greens. To my shock she took the Agriculture portfolio for herself. Talk about a poisoned chalice! Farmers were already protesting outside the gates of Leinster House.

But farming, which now made up far less than 1% of the economy, had made least progress on greenhouse gas reductions, and Ireland had no chance of meeting its targets without tackling that issue. The farmers had an extremely well organised lobby and weren't slow to bring their tractors and trucks up to Dublin to protest by paralysing the city's already overloaded traffic systems.

I asked Síle what on earth was she thinking! She would have half the country at war with her and the Greens. She said we were either serious about meeting our targets or we were not, and she wasn't in politics to have an easy ride. She had plenty of practice dealing with very obstinate people in her own constituency, and besides, there weren't too many farmers in East Belfast.

I thought she was taking a leaf out of Dr. Emerson's book and would run a coach and four through the agricultural industry. She certainly put the fear of God in the Irish Farmer's Association (IFA) leaders at their first meeting, talking about Ireland's Greenhouse gas emissions targets as being "non-negotiable."

In no time at all, and before the new government had had time to settle in, the farmers groups decided on a show of strength to show they were not going to be trifled with. A hundred thousand farmers and their families and supporters would invade the capital in their tractors, jeeps and trucks and paralyse the city. Síle would have to win that battle, or else she might as well resign from politics.

An emergency cabinet meeting decided on emergency legislation to ban all tractors from public roads without a permit. And permits would be denied to those who defied Garda instructions to turn around and go home if so instructed. Most farmers used public roads for their tractors to move livestock , produce or feed. Without the use of public roads, they couldn't operate their farms.

On the day of the protest the Gardai turned back all tractors heading towards Dublin. Those who refused were arrested and their tractors confiscated. There were quite a lot of violent confrontations, and the army were called in for armed support and crowd control. Quite a few farmers and Gardai were injured in the scuffles.

Sinn Féin made hay in the Dáil, and a sense of crisis enveloped the government, widely reported internationally. The Tribune wanted copious reports on the new government's travails. The farmer's case was not helped by the fact that the Government had yet to implement any specific measures. Their protest was largely pre-emptive.

Their case also wasn't helped by the fact that previous governments had dismally failed to reach their legally mandated climate change targets and were being subjected to heavy fines by the European Commission, payable by general taxpayers. Farmers worried that the new government would legislate to deduct EU fines from EU support payments to individual farmers who had missed their targets.

What was clear to all was that the new government had little choice but to face down the protests if it wanted to survive with any credibility. It was also clear that the government was only acting on commitments made by previous governments which they had failed to live up to. Climate change was becoming so extreme action had to be taken.

Sinn Féin's opposition was couched mainly in terms of police brutality and the government's "fascist" tendencies. The huge number of Gardai injured told a different tale. Most of the violence had been initiated by farmers. The Gardai were only doing their jobs to enforce the law and protect themselves.

But the DUP saw their chance to embarrass the new government. They had been criticised, for many years, for failing to represent northern farmer's interests properly ever since the Brexit debacle. This was their chance to rebuild that relationship and show their support for a "neglected group in society". No one could accuse them of sectarianism for standing with the farmers.

The Government was defeated, only a few weeks into office, with the support of the DUP for the no-confidence motion. Síle was accused of being a bull in a China shop or a fox in the chicken coop and all sorts of other less repeatable epithets. The kindest words spoken of her were that she had been naïve to take on the farmers so early in the administration.

The consensus was that the Greens would cop all the blame for the crisis and be decimated at the second election. Coalition partners moved to distance themselves from "the manner in which the Minister had pursued her brief." She had, apparently, been too "ideological".

But something very strange started to happen during this second election campaign. Far from being annoyed at having to go to the polls again so soon, opinion polls showed a high degree of voter engagement and support for the beleaguered Minister's stance. Síle had braved all the insults with great dignity. Polls showed support for the Greens actually increasing.

This left many seasoned political analysts scratching their heads. Politicians and parties who had caused great controversy in the past were generally punished by the Irish electorate. Divisiveness was not rewarded. How come the Greens seemed to be thriving? Three theories gained widespread support.

Firstly, the electorate were far more concerned with climate change than politicians gave them credit for. Secondly, farmers had ruled the rural roost for a very long time, had done very well out of EU income support payments, and now needed to do their bit for the environment. General taxpayers shouldn't be on the hook for fines Ireland was accumulating for failing to meet its targets.

But thirdly, the DUPs actions were seen as entirely opportunistic and negative, designed to frustrate all attempts at good government. If the DUP could be thrann, then so could the Irish electorate in response. Obstructionism and blatant opportunism were not going to be rewarded. The public had rights too, and using public roads to go about their daily business was one of them.

Whatever the truth of it, it was obvious the farm lobby had over-played their hand. Appearing to ally themselves with the DUP was not a popular move.

The second election was a resounding success for the Greens, who doubled their seats to 30 and became the third largest party. Both Sinn Féin and the DUP lost votes and seats.

Síle became Tánaiste in the new government which now had a small working majority not vulnerable to DUP attack. The people seemed to have decided they wanted firm and stable government and didn't like to see their Gardai beaten up on the streets. The DUP were not going to have a veto on future progress.

Síle was a hero among Green supporters. She had stood up for their policies and increased their seat count from 6 to 30 in two elections in a matter of months. Sinn Féin now had a serious rival as an all-Ireland party. Farmers had learned she was not to be trifled with, that legal obligations had to be met, and that the Greens had grown a spine. Northern Ireland politicians were making quite a strong and distinctive contribution to the governance of the island as a whole.

Even in East Belfast Síle was getting thumbs up signs from people she would not have classed as her supporters. For the first time she had been elected on the first count and didn't have to scrabble around for lower preference votes.

Dr. Emerson was going to have a rival for the title of the most ruthless Minister in the cabinet. I could have forewarned farmers about that. I couldn't recall when I had last won an argument with her! Ireland was going to be at the forefront of a new green revolution in agriculture.

I had helped Síle put together a comprehensive Green Party Agricultural Policy document much of which was agreed and incorporated into the new coalition programme for government. Called Ireland 2050, it focused on areas such as:

1. Sustainable agriculture for family farms rather than corporate industrial farming
2. Greater provision of urban allotments for city dwellers on public lands
3. Support for the chemical free Grow it Yourself (GIY) movement.
4. Banning of glyphosate containing weed killers, now present in 95% of human urine samples with increasingly widespread adverse health consequences.
5. Banning all carcinogenic additives and farm chemicals
6. Only approved genetically modified products could be sold within the state.
7. All Irish farms to become organic by 2050.
8. Encouraging greater biodiversity through native forestry and re-wilding
9. Reduced food surpluses and wastage – food wastage had reached almost 40% in Ireland.
10. Supporting reductions in global milk & grain surpluses
11. Supporting the grass fed bovine industry - now down to only 16% of total meat consumption.
12. Food labelled "Free Range" to be restricted to outdoor natural grazing habitats.
13. All farm animals to have access to free exercise in daylight at least an hour a day.
14. Increased monitoring of soil biology and effluents into water courses

15. Increased use of seaweed in animal feedstuffs to reduce methane emissions.
16. Support for methane capture systems from slurry pits
17. Support for anaerobic digesters for waste products only
18. Improved urban sewage treatment plants and recycling of waste products.
19. Grants for solar panels on all south facing farm shed roofs.
20. Grants for electric tractors and farm equipment
21. All new and 50% of old public car parking bays to have electric charge points by law.
22. Focus on carbon and energy balance accounting for grant assistance purposes.
23. Rewards for Net Zero farming at farm level
24. Increased carbon capture through afforestation with native species
25. Strategic move from meat production to tillage
26. Support for laboratory grown meat research.
27. Systematic culling of deer herds to sustainable levels consistent with afforestation on upland parks with mixed commercial and native species
28. Greater controls on potentially invasive species due to global warming
29. Diversification of fishing industry and fish farming to take account of ocean warming.
30. Mitigation measures for climate change induced increases in extreme flooding and wind speed events
31. Protection of coastal areas from sea level rises and extreme tides and storms.
32. Protection of inland approved farmlands and dwellings from river basin flooding including the restoration of natural floodplains where possible

It was quite an extensive and expensive agenda requiring good coordination between government departments and with the EU. Síle was able to tap into EU and Irish Sovereign wealth fund resources for many of the initiatives. Farming reaction was surprisingly positive when specific details of initiatives were announced. Most included grant or loan schemes for high capital cost initiatives. Many held out the prospect of new jobs in new or expanded industries.

Progress on particular initiatives was often slow, but there being so many, there was always progress on some to report. I had no end of material for newspaper articles enthusiastically received by my environmental editor, Professor Meekan. She also provided useful independent critiques of the efficacy of the measures chosen. There were often interesting divergencies between her advice and that of departmental civil servants, which I put down to the latter being too close to industry vested interests and lobby groups. I was sometimes able to enable Síle to challenge her official's advice.

Protests were particularly loud from battery chicken and pork producers whose animals were permanently caged in indoor facilities and who required extensive use of antibiotics and growth promoters to ensure rapid growth and disease free status. However, the harmful effects of such practices on human health were now well established, and Síle stood her ground. Those that couldn't adapt their production methods had to close.

Ireland led the way within the EU on many of these initiatives and gained a global reputation for healthy food and environments. This had huge benefits in marketing Irish tourism and produce which could command a price premium on global markets. There were always rogue farmers who broke the rules, but they were quickly isolated from their own communities as they put the health, reputation, and prosperity of all at risk.

Síle, Ciara and I were blessed with a second child, Pádraig, but somehow, she managed to balance the demands of an incredibly difficult job with family life. I did much of my work from home, and we also had the support of some au pairs who spoke French, Spanish, Italian and German and who were encouraged to speak those languages with Ciara and later

Pádraig. Síle's mum, Theresa, came to live with us much of the time, and shared our childcare burden.

I had also become reconciled with my own parents after our marriage, and they visited often, hence Pádraig's second name was a rather incongruous Sebastian, after my father.

In getting to know my father better, I was surprised to learn of the degree of Irish bloodlines in our ancestry. It had not been something discussed in our family.

I had always taken my father for a rabid imperialist and was surprised at his critique of British imperial history. "We weren't as bad as the Belgians, Dutch, Germans, French, Spanish and Portuguese, but we were pretty bad at times," was his considered critique. "When we conquered India with the help of feuding Maharajas, it was one of the richest countries in the world. We left it one of the poorest. We gave the Irish the Great Famine, which combined with forced evictions and emigration halved the population. Today that would be considered genocide and a war crime".

I suspected he knew rather more about recent Irish history than I did, but I shied away from discussing the Troubles with him. I was so focused on helping Síle build a better future. Nevertheless, he seemed to have a need to talk about it. "Síle's grandfather wasn't the only innocent person we targeted by mistake, there were a lot of cockups" he once said during the course of a more general conversation. I was shocked. I didn't know he knew. "Where do you think Naomi Long got that information?" was his only comment on that matter. But he went on:

> *"Northern Ireland was a total waste of time and resources. We had disengaged from Northern Ireland, strategically, long before Sunak had that brain fart... That Brexit mess only delayed things. It was all supposed to happen, smoothly, within the EU. We were going to sucker the Irish into taking it back".*

Again, I was surprised: "But I thought you were a Leaver?"

"God no! the EU was the only chance we had of remaining a world power. On our own, we couldn't even re-take the Falklands again, if the Argies could be bothered to take it back. Our armed forces are in meltdown. For show only. Military parades for old time's sake. My unit's been disbanded."

Do you miss Army life?

"Not at all. It all became a bit of a fantasy. Making plans we had no chance of carrying out because we had lost basic capabilities. If it weren't for NATO, bad and all that it is, we would be effectively defenceless. The last thing we needed was to piss off the rest of the EU. That Boris Johnson chap was a complete charlatan, fooling no one but our own people. I completely lost faith in Eton after that. I probably shouldn't have sent you to Uxbridge either."

Well, I did feel I had to unlearn everything I learned there. Conjugating a few Latin verbs is all I remember. It was a disaster from my point of view. All show and no go. The rugby was the only saving grace for me. Got me through college as well.

"Yes, I was surprised you even managed to get second class honours. Your Tutor said you were more interested in the rugby. You seem to have been able to pick up on the politics ok afterwards."

I'm a complete amateur. I can throw a few ideas together. Síle's the person who can get a strange mix of people working together. Where she got those 8,000 first preference votes in East Belfast I will never know. There isn't much of a natural constituency there for someone of her background and ideas. And yet I think that has helped her to mobilise the Greens into an organised force. They used to be all over the place.

Yes, a mix of Sinn Féin organisational discipline and Alliance idealism. The Greens have got a real gem there. An Emerald I should say! She could build the Greens into the natural ruling party of the country. Sinn Féin are too backward looking. All the other parties are basically still partitionist. It suits Ireland's interests internationally to be seen to be led by the Greens – an all island party, ecologically sound, leader in sustainable energy and organic food, in tune with global warming concerns, not tied to any church... Their problem was they were too urban and suburban based, but Síle is changing that with her focus on agriculture. That was a very astute forward thinking move".

I was surprised by the sophistication of his political analysis. I had always assumed he was a straightforward establishment law and order type. The type I rebelled against in College.

"I thought you were a natural Tory type?"

"You're not the only one who has learned a lot in recent years".

I was astonished. Humility was not a quality I associated with my father.

"I don't think I can ever remember you accepting you could be wrong before!"

He Laughed. *"I can do humility; just not very well."*

I think I forgave him all after that.

23.   Back to the EU

Sinn Féin left no stone unturned in trying to pick holes in government policy or exploit divisions between coalition parties. They were a very effective opposition. But somehow the coalition managed to stick together. Hang together or hang separately became the watchword. There were a lot of successes and failures. The successes were quickly taken for granted. The failures hung around your neck.

"Friend's come and go, enemies accumulate" is a phrase that comes to mind. Síle had a lot of successes in her term in office, but Ireland never managed to achieve its greenhouse gas emissions targets. Had the population or economy remained the same size, there would have been no problem. But the government was a victim of its own success. Economic growth sparked inward migration which generated more economic growth.

Even with significant improvements in sustainable energy production, energy efficiency, waste recycling, and emissions reductions per unit of production, Ireland's total emissions never achieved their targets. The earth continued to warm, storms and flooding increased, and some coastal areas suffered significant erosion. Someone had to take the blame, and it mattered not that what we were seeing was the result of 200 years of population and economic growth since the industrial revolution.

The Greens were the obvious party to take the blame, even if they were the party which had done most to mitigate the worst effects of global warming. Sea levels were rising ominously, violent storms were on the increase, and average global temperatures continued their rise.

Paradoxically Ireland was one of the few countries in the world that might actually experience a cooling in average temperatures. This was because the North Atlantic Drift, also known as the Gulf stream or, more technically, the Atlantic meridional overturning circulation (AMOC) was weakening and had almost come to a halt, due in large part to melting ice sheets releasing huge quantities of relatively unsalty water into the Arctic Ocean.

Warm water from the tropics was driven by the prevailing winds travelling north and westward past Ireland to the arctic, where it became saltier due to evaporation and cooled, thereby becoming heavier and sinking to the ocean floor and returned to the tropics as a deep undersea current to replace the water being driven northwards by the wind. It thus acted as a huge conveyer belt of heat from the tropics to Ireland. Without it, Ireland could become as cold as Labrador, roughly on the same latitude.

Ice sheet meltwater, being fresh, was much lighter, and mixing with the northward drifting water preventing it from becoming saltier and heavier and therefore slowed the rate of sinking, slowing down the entire circulation system. Longer term, this might even halt altogether and might even cause a new ice age in western Europe. There was much pessimism and fatalism that it was too late to prevent this. It was Síle and the Green's job to focus attention on the hugely damaging effects of climate change on the world as a whole and mitigate it as much as possible.

There were some green shoots. Global population growth had declined from its exponential trajectory, and looked like it could plateau and even decline in the next few decades. Japan, China, and Europe as a whole were already seeing significant population declines, and with it their carbon footprints.

But this led to new problems. Whereas, in 2024, there had been 5 workers for everyone aged over 65 in Ireland, now there were only 3, and this ratio was projected to decline further. Increased life expectancies and reduced birthrates had produced a huge imbalance in the structure of the productive economy. Even with the average retirement age veering towards 70, there were simply not enough workers to provide the health and social care services required. The problems were even worse in many European and Asian societies.

Automation, robotisation and artificial intelligence can reduce the requirement for many workers, but they are not so good at providing care for the elderly.

The Tribune was now sourcing most of its copy from news services, and the first draft of many a journalistic article was written by AI. I was accused of using AI for many of my articles, and always replied I was more interested in human stupidity. It was the foibles in human nature which interested me. Newspapers were shedding staff everywhere, and even though I was now covering all of Ireland, Politics, Environmental, Agricultural, and sporting beats for the paper, I dreaded the prospect of the axe falling on me as well.

Matt Casey assured me I would be the last to be let go. I had provided a lot of quality copy over the years. But it wasn't, ultimately, his call. It was the marketing men and the bean counters who would make the final decision. Where were the clicks coming from, which articles generated most clicks? I wasn't the most headline grabbing journalist around. Ireland had moved down the British agenda. There were sexier topics around.

In the end it was just an email from HR. Cutbacks were necessary to make ends meet. Statutory redundancy payments would apply. There was no mention of cutbacks in back room or administrative staff. Only front line journalists were being let go, including big names like Bill Featherstonhaugh.

I was devastated. Perhaps I had become too secure and comfortable in my role. I hadn't seen this coming. Getting another job in journalism would be hard. Every newspaper was in the same boat. I wasn't even sure I wanted another job. I liked the beats I was currently covering. There would be no shortage of work child minding and supporting Síle. She was under real pressure in her job as well. The opinion polls weren't good.

I had always assumed she was at greater risk of losing her job by not getting re-elected, and then my salary would act as a backstop for us both. I wasn't ready to become dependent on her. As Tánaiste she was, of course, well paid. But we had two mortgages and a young family. And she was one election away from the prospect of losing her job. We didn't have a mountain of savings.

I tried to maintain a public face of not being too bothered. I would have more time to support her. But she read me well enough.

I don't know if anyone pulled any strings, but I was offered a job as a columnist for the Irish Times. It wasn't much of an earner, but enough to keep my hand in. It would be a different challenge writing for an Irish readership, and moreover one which would treat me with suspicion because of my close connections with the government. I had no problem writing opinion pieces but preferred factual pieces and that often involved travel and research. The job didn't come with an expense account.

It was then that the idea for a memoire germinated, which eventually became this book. I wanted to write about how a united Ireland had become about, and about how the many subsequent challenges were addressed.

I would have liked to have been able to write about a widespread reconciliation process within Northern Ireland, but it never really happened. I'm not even sure many people wanted to be reconciled. People just ploughed their different furrows often in parallel to neighbours they hardly spoke to. People just seemed to be waiting for the direct combatants to die off. There would be no truth and reconciliation process. The funerals could be massive, but it was a whole history that was being buried.

The younger generation just yawned and turned away. They didn't want to know about ancient grudges. Oh, there were some high profile reconciliation conferences. Mainly self-promotion for the protagonists. The snake oil salesmen sold forgiveness and renewal. The real action was taking place elsewhere.

Real people were re-building the economy around real businesses selling real products and services. The vast majority just got on with it, moved on and made the best of it, and generally did quite well. Those who wanted to hold on to old grievances did so, damaging themselves in the process.

Sovereignty wasn't the issue. Power was. Some lost, some gained. And some never accepted their loss. I had been a player for a while, and now I was out.

Síle was still fighting her battles. She was going to go down fighting, if at all. The Greens were still implementing their agenda even when others within the coalition had lost interest, clinging on to power for the sake of it.

And then it came to me...

This journey wasn't about me at all. My job was to support Síle in her work. If she could make a success of governing Ireland, the past wouldn't matter all that much. The future was all that mattered.

I wrote most of her speeches, did some of her research, prepared meeting agendas, did advance work for her engagements. Yes, there were others who could and did some of that work, but it was my job now. I loved doing it.

Day by day, hour by hour, one problem after another was tackled. It wasn't glamourous. It was a grind. There were times when things seemed hopeless. But the tide was turned. The investments paid off. Confidence in the business sector improved.

Naomi fell by the wayside. Said she had had enough. She retired from the Alliance leadership and her cabinet post. Moved back to semi-retirement in East Belfast as a back bencher doing constituency work. She told Síle not to worry about her seat, she wouldn't be standing again.

But Síle wasn't going anywhere. She was on top of her brief, sharp as a tack in her exchanges in the Dáil. Always courteous, never scoring cheap points. Sticking to the facts. Some thought she was too nice for a tough job like Minister for Agriculture, especially if she was going to take on the farming lobby. But she got there making some good deals here and there.

The DUP were still there of course, loitering on the opposition benches. Always trying to ambush a minister caught unawares. But they learned to respect Síle. There were never any easy wins against her. She always had her factual ammunition at the ready.

And the bottom line was that everyone was better off. The economy was still growing. No one's civil rights had been impeded. The Barnett subvention was winding down, and the transition arrangements were coming to an end. Northern Ireland as a political entity would cease to exist, barely mourned by anyone.

The Good Friday agreement was due to expire unless agreed otherwise under the terms of the Transfer of Sovereignty and Cooperation Agreement, (TOSCA) but good relations with Britain were maintained. No one had been forced to change their identity, and many were embarrassed at what all the flag waving was supposed to be about.

That's what kids do. The adults were now running the show, and the objective was to improve living standards, public services, and the quality of life generally.

Ukraine reconstruction had been a huge drain on EU resources. Ireland, as a net contributor, had received some rebates to cover the increased cost of enhancing north south infrastructure. But even these had ended now, and there was some resentment at what was portrayed as wasteful spending by Brussels.

One visit to the Ukraine was enough to dispel that illusion. Large parts of the country were still devastated. Some areas hadn't even been cleared of mines. The Ukrainian economy had recovered substantially but was coming from very far behind the poorest of EU states. Attaining EU average living standards was still a far off aspiration for the future.

As Tánaiste Síle visited the Ukraine several times to promote agricultural and industrial cooperation, environmental rehabilitation, and the tourist sector. Irish companies were heavily involved. Irish people were buying holiday homes on the Black Sea coast. Ireland had benefitted hugely from EU membership during the first 50 years of membership and didn't begrudge Ukraine getting a leg up.

But Euroscepticism was on the rise throughout Europe, and the EU seemed to be only one major crisis away from a breakup or at least a damaging split between the northern and southern member states. Ireland was an anomaly, often siding with the "BlackMed club" against the more "prudent" northern member states and was always trying to act as an honest broker between the two camps.

It had taken Scotland 7 years to gain independence after Ireland had. They never achieved the sort of transition deal Ireland had with TOSCA. Scottish English relations were particularly soured when Scotland defaulted on its part of the UK national debt which it had been forced to take on with independence. It adopted the Euro instead of Sterling even before full EU membership had been granted when the Bank of England sought to impose sanctions. This caused further difficulties for Scottish/English trade.

There was much talk of England and Wales re-joining the EU to avoid all these trade difficulties. However, BlackMed member states were opposed because they were worried that England would join the northern camp within the EU and block wealth transfers to southern and poorer states. They tried to impose onerous conditions which England naturally baulked at. There had been quite a degree of regulatory divergence between the EU and UK in the meantime, and the EU was insisting on total compliance with EU standards.

England had tried to carve out a unique place for itself in world trade by focusing on research and development and innovation in pharmaceuticals, medical technology, information technology and financial services. However, it could never quite match the scale of the US and EU giants in these fields. Many of the England based companies in these sectors were in fact subsidiaries of foreign conglomerates, and even most of England's infrastructure was foreign owned.

In an ironic reversal of colonialism India and China had bought up many of the key players in British industry and services and key investment decisions were made abroad. Many innovative technologies, invented in England, ended up being commercialised and manufactured in other countries with limited benefits for England.

Most of the profits also left England and relative living standards continued to decline as a result. Ireland was a key competitor in all these sectors and was able to maintain a dominant position within the Single Market by continuing to attract key players from abroad. The difference was they declared their profits in Ireland because of the lower corporate tax rates on offer. England simply couldn't afford to reduce their rates to match Ireland.

From a purely economic point of view Brexit had ended up being a long and slow burning disaster. Despite the accession of Ukraine and other poorer states and an aging population, EU GDP/Capita continue to keep pace with England. Ireland's was now almost three times England's GDP/capita, and despite the distorting effects of multinational activity on Ireland's accounts, living standards were now almost twice that of England as well.

The Welsh independence movement was gathering strength as they looked across the Irish sea to Ireland. The difficulties with Scotland's Independence process had not been sufficient to put them off.

In a humiliating climbdown, England and Wales eventually re-applied to join the EU. It was the only way to avoid a further disintegration of the UK. They accepted that opt-outs for Sterling, Schengen, and various rebates enjoyed under their previous membership would no longer apply.

Despite being England's main and most direct competitor for investment, Ireland championed England's membership cause against considerable opposition from BlackMed members. Much closer British Irish cooperation once again became a British priority.

Mysteriously, I received a job offer from the Times to become their Ireland correspondent without even having applied for anything. I suspected my relationship with Síle, as Ireland's deputy Prime Minister, might have been a factor, but it was never mentioned in our discussions. I thought it might be a reprise of my old role in smoothing British Irish relations on the European Ultra High Voltage Supergrid as an advisor to Eamonn Ryan. I certainly had easy access for interviews with British ministers from that point on.

I like to think I played a small role in Ireland's campaign to allow England and Wales to rejoin. Certainly, my articles for the Times were widely quoted as an antidote to the still virulently anti-EU tone in some of the English popular press. I don't know if the British public ever appreciated how much such "gutter journalism" contributed to negative perceptions of England within the EU.

I had many a long drinking sessions with European journalists trying to persuade them that such coverage reflected the views of tax exiled billionaires rather than the general public. "Then why do the British buy papers containing such nonsense?" was a riposte I found difficult to answer. There always seemed to me to be some cognitive dissonance, bordering on schizophrenia in British attitudes to the EU. They bitterly resented its existence, in some ways, and yet couldn't do without it. I suppose it reminded them that Brittania no longer ruled the waves.

In any case Ireland's campaign to allow England and Wales to rejoin the EU eventually succeeded. It helped that Ireland had frequently acted as an honest broker between the northern and BlackMed members states of the EU. Some were puzzled that Ireland was so keen to allow its biggest and most direct competitor back into the EU. Ireland had done very well during the UK's absence, capturing a lot of the foreign direct investment (FDI) that might otherwise have gone to England.

But the structure of the Irish economy was now changing in any case. Ireland was becoming a lot less dependent on FDI and was generating its own investment momentum by Irish companies which had become major global players. Net Irish investment abroad now exceeded foreign direct investment in Ireland and Irish businesses now wanted a greater part of the action in England. Wage rates and costs had become too expensive for many companies in Ireland.

Another ironic reversal of colonialism.

24.   And so, to conclude...

I hope I have given you, dear reader, a sense of the turmoil in society, and the many twists and turns in relations between Ireland north and south, Ireland and Britain, and Britain and the world which occurred in the 15 years post Irish re-unification. It was a tumultuous time, and I was extremely privileged to be a close observer for much of it.

In retrospect very little of the action centred on the mean streets of Belfast. Like every other city it was transformed by business investment and gentrification, and the peace walls eventually came down. But it was technological and economic development, more integrated and better education and health care services, and the normal political processes of a democracy that effected much of the change.

Síle had been heavily involved in local community projects in East Belfast in the early years of her political career, and they certainly had an impact on local communities. But the really big changes came when big new businesses moved in, with advanced technological manufacturing processes or sophisticated service technologies that really transformed Belfast and the rest of Ireland over the years.

People were too busy achieving educational qualifications, working in advanced industries or services, and enjoying the fruits of their labour to become embroiled in ancient disputes. A few still marched in Orange parades or attended bonfires, but these had long become tourist curiosities rather than political protests.

Advanced surveillance technologies and electronic controls had put paid to a lot of anti-social behaviour and petty crime. There wasn't much point in stealing a car if it didn't drive without recognising your voice, iris, or fingerprint.

At Síle's behest I had taken part in a few "encounter group" style therapy sessions where people shared their trauma, repressed anger, anxiety, and fears. I even shared and dealt with a few of my own. At an individual level I'm sure they helped many to come to terms with their trauma and get on with life.

Not having suffered as deeply as many in Northern Ireland, I would be the last to tell them to "get over it and move on." Everybody is unique, makes their own decisions, and moves at their own pace. Some never "get over it" and bring their trauma, be it physical or psychological, to their grave. I would be the very last person to set myself up as their judge.

I can just record here that the vast majority of people of all traditions and backgrounds in Ireland did move on from Partition and the traumas it helped to create. The link with our neighbour, Britain was never entirely broken, to the benefit of both nations. Many physical and psychological traumas were overcome or at least managed to enable a better life.

The level and scale of suffering I encountered in Ukraine was of a different order entirely and it could be centuries before their relations with Russia are normalised. But I can only look to the example of Germany and France after centuries of conflict and two devastating world wars. It is possible to move on even after the most horrendous of war crimes and genocides.

With centuries of conflict between Ireland and Britan, and the 200 year anniversary of The Great Famine approaching, Ireland too, has had its share of suffering. Politics is a much maligned profession, but when done well it can do so much to alleviate the worst excesses of conflict and transform all lives for the better.

There is still a lot of performative anger, of course, particularly coming from the DUP. It is still almost *de rigueur* for unionist politicians to complain about Irish mistreatment of those with a British identity, particularly in the Dáil or if there is a TV camera about. The slightest perceived slight becomes amplified.

But one senses that, increasingly, their hearts aren't really in it. That it is being done almost out of a force of habit. Some even have a smile when they express it. The very fact we can even continue to speak of "unionist politicians" and parties gives the lie to any claim they are being actively repressed, beyond the normal competitive politics of a democracy. Disagreement does not imply disapproval.

So, this is ultimately a tale of success, told by a person very privileged to have witnessed so much of it. Many leaders have crossed these pages, and not all are remembered well. But insofar as they helped to resolve some ancient grudges and enabled others to build a better future, I salute them.

Peace is a reality often only fully appreciated when it is absent. Blessed are the peace makers, and let's hope they shall inherit the earth. Certainly, those who united Europe and then later Ireland, have made their contribution. It has not been an easy journey. It was full of sound and fury. But in the end, it also signified a great deal.

Printed in Great Britain
by Amazon

27323337R00139